Words to Win

Zubaan was set up in 2003 as an imprint of Kali for Women, India's first feminist publishing house, whose name is synonymous with women's writing of quality in South Asia. Zubaan has worked to continue and expand on the pioneering list built up by Kali, and many of the books published by us are today considered to be key texts of feminist scholarship.

To mark our tenth anniversary, we are delighted to offer you ten of our classic titles in bold new editions. These are a mixture of original fiction, translations, memoir and non-fiction on a variety of subjects. Each book is unique; each sheds a different light on the world seen through women's eyes, and each holds its place in the world of contemporary women's writing.

Zubaan is proud that these gifted writers have chosen to entrust us with their work, and we are pleased to be able to re-issue these titles to a new readership in the twenty-first century.

Zubaan Classics

Fiction
Temsula Ao *These Hills Called Home*
Kunzang Choden *The Circle of Karma*
Bulbul Sharma, *Eating Women, Telling Tales*
Vandana Singh *The Woman Who Thought She Was a Planet
and Other Stories*

Memoir
Baby Halder *A Life Less Ordinary*

Non-fiction
Uma Chakravarti *Rewriting History: The Life and Times of Pandita Ramabai*
Preeti Gill (ed.) *The Peripheral Centre: Voices from the Northeast*
Sharmila Rege *Writing Caste/Writing Gender:
Narrating Dalit Women's Testimonios*
Kumkum Sangari and Sudesh Vaid (eds.) *Recasting Women:
Essays in Colonial History*
Tanika Sarkar *Words to Win: The Making of a Modern Autobiography*

Note: Since all books are reprints, the bibliographical information they contain on authors has not been updated, and several titles mentioned in them as forthcoming are more than likely to have already appeared.

Words to Win

The Making of *Amar Jiban*:
A Modern Autobiography

TANIKA SARKAR

zubaan

ZUBAAN
an imprint of Kali for Women
128 B Shahpur Jat, 1st floor
NEW DELHI 110 049
Email: contact@zubaanbooks.com
Website: www.zubaanbooks.com

First published by Kali for Women 1999
This edition published by Zubaan 2013

10 9 8 7 6 5 4 3 2 1

ISBN 978 93 81017 90 6

Zubaan is an independent feminist publishing house based in New Delhi with
a strong academic and general list. It was set up as an imprint of India's first
feminist publishing house, Kali for Women, and carries forward Kali's tradition
of publishing world quality books to high editorial and production standards.
Zubaan means tongue, voice, language, speech in Hindustani. Zubaan is a non-
profit publisher, working in the areas of the humanities, social sciences, as well
as in fiction, general non-fiction, and books for children and young adults under
its Young Zubaan imprint.

Typeset in Bembo 11/14 by Jojy Philip, New Delhi 110 015
Printed at Raj Press, R-3 Inderpuri, New Delhi 110 012

For Sumit

Contents

Acknowledgments

The book had to be fitted into the interstices of many other responsibilities and commitments. A very long time, therefore, went into its making, and the tedium was relieved by the encouragement and support that I was fortunate to receive from my many friends. Urvashi Butalia had first suggested the idea of such a venture and Kali for Women gave me every help in realising it. I especially want to thank Jaya Banerji for her editorial suggestions. St. Stephen's College provided a pleasant work-environment where teaching has been a stimulus rather than an obstacle to research. Jasodhara Bagchi, Ania Loomba and Aijaz Ahmad helped at various stages with valuable suggestions. My association with Pankaj Butalia's film *Moksha* gave me insights into both bhakti and pilgrimage.

It is not easy to convince oneself that the writing of an obscure village housewife has any significance as a subject of historical research, since it cannot uncover new or significant "historical facts". Although history from below and histories of representations have elsewhere been acknowledged as legitimate areas of exploration, the world of the institutionalised discipline of Indian history still refuses to accept this. There were a few colleagues whose support was, therefore, crucial

in sustaining my belief in this kind of work. I am grateful
to Shohini Ghosh, Ravi Vasudevan, Radhika Singha, Parita
Mukta, Uma Chakravarti, Kumkum Sangari and Pradip
Kumar Datta for their endorsement of this project, at a time
when I had become deeply discouraged. Uma and Pradip have
also helped with very important observations on the book at
all its stages.

For obvious reasons, my mother was much in my thoughts
as I translated Rashsundari's recollections of her relationship
with her mother. Aditya was critical—especially about my
spelling—but interested throughout the long time it took me
to write the book. Since Sumit is far more involved with what
I write than I am, I think he should be the one to thank me
for at last finishing the book. It is dedicated to him.

1

Introduction

(*On getting married*) "I went straight into my mother's arms," crying, "Mother, why did you give me away to a stranger?"

(*After marriage*) "My day would begin at dawn and I worked till two at night... I was fourteen years old... I longed to read books. But I was unlucky, those days women were not allowed to read."

(*Learning to read at twenty-five*) "It was as if the Great Lord himself taught me how to read. If I didn't know even that much, I would have had to depend on others..."

(*Looking back on her youth*) "In the meantime the Great Lord had decked my body out just the way a boat is fitted out... How strange it all was: so many things came out of my body, yet I knew nothing of their causes."

These are some important words and themes from *Amar Jiban*, the first autobiography written by a Bengali woman, and very probably, the first full-scale autobiography in the Bengali language. Her writing and her life stand in a peculiarly significant relationship to each other, since the author, Rashsundari Debi, a housewife from an upper caste, landed family in East Bengal (now in Bangladesh), possessed none of the criteria that presumably render a woman's life noteworthy.

It was, on the whole, an uneventful, unremarkable life. Rashsundari was born around 1809 in the village of Potajia in Pabna district. When she was twelve, she was married off to Sitanath Ray, a prosperous landlord from Ramdia village in Faridpur. From the age of fourteen, she began to look after the entire household and she also gave birth to twelve children in fairly rapid succession. When she was twenty-five, however, Rashsundari made a daring departure. She secretly taught herself to read. Over time, she read through all the religious manuscripts at her home. Later, she taught herself to write.

Rashsundari was widowed when she was fifty-nine, and the next year, in 1868, she finished the first version of her autobiography.[1] She added a second part and a new version came out in 1897 when she was eighty-eight. We do not have any records of sales proceeds but it is significant that she was confident enough to go in for a second edition. It carried a preface by the well known literary figure, Jyotirindranath Tagore, elder brother to Rabindranath. Such propitious beginnings notwithstanding, we do not find any mention of her in the standard histories of literature,[2] nor is her date of death recorded anywhere.[3] *Amar Jiban* (henceforward *AJ*) was her single literary effort.[4]

Only one event of an exceptional kind had interrupted the even, quiet rhythms of a conventional domestic existence. Orthodox Hindus of those times kept their women illiterate, since there was a firm belief that the educated woman was destined to be widowed. In Rashsundari's own family, feelings ran so high against women's education that she would not so much as glance at a piece of paper lest she be accused of knowing how to read. The first tentative efforts by Christian missionaries and Indian reformers to educate women had produced a sort of an orthodox backlash against the move, and had hardened Hindu opinion. The meek and submissive housewife understood perfectly well that her secret effort went drastically against the grain of familial and social codes. This one act of disobedience, then, partially deconstructs the good wife—a script that Rashsundari otherwise followed with admirable success all her life.

Why did she, on her own, and in great trepidation, make this deeply transgressive departure? And what bearing does this desire and this achievement have on the fact that Rashsundari was the first Bengali person to write out her own life, to recreate, or, indeed, to invent it through the autobiographical act, and thereby gather it closely to herself and possess it more fully? What were the resources available to her that could have produced this desire and what are the new possibilities that we can read into women's lives and writings from the presence of this desire?

Rashsundari says that it was an inexplicable, yet irrepressible urge to read a particular sacred text that made her struggle in secret to learn to read. That book was *Chaitanya Bhagabat* (henceforward *CB*),[5] the first Bengali biography of Chaitanya, the Krishna-maddened saint of medieval Bengal, who had promised salvation to the wretched, the low caste, the women—categories excluded by brahmanical orthodoxy from higher spiritual aspirations and learning. She went on to read other manuscripts that dealt with the lives of Chaitanya and his beloved deity, Krishna, an incarnation of Vishnu, the Preserver of Creation. Her reading, then, had a lot to do with lives saintly and lives divine. When she wrote, she did so with a covert design and she audaciously structured her very mundane life story on a sacred pattern: she was the chosen instrument of God, who worked a miracle on her, the fruit of which was her wondrous mastery over the written word. As far I can see, it was she who had coined that magnificent word with which she proclaimed her own achievement:

jitakshara, or one who has mastered the word. *AJ* was proof
of the miracle, just as the miraculous events of saints' lives are
evidence of divine intention. Her life was meant to be read
as if it was enclosed within a divine purpose, as almost an
extension of God's own life. It was as if the two lives—God's
and the devotee's—were intertwined within a single narrative
frame, interanimating each other. In fact, the last sections of
her autobiography describe, without any apparent sense of
incongruity, not events from her own life, but from the lives of
Krishna and Chaitanya.

Rashsundari read from a fairly wide corpus of late
medieval Bengali devotional (*bhakti*) texts. Her reflections
drew upon terms that have long and multiple lineages within
Hindu religious discourses. Unless we refer often and in some
detail to this thick web of intertextuality, *AJ* would make only
limited and local sense.

Again, even though the history of her own times and place
seems remarkably absent within the text, the book itself. It
was a material product created by a woman, composed in
the new Bengali prose, and printed for a nineteenth-century
readership that was keenly interested in the life and self-
reflections of an ordinary woman who belonged crucially to
our first modern century. We need to explore the insertion
of the large historical processes into the life and into the
book, even though Rashsundari herself showed no overt
interest in them.

II

I was interested in *AJ* not only because it initiates the
autobiographical genre in Bengali, or because it is an early
example of a woman's writing in that language, but also

because *AJ* is a rare and early example of a modern woman's devotional quest that is articulated in her own words. My interest was sharpened as I came to realise how different the text turned out to be from what I had expected from a woman's autobiography, a woman's writing, a woman's *bhakti*.

It would be simple-minded to posit a straight connection between female subjectivity and female writing, to assume that the latter reflects the former in some direct, unmediated way. In fact, for the writing woman of her generation of the first-educated, the act of writing itself would have reconstituted her subjectivity in radically new ways. Yet, a woman's writing is far too easily folded back into the cultural world that it comes out of. Or, even more problematically, it is connected to her body—its phallic lack, its rhythms, pulsations, urges—as if it is the woman who alone has a body, or rather, her body is all that she has.[6] *AJ* seemed to be strenuously resisting the implications of both, as if through her writing, Rashsundari is declaring her emancipation from all the resources that have been conventionally allotted to her. Her resistance to her inherited and imposed world lies in her act of writing in more ways than one. In this sense, *AJ* is a very early text of modernity.

We find very little by way of the direct speech acts of the woman, or speech acts shaped entirely by female experiences: hardly any proverbs, riddles, tales, pungent or earthy idioms, through which women articulate their sense of the world.[7] Her writing is quite removed from everyday, colloquial forms—not only in the syntax and in grammatical constructions, but also in the very nature of the prose that she uses. It is not, in any noticeable way, gender marked.

It could be possible that one of her highly educated sons had brushed up the prose, or had edited the text. Yet, the market for the book would, if anything, have demanded some more evidence of the woman's speech, a specific, gendered writing. It is unlikely that the female writing traces would have been eradicated so thoroughly in any intelligent editing. Also, as we shall see, other women chose a similar mode of articulation, privileging the discursive, the reflexive, rather than the descriptive or the entirely emotional. They chose to do so even when the market would have preferred more self-evidently different and feminine modes. We have an example of such expectation of 'authentic' feminine writing in Rabindranath Tagore's short story, *Nashtaneer*. Here the woman first tries to emulate her literary brother-in-law's themes and ways of writing. Frustrated by the sterile mimicry, she then turns to her own rural past, observed custom, festivities, work, and she starts describing them in exactly the same words that she recalls them with. It was an immediate a hit with publishers, who took it as an authentic example of women's writing. In Satyajit Ray's filmic rendering of the story, her writing is dissolved in the act of her visual recalling, her hand merely traces out the pictures that her eye of memory conjures up. Writing is at no distance from visual or emotional experiences, it is merely a deposit left by those.[8]

It is remarkable that Rashsundari, and several of her contemporaries resist such expectations. It is true that very often they break into a highly emotionalised form of articulation which is integrated into the discursive. That, however, remained a characteristic of all modern Bengali prose, the boundaries between the emotional and the discursive being no more sharply drawn in male writings. It could be that with this new prose, that had been developed sufficiently to bear the weight of many different kinds of writing only in the first two or three decades of this century, women did not start writing too long after men had done so. There are, therefore, not yet any congealed, masculine ways of writing which would be inaccessible to the ways women would tend to write.[9] Another reason was that the new prose was quite fluid and not very rigidly structured in terms of syntax or patterns of articulation. There was an absence of very strict grammatical controls and regulations that made Sanskrit pandits extremely contemptuous of it. Even the great novelist and essayist Bankimchandra Chattopadhyay could not escape their censure. The flexible prose structure, then, was hospitable to the writings of those who had only recently been educated and who had had little experience in handling grammatical and construction rules in their own writing. That might be the reason why, among the genres to flower with the founding of the prose and the print from the early decades of the century, we find popular tracts, fiction and farces that were brought out by the cheap, pulp publishers of Battala in North Calcutta.[10]

The woman is generally supposed to be more sensitive to the concrete and the sensuous dimensions of everyday life, to the emotional complications of relationships rather than to abstract and cerebral matters. Rashsundari's book, however, is astonishingly bare of visual or sensuous content. There are few descriptions of exterior landscapes, of domestic interiors. There is no impression of taste, sound or smell. The objects she handled, the spaces she passed through, the faces she saw, bear no individual features in her narrative. The great rivers and waterways of Pabna and Faridpur—Padma, Brahmaputra, Ariyal Khan—are condensed into the single metaphor of a boat journey through the rivers of life. They also shape a dream sequence where her dead son comes to meet her on a tiny boat across the great, melancholy expanses of a river. The landscapes reflect her moods, her thoughts. Nature is merely a mirror to her interior states. Events that took place around her are similarly condensed. There is a brief poem on an epidemic fever that was raging at her village in Faridpur, but there is little about anything else that did not directly touch herself.

AJ is a curiously self-absorbed, non-dialogic narrative. Other people appear simply to make a specific point about her and then they disappear. They do not have an independent life within the text, nor do they live out relationships with one another. The husband, who had been given a few perfunctory references in the main body of the book, was granted a separate, brief section at the end, because, she said, people would want to know about him. A curiously impersonal obituary was, therefore, appended, for narrative requirements, not because she wanted to talk about him. Even that section concludes with an account of a triumph of her own writing skills.

She turned the narrative focus intensely upon herself, first of all, by abstracting herself from her lived world. "I came to Bharatbarsha and I have spent a long time here. This body of mine, this mind, this life itself, have taken several different forms." She lived out her life in two villages. They are, however, absent, except as mere names. Nor are there more intimate, familiar locales—the sub-division, the district or even the province. Her timescale is oddly precise. She deviated from popular, rural ways of patterning time and memory: pinning down a personal event by its contiguity with a natural one like a flood or a famine, or by referring to an event of local or family importance. There is no local time, village time, family time. She gives herself nothing less than a whole subcontinent and almost an entire century to live in.

In their larger, historical-geographical dimensions, these landmarks were remote to her lived life. Yet, evidently, they were meaningful to the design of her self-created, narrated life. They had an aesthetic purpose in conferring a rhythm to the movement of her life. At the time that she was writing, a united Indian empire had emerged, renewed and revamped after the 1857 Uprising. Bharatbarsha, then, was the effect of a new political reality. The name also occurs in *Chaitanya Bhagabat*. The Vaishnavite pilgrimage circuit, spreading from Nabadwip in Bengal to Puri in Orissa—which is a gateway to the south—to Mathura-Vrindaban in the north and Dwarka in the west, gave Vaishnavs a sense of a large, subcontinental sacred geography. Again, as the book was being written, the nineteenth century had self-consciously separated itself out from an undifferentiated mass of time, a recurrent replay of identical time-cycles. It had come to see itself as the site of a new and unique history, which gave time a direction, a teleology.

Rashsundari needed this very large background to abstract herself from her actual empirical life. She transcended its narrow limits, its inability to intersect with grand historical narratives, by giving herself the largest possible temporal and spatial frames that she could relate to. Her life thus acquired an adequate site where a great divine purpose could unfold.

Autobiography, as a genre, most obviously confuses the boundaries between the word and the world, deluding us that it is the actual life we are reading, and not a text. I found that *AJ* defeated the expectation continuously! In very many ways, its textuality is underlined by the distance it sets up between Rashsundari's lived experiences and her narrative preoccupations. It was through writing a book that the life that she wanted to express, could take on life. I have written about the text alone for I am not the biographer of Rashsundari, even assuming that it is possible to recover more facts about her life. The contexts and lineages that I have sought to gather, therefore, relate to the book and not to the life.

Bakhtin considers a fundamental tension as the constitutive principle of autobiographical writing: "...I must become *another* in relation to myself—to myself as living *this,* my own life in this axiological world—and this *other* must take up an essentially founded axiological position outside myself."[11] The aporia which is induced by this necessary othering of the self in order to narrativise it and render it into an aesthetic product in an inter-subjective situation, does not paralyse *AJ.* On the contrary, Rashsundari seems to have founded a theological-narrative stance that handles the paradox as a constitutive principle of her text. She underlines the distance and the difference between the writing self and the written self, pointing out the temporal gulf, the developmental process that intervenes and ruptures the unity of the two. The distancing, however, leads to no secure and final objective truth. Indeed, she is always at pains to insist on the impossibility of gaining a decisive purchase and hold on the meaning of her entire life. This is, as we shall see later, partly a function of her being a woman who necessarily lacks power and control over her life. It is also the hierarchical difference between God and the human devotee.

III

AJ is an indifferently written but superbly crafted text. The prose is not remarkable, sliced up, as it is, into short, somewhat jagged or trembling sentences which often sound like mild whining. The vocabulary is rarely extensive or very varied, a limited repertoire of words gets used insistently over large stretches of passages. Verse colophons are based on conventional devotional codes. As I have said before, people, landscapes and objects are sparsely drawn and do not come to life, except very rarely. What absorbs the author are her own states of mind, and her own life events are but a trigger to reflections on these. The text wallows in a kind of brooding introspection which, however, revolves round a fixed repertoire: pain, submission, obedience, fear, humility.

Yet, that is not all. Conventional devotional statements sometimes use a mix of metaphors or codes that are strikingly individual. They not only depart from pre-established patterns, but also subtly undo them. There are flashes of acute observations, descriptions that are deeply, though briefly evocative, reflections that pierce the drab, ponderous, pious prose with acid comments. Entirely unsuspected and jarring moods, emotions and reactions flash across the flow of the narrative, that relieve the prose and also deconstruct the dominant message and purpose. The disconcerting insertions are not accidental, spontaneous, an uncontrollable bursting through of the repressed, the silenced. They are carefully calibrated and highly controlled strategies that are worked deliberately into the text for maximum effect: the effects, again, are subtly framed so that the overt and explicit message sets up a strong but unstated tension with the occasional, the unexpected. Rashsundari proceeds through a magnificently controlled doublespeak that is facilitated by certain typically Vaishnav expressive conventions which I discuss later on.

Given these swift and insidious shifts in moods and language, I thought it best to follow the prose as closely as possible in my translation, allowing the impression of ponderousness and listlessness to come through fully so that the other, less typical parts may stand out all the more vividly. In other words, I do not propose to make the translation more pleasurable reading than the text itself, to tone up the drabness, to rectify the repetitions.

Of course, translations cannot be very literal. Particularly so, when the translation is in English, a language that occupies a very remote linguistic and conventional field from the original in Bengali. There are structured differences between one language and the other that cannot be naturalised in the translation. Bengali has a vast vocabulary, with a very large range of synonyms for most of our significant nouns and adjectives. Verbs, on the other hand, are limited in comparison to English ones.[12] When one word is preferred in the text against all others, it is because of its sound and meaning effects that will correspond most closely to the signified, for the particular resonances that sound and meaning will carry, and also for its allusive qualities, especially literary ones—when this word is placed in a particular arrangement. I have already talked about the fact that Bengali sentences are not as firmly anchored in a particular linear structure as they are in English. The relatively more loose and open-ended syntax opens up a field of considerable play on words. Such fluidity and structural variations had to be sacrificed in the translation, since they would sound unnecessarily idiosyncratic and experimental in English. But I have not interfered with the arrangement of paragraphs or the size of sentences, keeping them very long or very short, according to the original. That fidelity, however, was not possible with the verses, and I could not replicate the original rhyming or metrical patterns. I have also tried to preserve the repetitiveness by using the same English words in translation over and over again.

The autobiography, as we have seen, came out in two parts. The first part has been translated in almost its entirety, but only sections from the second part have been retained in translation. The other sections were particularly unreadable, enormously repetitive and there is very little about Rashsundari's own self. Some very typical samples have been translated, and so have those parts that seem to be very important to her self-reflections. I have also translated Jyotirindranath's Preface to the second edition, since I have frequently referred to it in my text.

I have had no previous experience with translating. Nonetheless, I felt that I needed to do the translation myself to acquire some intimacy with the text before I wrote about it. I have said that it is not a particularly pleasurable text to read. It was the constraints that drew me so strongly towards it. The compulsive yet hesitant moves towards self-disclosure and self-creation that this pious, modest and obedient housewife is engaged in are, I find, a profoundly modern possibility. They are even more a sign of our very distinctive and peculiar modernity where the good and humble woman so badly needed a space of her own, as well as a space in public view. The need troubled and touched me.

IV

Kalyani Datta's book on nineteenth-century Bengali women is full of rich insights and sensitive perceptions. In the preface, she cites a little verse from an anonymous nineteenth-century poet which, for her, sums up the world of women. The caged bird is an insistent motif throughout Rashsundari's text as well. Let me translate the verse here as something that I would like to address to her:

> Sitting in your cage, with your eyes shut
> Chained bird, what do you ponder on, within yourself?
> Or, perhaps, you alone have the right to think
> Since you must live through life as a bound prisoner.[13]

Notes

1. She writes, and it is usually thought, that her autobiography was
    published in the same year. Ghulam Murshid, however, thinks
    that it was published in 1875. The earliest edition that I have
    been able to locate in the India Office Library also bears that
    date. In her text, she certainly says that she finished writing the
    first part in 1868. See Murshid, *Rashsundari Theke Rokeya: Nari
    Pragatir Eksho Bacchar,* Bangla Acadamy Press, Dacca, 1993, p. 41.

2. See for instance, S.C. Sengupta, ed, *Sansad Bangali Charitabhidhan,*
    Sahitya Sansad, Calcutta, 1975, p. 487, which has a short note on
    Rashsundari but does not provide a date of death; or, Sukumar
    Sen, *Bangla Sahityer Itihas,* Vols 1 and 2, Eastern Publishers,
    Calcutta, 1965 and 1970.

3. There is a sparse mention in a more recent Biographical
    Dictionary. Apart from a reference to her book, the only other
    fact it offers about her is that her son was Kishorilal Sarkar.
    This, presumably, was the High Court lawyer, a man, it seems,
    of some importance. Subodhchandra Sengupta, ed, *Sansad
    Bangali Charitabhidhan,* Sahitya Sansad, Calcutta, 1976, p. 487.

4. The enlarged edition came out in 1897. A third edition followed
    in 1906 and a fourth one appeared in 1956, with an introduction
    by the famous historian, Dineshchandra Sen. For the translation,
    I have used a reprint of the second edition that was published
    in the *Atmakatha* series, by Ananya Publishers, Calcutta, 1981. I
    have also translated the Introduction by Jyotirindranath Tagore
    which comes in with the second edition.

5. According to Sukumar Sen, the biography was completed
    around 1541–42. Bimanbihari Majumdar, however, is of the
    opinion that it was around 1548. See Asit Bandyopadhya, *Bangla
    Sahityer Itibritta,* Volume 11, 3rd edition, Modern Book Agency,
    Calcutta, 1983, pp 348–50. Also Binanbihari Majumdar, *Shri
    Chaitanya Chanter Upadan,* Calcutta University Press, Calcutta,
    1959, Chapter I.

6. On such expectations from womens' subjectivity and its literary expression, see Elaine Showalter, "Feminist Criticism in the Wilderness", in Showalter, *The New Feminist Criticism: Essays on Women, Literature and Theory,* London, 1986.

7. Proverbs, especially, were a domain where women would have given a dominant shape to the cultural production. It is believed that if lullabies—another arena of female orality and creativity—expressed the tender and softer aspects of female subjectivity, proverbs reflected the hard contempt, the angry satire with which they interpreted the world and its patriarchal order. So closely were women associated with the making and use of proverbs that the first book written for their education—Gourmohan Vidyalankar's *Strishikshavishayak,* written about 1822—used about thirty-five of them in the first chapter. See Sushil Kumar De, *Bangla Prabad: Chhara O Chalti Katha,* Calcutta, 1947.

8. *Nashtaneer,* 1901. See *Galpaguchha,* Vishwabharati Publications, Calcutta, 1994, pp. 385–420. Ray's film that is based on that story is called *Charulata* and was made in 1963.

9. Christian missionaries began to translate their religious literature in Bengali and their needs of conversion gave an impetus to the development of vernacular prose, for which they utilised the services of pandits. In the first decade of the 19th century, men like Ramram Basu and Mrityunjay Vidyalankar wrote the first prose textbooks, but it was Rammohun Roy's translations of sacred texts in the second decade that brought Bengali prose into a usable and acceptable shape. Around the same time, the first Bengali newspapers, brought out under missionary auspices as well as under Rammohun's editorship, refined the prose even further. Ishwarchandra Vidyasagar's writings in the 1850s were still struggling with the problem of inrroducing a proper punctuation system into the prose. The first memorable work of fiction came out in 1858: Tekchand Thakur's *Aaler Ghare Dulal,* a proto-novel, followed by Kaliprasanna Sinha's

short fictional sketches, *Hutom Penchar Naksha,* which, however, used an outrageously earthy and colloquial form. Bankimchandra, who forced the prose into a chaste, more Sanskritised direction, remained the more dominant influence for serious fiction and discursive writings, while the *Hutomi* language got relegated more to the domain of farces and of pulp literature. See Sukumar Sen, *Bangla Sabitya Itihas,* Sahitya Akademi, Calcutta, 1965, pp. 160–72. Women's prose writings did not really lag behind. Kailashbashini's *Hindu Mahilaganer Heenabastha* appeared in 1863.

10. See Sukumar Sen, *Battalar Chhapa O Chhabi,* Ananda Publishers, Calcutta, 1984. Also, Bireshwar Bandyopadhyay, *Heto Bai Heto Chhara,* Calcutta, 1984.

11. M. Bakhtin, in Michael Holquist and Vladimir Lipunov, eds, *Art and Answerability,* trans. Lipunov and Austin; University of Texas Press, 1990, p. 113. For a discussion of the theme of autobiographical writing in Bakhtin, see Uday Kumar, "Bakhtin and Questions of Autobiographical Consummation", unpublished article. I am grateful to him for letting me look at his paper.

12. I am grateful to P. K. Datta for pointing out the specific difference between verb and noun/adjective usages.

13 Kalyani Datta, *Pinjare Bashia,* Stree, Calcutta, 1996, Preface. All translations from Bengali in this book are mine.

2

Her Times, Her Places

I
Bharatbarsha

Bharatbarsha and the large sweep of an entire century that Rashsundari evokes are curiously empty times, empty spaces. Time's flow is captured through her own physical and mental transformations alone—at the most, through certain very broad changes in the world of upper caste women. The evocation of masses of times and spaces, then, seems a gesture against the empirical limits of her own life. The limits, however, somewhere defeat the grand design that she tries to weave into her narrative. Having insisted on a huge spatial and temporal backdrop for herself, she can only try and fill it up with her own sparse body and mind.

Her Bharatbarsha is occasionally filled out in one or two verses as a Hindu—particularly, Vaishnav—pilgrimage circuit. Rashsundari says that she longs to see these holy places and to find out for herself what other pilgrims may seek there. She does not tell us if she did visit them. In all likelihood, she did, since Bengali widows, especially those with affluent sons, were routinely sent off on these highly organised, sacred travels. Nor did she describe any other places that she visited in the course of her long life. Obviously, it was the notion of a vast land mass that was important to her, it was precisely the abstraction of the concept of Bharatbarsha that made her naturalise it as her birthplace, not a more immediate, lived experience that connected her to it.

The long nineteenth century was a time of enormous changes, tribulations and possibilities. Rashsundari seems to have had a strong sense about the flow of time, a teleology that pointed towards positive changes: "Blessed, blessed be the kali age" (kaliyuga, the last age in the four-age cycle in Hindu cosmology). Apart from *strishiksha* or women's education, however, she does not talk much about what justified her confidence. Certain epochal changes—the uprising of 1857, for instance—would have, indeed, been remote to her world, although news of them would surely have percolated down to her village as rumours, as wondrous or horrible tales. Later, as a reading woman, she might well have had access to newspapers, especially since she had educated sons living at home. Some of the news must have stirred her imagination, engaged her sympathies. The work of the reformers, the orthodox and the revivalist resistance to that, the new laws about Hindu marriage practices, are packed into brief reflections on the educational and behavioural worlds of women, into changes that she ascribes to divine intentions and to the passage of time. She does not even talk about the happenings that erupted close to her, that affected her own class and caste: the "indigo riots" or the "Blue Mutiny", the Pabna peasants' uprising, the self-respect movement of low-caste Namasudra peasants of Faridpur, the administrative changes in Pabna and Faridpur that created these two districts in her own lifetime.

Entirely in passing, she does mention a few social facts.

There were the dreaded indigo planter *sahibs* against whom her intrepid husband fought and won lawsuits. There were the local Muslim landlords who encroached upon their tenants' lands. There was a low-caste Namasudra guest who sought their hospitality without prior warning. Her husband seemed to have spent all his time looking after his scattered landed holdings and the lawsuits over them. In contrast, her sons went to distant colleges, the first generation in the family to do so, and they also took up the new liberal professions: one became a lawyer at the Calcutta High Court. They would have swelled the band of absentee landlords. While the husband possessed and read the traditional handwritten manuscripts on sacred themes, the sons studied in schools and colleges and read printed matter. Rashsundari herself was sent printed books through the new postal system. There was also a noticeable spread of education for girls, some anger among the old-timers about it, and a sense that young women were acquiring more confidence and that they looked and dressed differently. We will fill out these details a little in the following section, so that the text makes more sense.

II
Pabna and Faridpur

Rashsundari lived in a Bengal that had been going through very large and long-duration changes in ecological and economic patterns. From the 17th century onwards, and particularly from the 18th century, parts of the land faced a major crisis. The western streams of the Ganga were silting up gradually, leading to the formation of a moribund delta in the region.[1] Agricultural productivity was markedly lowered because of infrequent inundation, and the stagnant waters produced an impressive spate of epidemics and fevers: Burdwan or the Hooghly fever that was a great killer, cholera epidemics from 1817, and smallpox that would rage virulently once every seven years. The silted-up waters, which became even more stagnant with the construction of railway embankments by the colonial state from the mid-century, generated the malaria-bearing annopheles mosquito, causing "intermittent" and "remittent" fevers that went undiagnosed and untreated till about 1897.[2] The dread of either prolonged and fatally weakening fevers or of sudden and unexpected epidemic killers structured the self-awareness of Bengalis by the mid-century, for the ecological changes and their consequences upon general health and mortality had been studied and discussed extensively by the 1830s.[3] Even Rashsundari, not otherwise given to such observations, left a verse on a fever epidemic in her village. She lost several children and grandchildren through illnesses contracted very early in life. In contemporary Bengali literature, contrasts between an earlier era and the present one were made most often in terms of impaired health and longevity. The changes were particularly marked in the western parts of the province which, for the preceding few centuries, had been the most significant and key economic and cultural zone.[4]

In contrast, substantial areas of the eastern parts were well-innundated by regular flows from great rivers whose annual floods left the soil remarkably fertile. The land had been relatively newly reclaimed, and much of it was highly productive, especially with rice and the new jute crops. Cultivation steadily expanded throughout the century. The great rivers and the many waterways provided excellent trading and marketing facilities: Sirajgunje in Pabna, and Goalundo in Faridpur being two notable instances. Pabna, the birthplace of Rashsundari, was bordered along its east face by the main stream of the huge Brahmaputra river and, along its south-west frontier by yet another great river, the Padma. The alluvial soil was criss-crossed with numerous natural waterways, and in the monsoons, villages could be reached only by boat. The regular innundations made the use of irrigation or manure practically unnecessary. Rice was grown in great abundance and jute was introduced in the late 19th century, adding very considerably to the prosperity of the district. *The Imperial Gazetteer* of 1883 noted that no uncultivated spare land was left for expansion, every part of the district now being maximally cultivated. The climate was mild and healthy, but for some relatively less virulent forms of malaria and dysentery. Cholera epidemics, however, were chronic and an annual occurrence. But taking everything into consideration, Pabna was one of the most fortunate of Bengal's provinces.[5]

Faridpur had a wilder landscape. While the northern part was comparatively well-raised and lay above water, at least in summer and in winter, the level below the Faridpur town dipped, until the southern parts that bordered on Barisal sank into a single vast swamp that was never completely dry. Villages were strung along the river banks, houses being constructed on raised platforms. They were surrounded by, in the words of colonial officials, "picturesque jungles of bamboos, betel palms and plantains." Boats were almost the only mode of transport throughout the year. The district formed a sort of a tongue between two huge rivers—the Padma and the Madhumati, and the intersecting land was cut through by innumerable distributaries, swamps and waterways, the chief of which was the massive Ariyal Khan. Faridpur shared with Pabna the magnificent river Brahmaputra along which Rashsundari must have travelled for three days to come to her new home after her wedding. With so much water around, fisheries were a major source of income and so was rice, but not jute. Neither the government nor the large landholders had, till the close of the century, done anything about draining the swamps and marshes. With the beginning of the rains, the greater part of the district would, therefore, go under water as the floods came in and left their deposits behind. The climate was very damp, and there was a great deal of malaria around.[6]

Rashsundari spent most of her life in village Ramdia which was located in the Rajbari subdivision, to the north of the district. The Padma flowed quite close to the subdivision while to the west of it a smaller river, Channana or Chandana, went by.[7] I came across a religious tract on the wanderings of a *sadhu,* Bhulua Baba, who was touring those parts in the 1880s, preaching, through *kirtan*-based songs, a form of anti-untouchability. He also preached more tolerance for women. There are vivid descriptions of his four-day stay in Ramdia, at a time when Rashsundari would have been composing the second part of her autobiography. Though she does not mention him, she would surely have heard him or of him. It seems that the village gentry was deeply involved in Vaishnav congregational activities—discussions, disputations, *kirtan*-singing and ritual feasting. Late 19th century Bengal witnessed a revival of ardent Vaishnavism, and the travels of Bhulua Baba capture some of its spirit. Bhulua Baba's host was a rich and devout Vaishnav of the Subarnavanik caste which suffered from low ritual ranking. Water from his hands was regarded as impure among the high castes in this village although he would be counted as a member of the higher echelons of the Shudra category who could offer water to brahmans elsewhere. He was a deeply pious man, much given to daily reading from sacred manuscripts, patronising holy men and going on pilgrimages.

Faridpur—in fact, most of Eastern Bengal—saw a compromise between ardent Vaishnavism and brahmanical orthodoxy. The strength of Vaishnav movements, sects, institutions and temple networks was considerable, but it depended on and reinforced the social leadership of conservative brahmans. Caste rules were even more rigid here among Vaishnavs than elsewhere.[8] It seems that ritual and caste observances were even more rigid at Ramdia and the Baba tried to wean away the villagers from it. He was able to defeat more conservative pandits at public disputations which were excellently attended by the village notables who must have included some of Rashsundari's own family members. He also organised recitations from *Bhagavat Puran* every night, preceded by collective devotional singing in the evenings.[9] The wave of devotional fervour and piety that swept over Bengal, at that time going through the peak point of Hindu revivalism, would have probably conditioned the declamatory enunciations in the second part of *AJ* which come close to the form of public *kathas* and *paths*, recitations and expoundings of sacred themes and passages.

It is significant that even though Pabna and Faridpur were Muslim majority districts, Rashsundari does not refer to any direct encounter with Muslim figures, though she mentions an epistolary exchange with a Muslim landlord of a rival family. At the same time, the absence of social interaction did not prevent cultural sharing. In a verse, she very easily brings in the *Koran* among Hindu religious scriptures.

III
Bengali Zamindars

Rashsundari moved from one landed, upper-caste household to another between Pabna and Faridpur. The landed gentry had a position of peculiar importance in the colonial economy of Bengal. In the first place, it was overwhelmingly Hindu and upper caste. Secondly, far from being a bourgeoisie in the established sense of the term, the Bengali middle class was singularly dependent on various categories of rent income from land. The connections of this class with productive forces were markedly passive. The Permanent Settlement—the revenue arrangement that prevailed in colonial Bengal—had generated a permanent gap between rent, which was elastic, and revenue, that was fixed. The gap ensured a wide spectrum of fairly comfortable parasitic rentier incomes at many levels. They also left tenants—often low-caste or Muslim—extremely vulnerable to arbitrary rent hikes, extra-legal cesses, and even eviction on charges of non-payment of rent.[10] Certainties of an absolute manipulative power over rent began to be breached— although in a very limited sense—from the mid-19th century, when the Rent Acts of 1859 and 1885 were passed. They were intended to give a measure of security to an upper category of tenants and to curb some of the arbitrary coercive powers exercised by the landlords' *cutchheries,* or unofficial courtrooms cum lock ups. *AJ* refers to the long hours that the *karta* or the master of the household, would spend there. The Rent Act of 1859 had come about partly as a result of missionary pleas on behalf of the tenant. After the Act had been passed, landlords started complaining that it had eroded their moral authority over the tenants and had affected rent collection.[11]

Men with surplus capital chose to invest mostly in landholding, partly because of the initial amenities that the unrevised Permanent Settlement had offered, but partly, also, because they lacked safe investment alternatives. Except for a few exceptional experiments, however, most of them were parasitic rentiers rather than active, improving landlords. Their relationship to property was non-dynamic, not properly entrepreneurial. Rashsundari's husband spent most of his "business hours" looking after rent collection at the *cutchhery* or fighting civil suits over property cases. This became the only function of resident landlords after the mid-century, while a substantial number would be, unlike the *karta*, absentee landlords, residents of Calcutta or district towns and combining earnings from rent with professional fixed incomes. Some of Rashsundari's sons would belong to this category.

After the 1840s, especially with the collapse of the Union Bank, major Bengali financial and commercial ventures went into a terminal crisis. By the end of the century, trade, manufacturing and industry, on any significant scale, had come to be controlled by Europeans and non-Bengalis.[12] Land was, therefore, much the safest field of investment, especially after the financial disasters of the 1840s, when profits and capital of many Bengali entrepreneurial families were wiped out, thanks partly to an extremely racially-structured colonial economy. A few large landlords were, indeed, trying to experiment with improving measures in agriculture that might, conceivably, have transformed them from parasitic rentiers to the first generation of capitalist landlords.[13]

The redoubled dependence on landholding after the spate of business depression in the 1840s, moreover, coincided with the onset of some changes in the untrammelled nature of the rent offensive that the gentry had so far been allowed to enjoy under the Permanent Settlement. While the new rent acts empowered the upper tenants with occupancy rights, from the early seventies, peasant organisations and movements created a great scare about the security of land investments among landlords.

In 1873, shortly before Rashsundari's book came out, her

birthplace Pabna witnessed an unprecedented form of tenant agitation. In the *pargana* (fiscal division) of Yusufshahi, that was now under five zamindari houses, tenants organised themselves to protest against illegal cesses and against the reduction in the standard of the measuring pole that was used on tenant lands. They resisted payments to zamindars and contested claims of enhancement in law courts. Even though the police counterattacked on behalf of landlords and arrested hundreds of recalcitrant tenants, the movement made some impact on colonial officialdom, inclining the Government towards a new rent Act.[14] The developments were deeply threatening to the class/caste hegemony of the Hindu gentry since it threw into sharp relief the pretensions of its paternalist self-image. In the agitation against the European indigo planters in the previous decade, the landlords had occasionally supported peasant refusal to cultivate indigo and had confronted the planters. Rashsundari wrote with pride about how her husband brought lawsuits against these planters: clearly, the memories of the rising would endow such action with a certain measure of heroism. With the Pabna uprising, however, the gentry's pretence to a symbiotic relationship with peasants collapsed.

At the same time, the caste authority of the landed gentry was challenged at Faridpur, and at other places, by a self-respect movement by untouchable Namasudra tenants that included, among other things, a refusal to cultivate the land of upper castes and a refusal to eat the food cooked by them.[15] The unexpected Namasudra guest who had deprived Rashsundari of her lunch, would no longer accept food cooked by her. Such developments were deeply troublesome in themselves. The government added to the profound discomforts of the gentry by beginning to ponder upon some form of affirmative action for lower castes.[16] One offshoot of such deliberations was the somewhat better educational facilities that Lt. Governor Campbell introduced for the Namasudras in Faridpur.[17] We shall later look into the visions of a comprehensive catastrophe that the prospects for education of the women of their class and caste had churned up among upper caste and middle class men. The education of low castes would, perhaps, indicate a greater crisis, for, in the late colonial period, higher education had already emerged as the principal gateway to social power, adding access to influential and well-paid professions to the existing profits from landholding. Access to education, therefore, was a major marker of social difference. Rashsundari's husband had been a full-time landlord. Her sons went in for the new education and the new professions. Any sharing of educational privileges with more deprived groups would be regarded as a serious diminution of hegemony.

IV
Women as Caste/Class Subjects

Rashsundari was a landlord's daughter and a landlord's wife. She, however, makes no mention of such stirring and disturbing events so near her own home. She does talk of her tenants, describing them as "subjects" (*proja,* the Sanskrit word, that in Bengali would mean both tenant and subject: the Persian equivalent was *ryot*) but the only incident that she mentions in that connection is the one where she intervened, at the behest of the wives of oppressed tenants, to save the latter from a tyrannical local landlord. She thus confirms the fact of oppression—albeit by a hostile neighbour—but she does not comment on the disobedient tenants whose rebellious actions in the 1870s must have struck terror into the hearts of the men of her class, her caste, possibly her family. Nor does she

refer to the bold defiance of the Namasudras, although such
an untoward tendency would have fuelled much talk about
kaliyuga among her contemporaries. From her significant
silence in this area, it seems that she did not share the anxieties
of the men of her class, at least not to a great extent.

One striking thing about her narrative is that she does not
begin it in the customary manner, with a verse colophon to
describe her caste, lineage and family details. The presentation
of these facts was a familiar mode of self-revelation, whether
in Vaishnav hagiographies or in most of the contemporary
women's writings, or in male autobiographies of those times.
Women's writings, however, had much thinner accounts in
this respect, often stopping with the father's name and the
mention of the place of the author's birth. Rashsundari has no
detail whatsoever on offer.

Under the *Dayabhaga* school of Hindu law that prevailed
in Bengal, women neither inherited their father's land nor
did they have definite or absolute rights to the land of their
husbands: at most, they had usufruct rights in the case of minor
sons when they were widowed.[18] The absence of right to land
inheritance, parental or matrimonial, the change of lineage
through marriage, the patrilocal custom of moving into a new
and unfamiliar residence would have probably combined to
create an ambiguous and thin integration with family and
lineage on both sides. The woman—even of a class and a caste
that enjoyed privileges, authority and power—might have felt
an inhibition about claiming the identity that class, caste and
lineage confer. She would remain a somewhat incomplete
class and caste subject.

E. P. Thompson has argued that the notations of class
derived from the categories of a fully industrialised set-
up would be misleading when applied to a different social

formation. If 19th century Bengal presented a more fluid
and inchoate picture of class relations than those which
obtain in an established capitalist structure, then we may have
something to learn about the ways of understanding the social
perspectives of subordinated groups in weakly industrialised
societies from him: "For what may define the consciousness
of these groups more clearly will be such factors as their *degree
of dependency;* that is, their dependence on or independence
of the lines of interest, influence, preferments and patronage
which structured that society from top to bottom." He
argues that tradesmen and artisans enjoyed a large degree
of occupational independence from interest and patronage
and hence were able to nourish "a more robust anti-court
and sometimes republican consciousness" in 17th and 18th
century England.[19]

With an upper-caste, affluent gentlewoman like
Rashsundari, we find a more compromised and complicated
relationship with the distribution of social and economic
power and influence. On the one hand, they were women of
high caste, important families and had a great deal of overall
economic security, whatever the daily small-scale personal
privations were. They certainly enjoyed an incomparably
higher standard of living than people from subordinated
social groups. They had power over their servants and even
over their tenants and day-labourers. On the other hand, they
had little money of their own, as the Dayabhaga system since
the times of Raghunandan had reduced the woman's access
to *stridhan* or bridal gifts.[20] They had no absolute ownership
rights over their father's or their husband's property. They
were people without incomes, more dependent economically
then the poorest day-labourer. Within the family, they were
objects of disciplining, they provided service and deference

through signs that were quite similar to those observed by low castes and classes vis-à-vis their social superiors. They were not as directly and actively implicated in relations of domination and exploitation of tenants, labourers and low castes as their men would be. In *AJ*, the *cutchhery* is a remote, distant place and her husband's property dealings take place without her knowledge, far less her consent. We also find her engaged in very heavy, daily labour at home and she was as familiar with starvation as her poorest tenant would be. Perhaps, that is why she made friends with the maid-servants of her new family so quickly as a young bride, despite the great gap in status.

These extremes of privation and labour—even within the privileged order—detached the woman somewhat from processes of exploitation and full class and caste membership. It aligned her to some extent with the worst-exploited social categories of that order. It is significant that the great 19th century reformer of low castes, Jotirao Phule, had bracketed the brahman woman along with shudra and untouchable castes as victims of brahmanical domination.[21] So her subordination ensured a space of relative autonomy, unmarked by the vested interests of her family.

The alignment, again, was limited as well as temporary. We have just looked at some of the limits. It was also often a passing thing. With the onset of middle age and the acquisition of that most important form of human capital—sons—the woman from a privileged family may enter a time of power, authority, decision-making, larger freedom and mobility. She is then exempted from much of the burden of household labour and the manifold restrictions that younger wives have to observe. She can exercise considerable disciplining power herself on a new generation of subordinate women of the family—the daughters-in-law. Moreover, even young wives were better off in material and status terms than widows, infertile women, women without sons or improvident, dependent kinswomen who usually suffered from a much sharper degree of material deprivation, ritual dishonour and labour burden than even the young wives. When talking of her happy middle age when she is relieved of the burden of childbearing, Rashsundari talks of "her" household. The woman then gets stitched into the fabric of her class, caste, lineage.

We tend to absolutise male and female domains in much feminist writing and see them as seamless blocs, forming opposites of total power and total powerlessness. Patriarchy, however, operates through far more complicated trajectories, with criss-crossings of powerlines according to various subjectivities within class, caste and privilege. Even within the female world, sharply delineated, internal powerlines run that shift course according to domestic status, changes in the life-cycle and material circumstances. The same woman goes through extremes of helplessness as well as great authority in the same lifetime, as we have seen in Rashsundari's case. She gets to know both subjection and the taste of ruling. That is why and how, perhaps, women are, most of the time, complicit subjects of patriarchy.

V
The Domestic Sphere

Let us get back to the makings of the profound sense of crisis for the Hindu upper caste, landowning middle class. Colonial rule had deprived it of political/military/administrative authority. Activism, whether in land relations, or in trade, finance or manufacture, had been definitively eroded by the 1870s. Since an autonomous sphere did not develop within civil society where the middle classes would dictate their terms to production forces and relations, their social privileges and claims for self-rule and autonomy could only be confirmed in the sphere of human relations within the Hindu home, the Hindu joint family, Hindu conjugal norms. They would require an assertion of full authority over the lives of its women. Women were also the signifiers of the autonomy of Hindu laws and their discipline, whereas colonial rule had allegedly compromised the man through its education and culture. The woman, as ruled entirely by Hindu scripture and Hindu custom, was perceived as the site of a past freedom as well as of an emergent nationhood.

And, it was precisely in the nineteenth century, that the Hindu woman became the most disturbing site of a possible challenge to their hegemonic claims. Upto the 1870s—when *AJ* came out for the first time—the standard domestic regulations would include a very early marriage before menarche could set in, so that the *garbhadhan* ceremony or ritual cohabitation with the husband would be performed as soon as the girl entered puberty; an indissoluble, non-consensual marriage with a man who could be of any age at all and who might well have more wives, for male polygamy was permitted but a woman was allowed only one husband in a lifetime. Widow remarriage was legalised by mid-century, but the ritual repugnance against it remained and it was extremely uncommon even for child-widows. Life in the matrimonial residence implied a battery of severe restrictions on movements and gestures and speech, while widowhood meant a draconian disciplining of diet and dress: fortnightly ritual fasting without even a drink of water was often mandatory. Originally emanating from upper caste households, such norms had become fairly widespread among households from lower subcastes that aspired towards respectability and that could afford to pull out women from productive labour outside the home.[22] Within the household, women still continued to perform a number of tasks that completed agricultural or artisanal work—threshing of grain, for example, or spinning—but these did not generate any income. Quite a few times, *AJ*, too, confirms the dark landscape of upper-caste domesticity.

The entire century was deeply preoccupied with a number of fundamental changes in the practices and the mode of being of the upper-caste Hindu woman. Changes had been inaugurated with the agitation for the banning of widow immolation and they were continued by social reformers and dissident religious sects like the Brahmo Samaj from the middle classes. The movement for widow remarriage threatened to split Hindu society right down the middle. The 1870s saw the introduction of a most radical civil marriage law. There were moves to abolish child marriage, to give the woman the fight to divorce, to give her an education. Finally, in the last decade, the Age of Consent debates over raising the age to twelve from ten, created something like a mass level anti-colonial agitation. It was argued that since in the hot climate of Bengal, a girl could reach puberty before she was twelve, the new law would interfere with the performance of *garbhadhan* at the ritually appointed time. All sons, born to such a woman, would be incapable of making the ritual offerings to ancestral spirits, for the purity of the mother's womb had been compromised.[23]

The non-consensual, indissoluble, infant marriage system, with its attendant ban on widow remarriage and its tolerance of polygamy, was a structure that was now continuously under siege. The debates between the reformers and the orthodox and the late 19th-century revivalists gradually clarified the ideological basis of the norms and the injunctions. There was a keen sense of the fragility of the economic and the domestic privileges of the Bengali elite. This was the kaliyuga that Rashsundari heard men around her talking about. And this is the age that she celebrates, along with many other women writers, again and again. The woman's consent to the discipline of her own men—like the supposed consent of peasants and low castes to the social order—could no longer be taken for granted. Clearly, the moral order of Hindu patriarchy was at peril.

In the course of the 19th century, then, through social and religious reforms, through movements for women's education and through the new laws around Hindu marriage practices, we witness a shift away from an order of interdictions under which virtue was defined as strict adherence to prescriptions without active ethical self-creation. We find the evolution of a situation where Hindu patriarchy had been exhaustively discussed, thoroughly problematised and rendered uncertain— both in its orthodox residue and in its emergent reformist manifestations, since both questioned each other ceaselessly. Now both defenders and opponents of all systems needed active forms of self-subjectivisation and a far more engaged assessment of the morality of the practices. We have something corresponding to what Foucault might describe as a transition from "code-oriented moralities" to "ethics-oriented moralities."[24]

Notes

1. See Peter Marshall, *Bengal: The British Period in Eastern India 1740–1828,* CUP, 1987, p. 4.
2. See Frank Perlin, "Proto-Industrialisation and Pre-Colonial South Asia" in *Past and Present,* 1983, p. 56; also, Marshall, op cit,

pp. 5, 18-19. Also Benoy. B. Chowdhury, "Agrarian Economy and Agrarian Relations in Bengal, 1859–1885" in N.K. Sinha, ed, *The History of Bengal,* Calcutta, 1967, pp. 241–43.

3.   Marshall, op cit, p. 4.

4.   See Rajnarain Basu, *Sekal O Ekal,* reprinted, Calcutta, 1988, p. 31–36. I have discussed this trope in Bengali writings on colonialism and modernity in my "The Hindu Wife and the Hindu Nation: Domesticity and Nationalism in Nineteenth Century Bengal" in *Studies in History,* New Series, July-December, 1992.

5.   W.W. Hunter, *The Imperial Gazetteer of India,* Vol.V, ii, London, 1883, pp. 238–244.

6.   Ibid, pp. 242–247.

7.   L.S.S. O'Malley, *Faridpur District Gazetteer,* Calcutta, 1925.

8.   Ramakanta Chakravarti, *Vaishnavism in Bengal, 1486–1900,* Sanskrit Pustak Bhandar, Calcutta, 1985, pp. 275–304.

9.   Bhulua Baba, *Haribol Thakur,* Pabna, published circa 1935, pp. 61–70.

10.   See Ranajit Guha, *A Rule of Property for Bengal: An Essay on the Idea of Permanent Settlement,* Monton & Co., Paris, 1963, Ch. 6, pp. 187–99.

11.   Chowdury, op cit, 295–99.

12.   See Amales Tripathi, *Trade and Fmace in the Bengal Presidency, 1793–1833,* Calcutta, 1979, ch. 5.

13.   See Nilmoni Mukherji, *A Bengal Zamindar: Jayakrishna Mukherjee of Uttarpara and His Times,* Calcutta, 1975, chs 5–12.

14.   See W.W. Hunter, op cit, p. 239. Also K.K. Sengupta, *Pabna Disturbances and the Politics of Rent: 1873–1885,* Delhi, 1974.

15.   See Sekhar Bandyopadhyay, "Social Mobility in Bengal in the Late 19th and Early 20th Centuries", unpublished thesis, University of Calcutta, 1985, ch 5.

16.   Sekhar Bandyopadhyay, *Caste, Politics and the Raj: Bengal 1872–1937,* Calcutta, 1990; also his *Caste, Protest and Identity*

in Colonial India: The Namasudra of Bengal 1872–1947, London, studies on South Asia, Curzon Press, 1997, pp. 30–64.

17. W.W. Hunter, op cit, p. 248.

18. See Roop L. Choudhry, *Hindu Woman's Right to Property (Past and Present),* Firima K.L. Mukhopadhyay, Calcutta, 1961. pp. 1–6.

19. E.P. Thompson, *Witness against the Beast: William Blake and the Moral Law,* New Press, New York, 1993, pp 110–11.

20. Sureshchandra Bandyopadhyay, *Smitishastre Bangali,* A. Mukherjee & Co., Calcutta, 1959, pp. 8–18.

21. Rosalind O'Hanlon, *Caste, Conflict and Ideology: Mahatma Jotirao Phule and Low Caste Protest in Nineteenth Century Western India,* Cambridge University Press, Cambridge, 1985, pp. 189–206.

22. On the downward percolation of the custom of infant marriage, and the ban on widow remarriage, throughout the 19th century, see H.H. Risley, *The Tribes and Castes of Bengal, Ethnographic Glossary,* Vol. I, Calcutta 1891. Calcutta reprint 1981, Introduction.

23. See Tanika Sarkar, "Rhetoric against the Age of Consent: Resisting Colonial Reason and the Death of a Child Wife", *Economic and Political Weekly,* 4 September, 1993.

24. Michel Foucault, *The Use of Pleasure: The History of Sexuality,* Vol 2, New York, 1986, pp. 29–30.

3

The Changing World of Religion

I
Sansar and Ways Beyond It

Rashsundari was born and brought up to live out her life as an illiterate, upper-caste, rural housewife. Two things, however, worked on her and set her apart from her inherited conditions. One was her own times when a few women like her were able to acquire a new kind of education—a development that we shall explore in our next chapter. The other factor—our present concern—was her active, restless and questioning *bhakti* that drew together broken, fragmentary, half-familiar strands from multiple Hindu religious discourses. Her intellectual efforts succeeded in pulling them together into a whole narrative, though it was not a distinctive system or cosmology that emerged out of them. What is striking is the relationship she establishes between her individual understanding and her life—something that she brings out through a series of questions addressed to God. At first, they seem to lead nowhere in particular. In the end, however, we realise that entirely through the manner in which she poses the questions, she has been able to build up a striking vision of God and his designs for the human devotee.

By making her autobiography and her piety dependent
upon each other, Rashsundari tried to make two statements.
The fact of writing her life proved that it could not have been
done without being the Chosen One of God. At the same
time, she needed to problematise her relationship with her
household or *sansar* since, on the face of it, *sansar* seemed to
define her entire identity. We need to explore the different
meanings of *sansar* in Hindu religious discourses and also locate
the forms of excess beyond it that were held out by strands
within various theological traditions. We can then identify the
ways in which *AJ* drew upon as well as departed from them.

Sansar is the realm of the householder, the stage of *garhasthya*,
a vital middle phase in the four-stage life-cycle. Only an ascetic
may renounce the domain of worldly responsibilities. Rules for
this life vary according to caste and gender differences. They
are spelt out by the *Vedas* or the *Sruti* and by the subsequent
sacred law codes—the *Smriti* literature.[1] The rules of
prescribed and forbidden behaviour *(vidhi-nishedha)*, constitute
the essence of *dharma* or a pious existence for the householder.
The woman enters *sansar* through the sacrament of marriage,
the only sacrament that is available to her. For her, *sansar* is the
unending flow of domestic work and responsibilities and of
female rites and ritual observances.

In a broader theological sense, *sansar* is sustained by the
rule of *karma*. This is the conviction that actions performed
in one life bear results in subsequent ones, through a chain
of rebirths. Only a strict adherence to the rules of *sansar* will
eventually wear out the fruits of past action and release the
human being from the *karmic* order and the chain of rebirths
which is fundamentally painful. *Sansar* is thus the site of *dharma*
as well as a site of trials. Rashsundari accepted this definition
of *sansar* but there is surprisingly little use of the key term of

karma in her text. She, however, uses some of the influential concepts connected with the various forms of excess beyond *sansar,* while modulating them in rather distinctive ways.

The *Upanishadic* sequels to the *Vedas* lay down the basic parameters of metaphysical speculation: the true nature of and relationships between the human self-soul, and the Creator. While they do not contradict at all the rule of *vidhi-nishedha,* they do go beyond it. They postulate an ultimate and fundamental identity between *Brahman* or absolute reality and *Atman* or the individual self. The enlightened sage may, in a flash of revelation, grasp the non-division of experience, experiencer and object of experience. The revelation lifts him above time and space and the law of causation and fills him with bliss. Here is a latent possibility that spiritually the *karmic* order may be inverted and the absolute validity of a stratified world order undermined. The possibility, however, is immediately undercut by the explicit endorsement of the *karmic* order and its injunctions. It is also undone by the fact that the possibility of transcendence is entirely in the realm of ideas and is accessible to the enlightened sage alone.[2]

Post-Vedic brahmanical thinking also begins to introduce a very different theme; the reality of a personalised God, of the validity of human devotion for a separated and irrevocably-distanced Creator for whom the distance opens up a space for intense adoration or *bhakti.* The state of adoration is occasionally privileged even over the blissful realisation of non-separation. This strand was elaborated by yet another sacred text *(Bhagavad Gita)* that was a part of the *Mahabharata* and that was narrated as an event within the epic. Yet, simultaneously, the *Gita* was and remains, a text of great importance in itself. Its presence is essential for sanctifying spaces and times. Modern Hindus, for instance, take their oath in law courts on the *Gita.* On the one hand, it tried to shore up the *karmic* order, insisting on unquestioning adherence to injunctions on appropriate caste and gender roles, and prescribed such actions as the only basis for a religious life: *Karmanyevadhikaraste ma phaleshu kadachana* (you can only perform the prescribed action, you may never consider its consequence). Overarching the given, inflexible prescriptions, on the other hand, is the exalting faith in a personalised God, embodied in Krishna who has a life story for the devotee to reflect upon and to adore. On the eve of the apocalyptic, epic battle among brothers, Krishna admonishes a demoralised Arjuna who hesitates to strike against his own kinsmen. He convinces Arjuna of his purely instrumental role within the *karmic* order that is ordained by Krishna himself. He physically demonstrates that it is his maw that continuously issues forth and swallows up all creatures, that Arjuna can cause nothing to happen, that Krishna himself is Time that destroys all. Arjuna's response to the revelation is devotion, not the intensely emotional kind that is associated with later Krishnabhakti, but a form of devoutness that is grounded in intellectual comprehension, in a form of *yoga*. However, the commitment to a particular person can open the doors to more emotionalised forms. Rashsundari, especially in her verses and her reflections, chooses an emotionalised articulation. Yet, she insists, her way to God was first found through intellectual understanding, through a reception of difficult religious concepts conveyed by her mother. Since the recitation of *Gita* would be an essential feature of life-cycle rites, especially the funerary and ancestral rites, Rashsundari would surely have received some knowledge about the inexorable rule of *karma* which functions through caste-ordained prescriptions, whose violation constitutes the fall of *dharma* or virtue, piety. She, however, does not derive any of the basic terms of her religious vocabulary from them. *Karma,* in her verses, refers to the weakness of devotional life in this birth and the resultant sinfulness; it does not refer to the essential category of caste-related *dharma.*

The note of intense adoration is framed by a yet higher order of truth: the true origin in and ultimate return of all selves to an undivided Absolute Reality. In her very first lesson on the nature of divinity, we find Rashsundari's mother referring to several distinct levels within the notion of God. We have here a play on several different comprehensions of truth, none of which negates the other, but each being available to a particular kind of devotee, prescribing a different order of knowledge, action and social existence. Contradictions are acknowledged yet dissolved in the same move, without reaching a synthesis as a singular truth.[3]

Buddhism, from the 6th century onwards, had held out the possibility of a non-divided order of moral conduct, knowledge and action. It had also questioned the Vedic forms of religious life that centred around the performance of sacrifices and the social and caste hierarchies that were organised around them. With a fast-developing division of labour that saw a growth in the importance of classes engaged in agriculture and trade, Buddhist doctrines had some potential for social levelling.

Shankara's monistic philosophy tried to grapple with the social and intellectual challenges of Buddhism on two simultaneous registers, denying, however, the softer alternative of devotion to a personalised God. He reinstated an authoritarian rule of *vidhi-nishedha* as the only *dharma* in the material, empirical world. While nothing at all may soften or modify the injunctions of the *sniti* and *smriti,* for one striving towards a higher order/meaning of existence, the *Upanishadic* parts alone are relevant. So we have a gradation of aspirants as much as a gradation within knowledge—the notion of *adhikarbhed,* fundamental to Hinduism. For one who seeks to understand the relationship between the human soul and Absolute Reality, *shabda* or the words of the *Upanishads* constitute the only appropriate source of knowledge *(praman).* Sense perceptions cannot comprehend *Brahman* or Absolute Reality since *Brahman* is entirely formless and attributeless. Any attempt at understanding through the senses will, therefore, impose a false form. The Vedic *karmakanda,* being preoccupied with empirical reality, is also inadequate for a sense of a reality unconnected with materiality. *Brahman,* moreover, is the eternal subject, the sole repository of pure awareness *(chaitanya).* The knower cannot be an object of knowledge since it will be absurd to conceive of the subject as object. It is equally absurd to conceive of *Brahman* as both subject and object since the two are, by nature, entirely opposed. What *shabda* can do is to rectify false knowledge or *abidya* and correct the boundaries of what is already known within limits. It cannot demonstrate *Brahman.*

If *Brahman* as self is not an object of perception, neither is he entirely unknown: Rashsundari says, who can have perfect knowledge of you?, implying that some kind of knowledge does exist. Shankara grounds this imperfect knowledge in the universal sense: "I exist". Had there been no self, the feeling could not have existed. That self is *Brahman.* However, such apprehension is limited or *samanya gyan.* More precise knowledge or *vishesh gyan* would resist the imposition of a sense-apprehended notion of the self (I know or I exist) on an understanding of *Brahman* who is beyond and without the senses.

Shankara also creates levels within truth. We begin to understand why an erudite scholar like Jyotirindranath was so excited by the nature of Rashsundari's mother's instructions: the terms of a graded religious truth reach out to the realms of the most complex philosophical traditions. At the lowest rung, there is a divine creator or *Ishwar,* but a higher truth lies with the conception of *Brahman* who is without form or attributes *(nirguna* and *nirakar)* but who is pure existence, pure consciousness, pure bliss—*sacchitananda.* Yet, there is an even higher reality that strips *Brahman* of these qualities, or rather, adds to them what is not existence, not consciousness, not bliss. That *Brahman* is a single essence, without any distinction between creator and creation. The world and the individual selves that seem to populate it are the function of *Brahman's maya,* an illusion-bearing power which creates appearances. Owing to its operations, the self erroneously identifies itself with a being—material, finite, separated. One who has attained freedom from all bonds of attachments, who can distinguish between eternal and temporal things and has control over the senses and the mind, may recover the forgotten truth of the essential oneness of all being. He can attain liberation from the *karmic* order *(moksha)* and he can even achieve it while he is still living in this world *(jivanmukti).* The attainment depends on a course of instruction from an enlightened preceptor.[4]

In the nature of things, the enlightened preceptor who has access to Upanishadic knowledge and the aspirant are both brahman males. Shankara's insistence on the absolute validity of the laws of the social world rules out the possibility that it may be otherwise. If eternal truth demonstrates the falsity of divided and conflicted egos, if it is grounded on the non-division of all beings from one another and from Absolute Reality, then the other part of Shankara's teaching makes sure that such knowledge is withheld from women, from low castes, according to *vidhi-nishedha.*

It is interesting that while the source of human sorrow is located in a stratified and self-divided world order, a transcendence is sought only in the realm of metaphysical knowledge. At the same time, the more the empirical world is left intact, the more intense is the metaphysical emphasis on the essential oneness of all selves. While Shankara's monistic philosophy belongs to the regions of immensely erudite speculation, the sense of a dichotomy between appearances and reality that is obscured by the force of *maya,* slid into a popular common sense, into a familiar vocabulary for talking about religious matters. Rashsundari's verses are resonant with this notion. Her religion, however, is entirely dualistic, postulating a firm division between Creator and creation. Nor is her Parameshwara without attributes or beyond the senses.

If ultimate knowledge is for the initiated, then what remains beyond it for the spiritual needs of the ordinary folk? Post-Shankara devotional traditions or *bhakti*—with their accommodation of a personalised divinity with a form, attributes and a mythological life-story, provided the same excess beyond *sansar* that knowledge is meant to provide to the initiated. Both allow the aspirant to partly create her own religious life and thinking beyond the terms set by *sansar,* to found a realm of individual creativity and spiritual labour, the fruits of which cannot be expropriated.

Medieval *bhakti* movements, fructified by creative encounters with Sufi mystical traditions, restored the gap between the Creator and creation to allow devotional emotions to come into play. By the 15th century, there were four major modifications of absolute monism, leadng to four major *bhakti* sects. Ramanuj's *vishishbtadwaitavad* (circa 11th century) claimed that the self is a part of *Brahman* but it is temporarily separated from it by *maya* whose removal through *bhakti* would lead to a reunification. Maddhvacharyya's *Dwaitavad* (circa 12th century), on the other hand, claimed that the self and the world are as real as Brahman and, within this duality, they are subordinate to Brahman. Nimbarka's *Dwaitadivaitavad* (circa 11th—12th centuries) posits a dualistic non-duality which sees the self as different from Brahman in attributes and functions, yet it is dependent on Brahman, sharing in part of his attributes. The Bengali Vaishnavite canon—*achintyabhedabhed* of Gaudiya Vaishnav theology—was a variant of this school. Around the 15th-l6th centuries, Ballabhacharyya proclaimed *vishudhhadivaitavad* which denied *maya* and restored all appearances to the single reality of Brahman, who, however, is merged in the figure of Krishna.[5]

In *AJ* we find fragments of all this at play, demonstrating not simply the circularity between erudite theological systems and popular beliefs, but also the operations of a self-created religious life that each *bhakt* may compose out of more dominant and coherent systems. What we have here is not the unconscious, long-term assemblage—bricolage—by collective "savage" minds, but a highly deliberate and individualistic composition. Rashsundari seems to take a fundamental duality for granted, that is more extreme than that accepted by any of the major schools. Not only does her life stay separated from God's till the end, she is at pains to underline the contrast between the two at every point. All she hopes for is not a merger at the end of life, but "the attainment of his lotus feet"—recovery of a closer arid more intimate form of subordination. It is, in fact, the contrast, the hierarchised differences in attributes, that compels devotion.

She uses *maya* in a very specific sense. At its source, it is more akin to the other, non-theological meaning of the Bengali word that denotes fondness, attachment to things or persons dear to one's life but who are, nonetheless, elusive. The poignancy that is associated with this kind of attachment is underlined through the entry of death, again and again, to terminate the precious and fragile attachment. It is the divinely ordained cruel finality of death, rather than *bhakti* or knowledge that teaches her to acknowledge this attachment as fundamentally transient and hence, illusory; to recover, in other words, the theological meaning of *maya*. The removal of the curtain of *maya*, however, reveals ultimate reality not as bliss or non-separation, but as a mangled human life whose every attachment has been hopelessly mauled by an inflexible, unalterable and inscrutable divine will.

II
Krishnabhakti

Bhagavat Puran (henceforth *BP*), composed sometime between the 9th and 10th centuries, tried a synthesis between monistic Advaita and theistic *bhakti*, in the process, however, giving Krishnabhakti its strongest emotional and aesthetic form. The Krishna cult itself is far older than this text and the notion of his divine sport or *leela* has been elaborated through *Harivamsa, Vishnupuran, Padmapuran* and *Brahmavaivartapuran*. The *BP*, however, introduced crucial reorientations and emphases within the cult which makes it the most sacred text for Bengali Vaishnavs. It also renders Vrindavan—the pilgrimage on the Yamuna banks where Krishna's childhood and erotic *leela* was performed—the most sacred space for them.

We have, yet again, a spiralling of very different and simultaneous conceptions of divinity or Absolute Reality. The outer and final concentric circle is the notion of non-dual consciousness which is both immanent and transcendent and which is designated as *Brahman* or *Pammatman* (supreme soul). Rashsundari's usage of the word Parameshwara comes close to this word and its meaning. Yet, within an enclosed, second circle, the Supreme Soul is also the human self as well as all that which lies beyond it. It is all that the human self can be but be so only in broken snatches, through and in right knowledge. While asserting the primacy of knowledge, this level also creates the point of contact between the ultimate reality and the finite individual self. The contact is filled out when the self merges itself in the contemplation of Krishnaleela at Vrindavan. For, at the third, yet the most significant level, the supreme soul is apprehended as Bhagawan Krishna.

Creation comes into being when the creator wants to play with his own shadows. This desire is fulfilled through *yogamaya* which denotes the principle of plurality charged with divine majesty and with the potency of the Absolute. In *BP* the play is given a sensuous, continuous form. Krishna sports with humble cowherds of Vrindaban whose simple devotion and total surrender he finds more pleasing than the arrogance of learned brahmans. He also engages in a highly charged erotic play with thousands of *gopinis* or milkmaids who renounce their inhibitions and shame, the pull of *vidhi-nishedha* and of sanctioned relationships and norms, their possessive instincts, in their love for Krishna. What provides the charge to this image is the power and beauty of the arcadian chronotope, what Bakhtin would have called "a time of honey".[6] The eternal love, the blazing youth and beauty of the participants of the *leela,* the poignant sweetness of Krishna's flute as he calls out to his lovers, the emotional and erotic intensity of the contact are played out among landscapes of unsurpassed beauty—making, subsequently, poetry and music the most effective medium of Krishnabhakti rather than theological canon.

Vrindavan is simultaneously a place in time and space as well as an eternal condition where the *leela* continues unendingly, playing on the themes of love, fulfilment and separation or *viraha*. For Krishna leaves Vrindavan for Mathura to claim his patrimony. He settles down as king and husband of many queens and as the agent who decides the course of the epic battle of the *Mahabharata*. He never returns to Vrindavan again. The pilgrimage differs from traditions associated with other major pilgrimages where the ritual journey and performances lead to certain concrete benefits for the pilgrim's lineage. The chief benefit of coming to Vrindavan, however, is to come closer to the sources of remembrance, to attain a more vivid sense of the sweetness and pain of that divine experience.

The *BP* introduces a pastoral idyll of endless love and ecstatic pleasure, of eternal music and fragrant flowers where *sansar* and its unbending *vidhi-nishedha* stand suspended. More, they seem to be inverted, for Krishna finds low caste cowherds better companions than brahmans, he invites married *gopinis* to seek pleasure with him. The devotee, through mere contemplation of such bliss, finds access to an image of surfeit. Would she even find the resources for a fundamental questioning of the laws of *sansar*?

I think that ultimately, the laws are not cancelled out. What the image of surfeit promises is, rather, a dream of the values of *sansar*, taken to the limits of their possibilities. We have God as a male lover who brings pleasure in equal measure to his many women devotees, a king who plays with shepherds. Here power dreams of such absolute hegemony that it can translate itself as love and fulfilment for the powerless—the human devotee, the low caste, the woman. God, however, remains a polygamous male king who will eventually leave the play behind. The devotee, the low caste, the woman will remain trapped in an inescapable condition of helplessness, *viraha* and pain where they had always been placed. For them, there is no other way to God. The fleeting image of fulfilment was a rich surfeit, indeed. Its withdrawal and the eternal longing for a return to that blissful state of merger where all Vrindavan was united with Krishna, remains the closest possible encounter with the Absolute.

It is generally considered that the *advaita* principle of non-separation between Creator and creation relegates the theme of separation to the realm of transient phenomena, that the purpose of *BP* is to create the image of non-separation or non-dualism through the erotic spectacle of *leela*. Freidelm Hardy, however, thinks that *viraha* induces an excess beyond this, that separation is no mere transient, purely human experience. *BP* goes beyond its predecessor *Harivamsa* to insert a final section on *viraha* with some deeper purpose that partly unwinds the design of ultimate non-duality. The whole *leela* expresses more than the reflection of Krishna upon the mirror of *maya* and the events signify more than mere games that he plays with himself. Hardy points out the sheer physical quality of eternal longing which is not to be found anywhere else in Sanskrit literature. He also underlines the fact that there is no image of a final union.

Rashsundari, as we shall see, does not use the imagery of the erotic play which might, then, carry on into a theological concept of non-separation. Yet, she reaches, perhaps, the same conclusions, from a contemplation of her own life, rather than God's. Her religion is essentially dualistic. In a novel departure as well as a retention of the form of *tatastha bhakti* that her autobiographical mode enables her to undertake, she is transfixed at the shores of her own life, she contemplates—not with bliss but with considerable pain—the games that

God is playing with it. She is left with an inexorable sense of an insurmountable division within reality that is, moreover, structured by divine power on the one hand and by human suffering on the other.[7]

The Krishna of *BP* is a male figure who fills thousands of *gopinis* with equal bliss. Radha, as a separate, privileged figure, has not made an appearance as yet in this text. Religious imagination could not indefinitely sustain this unproblematic idealisation of polygamous patriarchy. Inexorable existential and social problems of pain and inequality re-enter subsequent narratives of Krishnabhakti and fracture it at different points. Later devotional texts, especially medieval Bengali *bhakti* lyrics, introduce the figure of Radha—splendid in her demanding love—who breaks up the undifferentiated mass of loving womanhood. She approaches Krishna with an angry, resentful love, straining against the basic asymmetry of the relationship, since Krishna must love others and must eventually leave her to eternal *viraha*. Her resentment forms a language through which the devotee articulates a sense of the arbitrariness of God's power over the world and of a human condition that is marked by inequality and *viraha*. A Sanskrit couplet, ascribed to the *bhakti* saint Chaitanya, expresses this resentful devotion in a language of unusual violence: "Let that immoral, faithless one come and ravish me."[8]

Even in the *BP*, and much more so in the later texts, problems of a patriarchal social order clash with the articulation of *bhakti* through an erotic mode. If an endless love play becomes the ideal repository for the most perfect relationship with the most desired being—that is, with God—then to be adequately demanding and challenging, to be worthy of a lifetime of yearning, that desire cannot be expressed through the conjugal condition where the love object is already attained. In *BP*, the *gopinis* were married women and post-Chaitanya Vaishnavism in Bengal adhered to the theory of *parakiya* or the adulterous nature of the Radha-Krishna relationship. At the Jaipur royal court, this school won a major victory over the *sivakiya* or licit love school. Interestingly, the debate was repeated with the same results, at the Murshidabad court of Murshid Quli, the Muslim Nawab in early 18th century Bengal. The Nawab was a keen listener throughout the debate, and he concluded that the *parakiya* school had offered better arguments.[9]

Through the theory of illicit love or *parakiyatattva, sansar* acquires yet another meaning. It is the ensemble of licit relationships and sanctioned norms that bars Radha's way to Krishna. A paradox is set up: the world of patriarchal injunctions, insisting on the woman's unconditional surrender to unrequited monogamy, is her true *dharma;* yet her desire for Krishna is a call coming from God himself. The erotic situation corresponds to a spiritual problem, which it is meant to exemplify. Karma enjoins submission to *sansar,* yet *sansar* with its unendingly trivial demands and rigid prescriptions, is an impediment that thwarts a complete surrender to God, that makes God recede from the devotee. God calls out to her and goes back empty-handed since *sansar* is an obstacle that is divinely ordained. The paradox makes both God and the devotee weep. *AJ* introduces a mediated version of the paradox, since Rashsundari's *bhakti* must be expressed through an illicit desire for the written word which has an independent existence as an autonomous object of desire in itself.

Parakiya might be an adequate and effective vehicle for the logic of intense devotional imagination, but the form carries an ineffable and transgressive excess beyond the theological message, The *BP* itself tries various ways to contain it by furnishing several safe explanations. For instance, it says that the *gopinis* were first married to Krishna and then to their worldly husbands, so Krishna had prior claims to them. We find a curious echo of this belief in the marriage practices of a Vaishnav landlord family from Taras in East Bengal. Every daughter of the family is first ritually married to Krishna and is then wedded to the human husband, on the wedding day.[10] The *BP* also says that Krishna inhabits the bodies of *gopinis* as well as of their husbands, so it is always he alone who enjoys the women in a dual capacity, and no real adultery, therefore, takes place. And, of course, the whole episode is also considered as a metaphor. In the late 19th century, Bankimchandra used elaborate linguistic sophistry to argue that Radha is a linguistic device rather than a mythological person.[11] The *BP,* moreover, warns that the episode cannot be taken as a model for human behaviour since extraordinary lives are entitled to extraordinary privileges. We are given, therefore, a divine biography which is the cornerstone of religious belief, but which carries no moral lesson for the devotee. On the contrary, it seems almost a summation of all possibilities that are put beyond the reach of the human devotee.

III

Chaitanyabhakti

Vaishnav faith in Bengal was conveyed very largely through a rich and evocative tradition of lyrical songs, composed between the fourteenth and the seventeenth centuries, and sung according to the Bengali musical genre of *kirtan*. Chaitanya had expounded on the importance of congregational singing of *kirtan* as the most significant and effective mode of worship that promised equal access to salvation to all manner of devotees. He emphatically denied the efficacy of caste-differentiated ritual or worship and he asked all devotees to join together in ecstatic singing and chanting of the holy name. Salvation was, in fact, to be easier for the lowly and ignorant, for women and shudras, for their hearts were not hardened by pride as were the hearts of arrogant brahmans. Salvation was also more easily available in this last and most degenerate age of Kali. In his own lifetime, Chaitanya had invited the combined wrath of the brahman pandits of Nabadwip who tried to forbid the multi-caste congregational singing that Chaitanya had initiated as a public activity: the Muslim qazi favoured the brahmans and nearly brought about a riot-like situation by trying to enforce the ban on Chaitanya's followers who looted his property and burned his house in retaliation. The promise of spiritual equality through a shared and a collective ritual enabled Chaitanya and his largely upper-caste acolytes to undertake a massive proselytisation campaign among low-caste, yet socially and politically important groups—artisans, traders, manufacturers, tribal chieftains. Possibly, the success of Islamic proselytisation was seen to lie in its congregational life and its conviction in an unstratified spiritual order.[12]

Even though some post-Chaitanya sects and groups did violate brahmanical injunctions about caste and gender, on the whole, Chaitanya's *bhakti* was not meant to transform or significantly reorder social relations and practices. Unlike most *bhakti* saints of medieval India, he and his disciples belonged to upper-caste, affluent families. Chaitanya asked the brahman and highly erudite Goswami theologians settled in Vrindaban to compose a theological canon that would have authoritative power over Bengal Vaishnavs. The canon eventually curbed much of the rather anarchic, ecstatic tendencies that some of Chaitanya's own acolytes manifested in Bengal. In exchange for receiving canonical status for the Goswami doctrines, the

Goswamis eventually agreed to accept Chaitanya as a deified object of worship who was supposed to be an embodiment of Krishna and Radha together within the same body-mind. In Bengal, the Gauraparamyavadi groups saw him as a deity in his own right. He was widely worshipped as an incarnation of Krishna and Rashsundari also refers to him as *avatar.*[13]

For the Vaishnav householder, brahmanical norms continued to rule.[14] Mendicant and deviant orders were looked down upon, even by respectable Vaishnavs who were careful to tighten up the order of *vidhi-nishedha* even further to indicate their difference from the mendicants. Individual devotion was to be initiated and carefully modulated by gurus, mostly from upper castes. On the whole, caste hierarchies were observed. Around the early 19th century, an intermediate caste Vaishnav *bhakt* in Khulna came to acquire great fame and power among local traders and merchants for his preaching of *bhakti*. He owned the idol of a child Krishna who, on a stormy night, asked him to build him a house to keep out the cold. When Balakdas, the *bhakt,* chastised his deity for trying to turn his mind to material possessions, the holy child, according to Balakdas' hagiographer, simply burrowed into his bosom and whispered: "Father, I am so cold." The devotee then gave in and inspired his wealthy disciples to build a fine temple. This is a rather unusual example of *bhakti* where the adult male's activist devotion is inspired by fatherly love towards the child-Krishna. Generally, the child-Krishna is associated more with the worship of women devotees. The Mahishya guru also preached unequivocal devotion to brahmans and taught his low-caste followers about how to observe proper deference to upper castes.[15]

Chaitanya had asked brahmans to cultivate humility and service as part of the techniques for the formation of a

Vaishnav self. The attributes of an ideal woman or peasant, thus became the attributes of an ideal Vaishnav. Moreover, his hagiographies describe his frequent bouts of anger against arrogant brahmans who are ensnared by sterile learning or by empty ritual and who have no love in their hearts: they are called *"pashandis"* or sinners.[16] However, the spirit of service and humility, when enjoined upon brahmans, did not entail actual social levelling or renunciation of power. It was restricted to a certain style or mode of address to the world. On the other hand, the shudra and the woman, for whom humble service was, in any case, socially obligatory, had to undergo a double confirmation of their appointed stations and gestures: as shudra/women and as Vaishnavs for whom lowliness is a condition for salvation.[17]

Though the *raganuga bhakti* of Bengali Vaishnavs, patterned on the unbearable longing for Krishna among his Vrindaban associates, was the most privileged form of devotion, *Vaidhi* or more ritualised forms were also enjoined upon householders: services to the household deity, worship of the family guru, fasts, chanting and singing holy names, congregational feasts and music and pilgrimages. These would often constitute all of women's devotion and even women in the mendicant orders would engage primarily in the idol's daily services. Though they were often literate and some of them were reputed to be learned in theology, there is no evidence that they wrote or contributed to the substantial corpus of Bengali Vaishnav literature. Sects were sometimes led by the wives of the founders and the wives of Nityananda were prominent organisers. One of them was credited with miracle-making powers. Several hagiographies of Chaitanya describe women's adoration and record moments of obeisance.[18] Women themselves, however, have not left records of their spiritual quest, their states of devotional experience. *AJ*, in fact, is a rare and important articulation of that.

V
Other Modes of *Bhakti*

Rashsundari's sensibilities possibly drew from non-Vaishnav sources of belief as well, since no hard boundaries segregated the two dominant sects—the Shaktas and the Vaishnavs—from each other. She, in fact, deliberately feminises divinity once or twice, addressing her as the principle of Shakti or fundamental energy that is embodied in the Great Mother who presides as either Durga or Kali, the two aspects of the consort of Shiva.[19] Shakta devotional traditions are chiefly iconic—the two great annual worships in Bengal relate to the worship of Durga and Kali—and musical, with a rich corpus of songs especially from the 18th century.

Durga is a figure of majestic splendour, both as a divine mother and as demon slayer. A particular category of Shakta songs, known as *agamani,* however, also visualise her as a little girl, the beloved daughter of the mountain deity Himalaya and his wife Menaka. Married off to Shiva who chooses to live like a feckless mendicant surrounded by spirits, she can visit her parents only for three days a year. For the rest of the year, her mother yearns for her, alternately worrying about her plight and recalling the happier days of her charming infancy. In a land where the male child is practically a god, and the daughter is doomed to be an outsider to the natal lineage, whose compulsory, preferably hypergamous marriage is notoriously hard to fix, the mother–child relationship is almost universally celebrated as a mother–son connection. Agamani songs were the only trope which accorded the daughter a place within the affective/imaginative order.[20] Rashsundari's references to her absence from her mother's life are filled with the bitter longing of the daughter together with the vicariously experienced emotions of her own mother. However, curiously enough, she makes no mention of her own emotions about parting from her married daughters, one of whom had died in childbirth. This seems related to a carefully organised narrative economy where the strongest emotional experiences are carefully distributed, so as to avoid repetition and blurring. About *viraha* or separation, the earlier sections, centred on her own relationship with her mother, have all that she needs to convey. For the later sections, the most powerful human experience of pain is that of death— and, curiously enough, her love for her children is described almost exclusively through her experience of their death.

The Shakta tradition, therefore, allows a fuller and more rounded configuration of both the woman and of viraha than do Vaishnav lyrics which confine both to the erotic realm alone. Shakta songs contain yet another genre which similarly concerns itself with a different, and possibly more extended relationship between God and the devotee than is captured through the erotic devotional emphasis of Vaishnavism. Vaishnavism, too, has a rich vein of devotional experience around Yashoda's love for the enchantingly mischievous infant Krishna. That, nonetheless, is a one-dimensionally happy mode, without the more complicated expressions of Agamani songs, where similar descriptions of a naughty little girl are always overlaid with the pain of imminent separation. Nor is the filial mode most privileged in Gaudiya Vaishnav canon and in the lyrical/musical tradition whose most memorable achievements are in the erotic mode.

The 18th century was a particularly troubled and uncertain

time for Bengal: quick dynastic change, repeated invasions
by Maratha marauders, transition to colonial rule, decline
of handicrafts, a catastrophic famine and the prolonged
devastation of agrarian life that began with colonial rule. A
magnificent crop of *shyamavishayak* or songs dedicated to
Kali were composed at the time that focus on the terrible
uncertainties of human existence. Kali is the fierce aspect
of Shakti, embodied in a goddess who ranges around the
cremation grounds with bands of skeletal spirits. She is lean,
black, terrifying to look at, voraciously hungry and feeds on
human sacrifices. She is portrayed as standing on the body of
her husband Shiva. She is the exact reverse of all aspects of the
nurturing mother figure who has her beautiful breasts, flowing
robes and associations with bounteousness: in Kali, they are
replaced with a cadaverous nakedness, a prominent lolling
tongue that some scholars identify as a substitute penis, with
absence of feminine shame or sensitivity to polluting elements.
Yet, for the devotee, she is quintessentially the mother, the
true mother.[21] In an utterly amazing move of inversion, all
accepted meanings of motherhood are turned askew. She is
not so much the wicked mother who will be replaced by
the nurturing one. She is the only mother that the devotee
acknowledges, that he longs for. He is completely uncertain
about the possibility of her mercy or grace, he complains about
her terribly inscrutable will and her total capriciousness that
does not discriminate between the good and the bad child.
Yet his surrender to her is complete and so is his love for her.
He wants no other mother.[22]

    While this an exemplar of the nature of devotion
which must know the inscrutable and unjust condition of
divine power prior to the act of surrender, it is also perhaps
an acknowledgement of the nature of human existence itself

if it is taken out of a religious teleological frame. It affirms the insatiable thirst for this very life among human beings. Shyamavishayak songs range across a diversity of concrete human experiences: poverty, starvation, social hierarchies and human disregard and indifference. Rashsundari, as I said before, overturns the meaning of *tatastha bhakti* by contemplating her own life more than she dwells on God's sports: or, rather, she examines her own life as evidence of his *leela*. The descriptions through which she links her life with divine sports are very often drawn from the stark, terrifying, dark world of Shakta images rather than the fragrant and erotic pleasures of Vrindaban. They have more to do with the tears of cruelly separated mothers and daughters, with starvation, with loneliness and unspoken fears, with the terror and the pain of death. They have nothing to do with the everlasting, idyllic unions and lovers' quarrels that resonate in the Vaishnav songs and lyrics.

A final form of excess beyond *sansar* was constituted by body-centred cults and sects. Their base is constituted by Tantric philosophies which have a Shakta as well as a Vaishnav variant. Certain *sahajiya* lower-caste, esoteric, popular religious sects, some of which were loosely affiliated to Vaishnavism, also aspired to trap divine energies, even divinity itself, within the human body, through ritualised violations of purity-pollution taboos, and through secret and forbidden forms of sexual rites. They proclaimed the primacy of bodily sense-perceptions over scriptural knowledge. Propagated largely through songs that encoded their rites and theories, their philosophy of *dehavad* had become familiar to 19th century villagers, even though upper castes, on the whole, considered them deviant and contemptible. The full extent of their lore would be known only to the initiated, but their songs and the broad outlines of their movements would not be unfamiliar to most.[23]

AJ, as we shall see later, uses fragments from *dehavad*, but the influence is limited. Even though the body-centred philosophy, with its defiance of caste and pollution taboos seems an attractive and liberating form of excess over *sansar*, a lot of their texts reveal that the female body and emotions were supposed to be used in an instrumental capacity, for filling the male body with extraordinary powers which would eventually liberate it from all desire for the woman. Nor were they unmarked by the deep-seated conviction in the innate depravity of the woman which characterised upper-caste codes.

IV
Vaishnavism in Modern Times

The routinisation of charisma that had begun in Chaitanya's own lifetime, proceeded vigorously in the next few centuries. On the one hand, there was a consolidation of canon, of institutions, of ritual and of temple-building. On the other hand, there were waves upon waves of proselytisation in new regions, among fresh social groups. A "Hinduisation" of pantheistic or tribal and untouchable religious practice was accomplished through Vaishnav preachings. As segments that were as yet weakly integrated with the brahmanical mainstream were incorporated, some low-caste sects and popular religious movements—loosely associated with Radha-Krishna worship—developed radical cosmologies and deviant ritual practices. They overturned pollution taboos but were otherwise quietist. In the early 18th century, the dissident Sahebdhani sect that grew up in Nadia and subsequently spread to Jessore and Burdwan, took Chaitanya as the ruling saviour figure. But it composed a highly intricate web of deviant ritual and openly mocked caste taboos.[24]

In the 19th century, the new middle classes would often move across class and caste barriers to experience the forbidden pleasures of the more libertarian orders. The Kartabhaja sect, first popularised among low castes in Nadia, also attracted extremely erudite sections of the *bhadralok:* the poet-cum-bureaucrat, Nobin Sen, visited the festival. The newspaper *Somprakash* reported in 1864 that about sixty-five thousand people had attended the annual festival of the sect at Ghoshpara where Calcutta literati would mingle with crowds of prostitutes. (Benoy Ghosh) The sect trained women preachers—*ma-gosains*—who radiated out into Calcutta middle-class households. The leader of the sect was invited, along with Vivekananda, to attend the World Conference of Religions in 1893, but he could not go since he did not have the resources.[25] Wandering Bauls, whose esoteric practices were encoded in songs of great beauty and mystical resonances, began to attract a middle-class following.[26]

While the tension between respectable and deviant orders that the Chaitanya movement had produced was one kind of paradox that accompanied the growth of Bengali Vaishnavism, there was yet a deeper paradox in the relationship between the inner and the outer in the Vaishnav construction of the self. A new and deep emphasis grew about the inner light of faith, a self-realised conviction, often to be held on to against the disapproval of the world, similar to the love that Radha had for her lover. A great deal was made of the continuous and private relationship between the devotee and his God. So we may say that Vaishnavism stimulated a radical sense of interiority and a highly individuated form of devotion—or, conversely,

a devotion-centred selfhood in the individual. At the same
time, the parameters of the devotional imaginary were already
worked out in detail by the sectarian gurus through a highly
developed textual tradition of the aesthetics of religious feeling:
the several *bhavas* or moods induced by the categories of *rasa*
or aesthetic stimuli. So was a behavioural model—supposed to
reflect the inner qualities of the transformed Vaishnav self—
worked out in detail.

Through a circular movement, then, canonical paradigms
of belief, practice and mood were laid out, according to
which the devotee would regulate her inner life as well as
her external behaviour. At the same time, the devotee's altered
belief and practice would supposedly indicate and reflect
inner convictions. While this enables a reliance on external
authorities—texts, temples, gurus, idols—it simultaneously
creates a perception about the possibilities of self-fashioning
as well as the fashioning of a faith of one's own.

Nineteenth-century metropolitan Calcutta, however,
reoriented Vaishnav practices and aspirations in novel directions.
In early colonial Bengal, the new revenue arrangements under
the Permanent Settlement had massively disrupted the older
zamindari establishments that used to be predominantly
Shakta in their religious orientation. The new landed fortunes
were very often founded by affluent Vaishnavs—the rajas of
Cossimbazar, of Posta, of Shobhabazar. Some of them funded
a spree of temple building in the new colonial metropolis of
Calcutta where most of the temples were, indeed, Vaishnav
ones. They also undertook the construction of notable temples
at Vrindaban. Occasionally, the new and somewhat small-scale
landed patrons would come from relatively low castes. They
would try to manipulate brahmanical establishments to reduce
the ritual gap between themselves and the upper castes, to

introduce a modicum of ritual levelling of status. Motilal Sil, for instance, asked a Brahman Sabha in the mid-century to modify hierarchical extremes. When the Sabha refused to consider his request, he tamely accepted their decision. A more robust Vaishnav, Bhairabchandra Datta, however, challenged and repudiated brahmanical authority through his radical tract, *Vaishnavbhaktikaumudi*. It was appropriately printed by the Pashandadalan Press in Calcutta in 1834, for *pashanda* was the name given to brahman opponents of Chairanya by his disciples and the name of the press meant the Oppressor of Pashandas.

In outlying towns, important festivals were financed by low-caste but rich devotees as a way of acquiring status. Vaishnavs were very visible, even combative in the emergent modern public spaces. In 1834, the colonial government had imposed a ban in Calcutta on noisy Vaishnav processions and public singing. In 1835, however, the ban had to be withdrawn, thanks to the intercession of Radhakanta Deb. Vaishnavs also learnt quickly about how to become adept with the new communicational and institutional modes of public life. Print culture soon became a major resource and between 1818 and 1829—just at the moment of its emergence—several Vaishnav classics were printed. A little later, the cheap Battala presses began to turn out translations and new religious writings in great profusion and at low prices, for low-income and rural markets. Dissident sects like the various Sahajiya groups printed their literature on a vast scale. In the last decades of the century, the *Amritabazar* group of Sisir Ghosh, began to compile, edit and publish sacred manuscripts. A Vaishnav journalism developed quite early. In 1831, Brajamohan Chakravarty founded the weekly paper, *Bhagabatsamachar,* and he was followed by several others in Dacca, Tripura and other places.

As Vaishnav monastic orders or *akharas* grew, so did more modern forms of urban religious association. They had a formal membership and organisational structure, rather than the loose, ad hoc congregations of older times. Calcutta formed the *Haribhaktipradayini Sabha* in 1852. The plague scare in 1898 stimulated a large crop of *Harisabhas* in Calcutta and its suburbs.[27]

Proselytising acquired new teeth and made fresh conquests through modern forms of social service and philanthropy. The Vaishnavs moved towards the marginalised and dishonoured groups of society to knit them into the Hindu fabric. In the late 19th century, Vaishnav reformers were working among Calcutta scavengers and prostitutes and others were spreading the faith among untouchable peasants in Faridpur and Jessore. Namasudra peasants, inspired by a variant of Vaishnavism, developed their own self-respect movement around the Matua religious sect.[28] Modern Vaishnavism, therefore, had a large sprawl, spanning very diverse social segments, assuming widely different shapes and purposes and adapting to new technological and organisational possibilities with considerable confidence.

V
New Religious Orientations

Contrary to received wisdom, the religious world of the modern, English-educated *bhadralok* did not arrogantly insulate itself from plebeian, popular religious culture. In fact, as we have seen, sections of the middle class sought out their festivals, their songs and their gurus. An educated landed family in the village of Doyhata in Bikrampur put itself at the service of a low-caste preacher with a violent, chiliastic vision and performed a form of human sacrifice to usher in a golden age.[29] Ramakrishna, an illiterate poor brahman, found eager disciples among the most active and famous social reformers and literary figures of Calcutta.[30]

Rashsundari seems equidistant from the plebeian as well as from the middle-class forms of devotion. There are a few fragments of *dehabad* in her book. And yet, a scion of the reformist and literary family of the Tagores wrote the preface to her book. Obviously, she knew of one and she had a lot to say to the other.

In a series of interlinked studies of 19th century middle-class religious movements, Sumit Sarkar has established an interesting pattern. He shows a regular oscillation between a this-wordly, dynamic, practical activism and high reason on the one hand, and a softer, fervent, ecstatic, quietist religious expression on the other. Rammohun Roy moved away from an early rationalism that derived largely from Islamic monotheism to a more tempered and pragmatic theism. The shift occurs among the iconoclastic defiant young Derozians whose uncompromising adherence to the rule of reason got softened, in their old age, into more acceptable forms of mainstream religions. The pattern reached a peak in the 1870s and '80s, when a childlike, instinctive and emotional form of devotion, conveyed through the quotidian images and metaphors of an inspired and illiterate guru, Ramakrishna, were valorised over textual knowledge and activism.[31]

AJ and other statements on religion by 19th-century women, however, indicate another trajectory that is not aligned to this pattern, and that, in fact, deviates sharply from it. For they search for texts, for understanding reached through the path of knowledge, for the ability to express their dialogues with God through writing. The divergence is immensely significant, for women's religion is supposed to be spontaneous, unlearned, instinctive. Moreover, they—again, supposedly—inhabit more comfortably the regions of seeing and hearing rather than reading and writing. We shall come back to the implications of this difference in the section on education.

The movements between a practical religious activism and a self-absorbed emotionalism had combined to create a new possibility in modern religion: the saturation of the profane world and of practical action—philanthropy, social work, reform—with religious significance, their encompassing and absorption within the religious domain. The secular public sphere understood itself as essentially religious. This was something radically new. Older notions of *dharmic* behaviour had, indeed, ruled over householder existence, but those had been externally prescribed regulations. Now, the connection between the everyday and the sacred had to be understood and worked out by individuals. This was quite different from a more mechanical pantheistic understanding that postulates that everything in this world contains a part of God. For the new understanding was intrusive, transformative, and sought to change the self and the world to bring them in conformity with God. We have something like a re-enchantment of the world, the packing of the mundane with the sacred—but this was something that each devotee had to accomplish in each lifetime. Modern religion becomes, thereby, a constant intellectual effort, a ceaseless cognitive activity.

VI
Hagiographies, Manuscripts and Recitations: Vernacular and Popular Modes of *Bhakti*

Chaitanya *bhakti* introduced a new form of religious literature in Bengal—hagiographies celebrating lives of saints and of great devotees. Chaitanya, however, was revered by his hagiographers as more than a saint—he was called a reincarnation of God in his own right. Rashsandari's secret reading was inspired by an unquenchable thirst for the Bengali hagiographies of this genre. It was a desire shaped by three elements. For Vaishnav households, manuscripts were freely available and were regarded as the heart of their sacred canon; they were Bengali texts, deliberately written to educate a wide cross-section of devotees in matters of Chaitanya's life and Gaudiya Vaishnav teachings; being sung, recited, explained and amplified continuously, they could reach out to non-literate devotees most successfully.

There were earlier biographies of Chaitanya that were written in Sanskrit by Bengali poets in the early decades of the 16th century. Their impact, however, was extremely limited. Vrindaban Das' *Chaitanya Bhagabat (CB)* was the first three-part biography written in Bengali and it was a momentous event in the religious and literary history of Bengal. Worshipped as a sacred text and renamed as *CB* to indicate its closeness to *BP,* it self-consciously structured the early part of the narrative to evoke memories about Krishna's childhood, so as to reinforce the divinity of the saint. Part of its veneration seems to derive from a new concern about historicity that might have something to do with Muslim court chronicles. Dates and places are precisely mentioned and the authenticity of sources is carefully vouched for. Vrindaban Das himself was close to Chaitanya's lifetime, his mother had been personally blessed by the saint as a child, and the poet belonged to a Vaishnav family of great importance. He heard tales about Chaitanya's childhood from the saint's oldest disciple, Advaita, and he attributed the importance of his narrative to the privileged oral accounts that only Advaita could have recounted.[32] Vrindaban Das often insisted: "I write only what I have heard from *bhakts*"—that is to say, heard from men in the know.[33]

Each *adhyay* or section in *CB* begins with a hierarchised invocation of sacred Vaishnav names: *Shrikrishnachaitanyanity-anandadvaitachandraya Namah*—Salutations to Krishna, Chaitanya, Nityananda and Advaita, the last two being foremost disciples of Chaitanya. The importance of the sect and of its gurus is evident. In fact, *CB* is also a biography of most of Chaitanya's disciples. Next comes an obeisance to the sect— *Shrichaitanyapriya gosthi*—to the sect dear to Chaitanya. We have an acute understanding of the organisational importance of the sect and its proselytising leaders. *CB* is a deeply sectarian text, full of violent fulminations against faithless opponents of Chaitanya and the Muslim qazi of Nabadwip who tried to curb the sect. Chaitanya himself appears to be violently dogmatic, ready to smash his opponents in argument and disputation and to physically coerce brahmans, Muslim qazi and disobedient disciples alike. He carries a metaphorical sword in his hand. It is significant how little Rashsundari's narrative derives from the book that she was longing to read. Her devotion valorises the path of understanding, it is completely non-sectarian and she refers neither to Krishna nor to Chaitanya in her colophons: she solicits help from Saraswati, the goddess of learning who carries a book in her hand. This is a most un-Vaishnav invocation. There is never a mention of the order of Vaishnavs, to congregations or sects or to gurus. On the other hand, *CB's* celebration of the Kali age as a time when the saviour is born, is carried into *AJ* and is recast as the praise for her own times when women are freer.

CB was meant for teaching the ordinary *bhakt* the story of Chaitanya's life in simple, vivid poetry. *Chaitanya Charitamrita* (henceforward *CCM*), on the other hand, was commissioned by theVrindaban theologians to narrate Chaitanya's life, as well as to communicate and explain the doctrines of the Goswamis in Bengali. Krishnadas Kaviraj was sent to Vrindaban by Nityananda to form a bridge between the movement and its theology. *CCM* is the most authoritative and exhaustive account of the life of Chaitanya and of the religion.[34] It discusses the preferred *raganuga* model of devotion and it explains the theology of *parakiya* love. Although Radha is missing in *CB,* she is an important figure in *CCM.* It also is a detailed history of sect-formation and of the different strands within theVaishnav faith and movement. Krishnadas retains the invocations from *CB,* and he also cites short, Sanskrit couplets and amplifies the meaning in Bengali. He puts down the various Sanskrit couplets that are ascribed to Chaitanya and that comprise the core teachings of the prophet. The book conveys a strong sense of the land of Bharat where people have a special vocation: to be good and faithfulVaishnavs. Rashsundari talks of the futility of her own life every time she mentions her birth in the land of Bharat. Obviously, she has in mind the vocation that she thinks that she has failed to live up to. *CCM* condenses this vocation into the recitation of the holy names of God and his incarnations which are enough, in the age of Kali, to bring salvation: *Harenama harenama harenama kevalam; Kalou nastyeba nastyeba* (Only the name of Hari, there is no other way out in kaliyug). All scriptural knowledge is thickened and dissolved into the name. Chaitanya himself had mastered the path of knowledge, had transcended and had left it behind for simple faith and love. His devotees need not repeat the effort, they may adhere to the end-product of the long process.

The explicit message is, nonetheless, undercut by the medium through which it is communicated—a learned theological tome. This instantiates the paradoxical relationship between knowledge and unlearned faith that is forever unresolved in Vaishnavism. For we have here texts that are meant to be read—and not by pandits alone, but by the common folk. Both texts are fast-flowing, easy to understand and to memorise. Written in the *payar* metric structure, each line of the verse has twelve words and every two lines compose a complete statement—in form, very close to prose sentences. Rashsundari's unfamiliarity with prose texts could have been offset by the structure of these verses.

Neither text was printed before the end of the 19th century, and Rashsundari could only have read them in manuscript form. We have no way of knowing how old the manuscripts at her home might have been, but sacred texts were being copied by hand well after the introduction of print, down to the end of the 19th century.[35] Her versions might, however, have been quite old ones. Vaishnav manuscripts began to be copied in great profusion by the 17th century, and quite a few of them were later unearthed among low-caste and poor rural households. According to Hiteshranjan Sanyal, low castes, indeed, were the most numerous consumers for such manuscripts.[36]

Dineshchandra Sen claims that he began to look for manuscripts when he wanted to write an essay for a prize that had been instituted by the Calcutta University in 1891. His initial searches found rich rewards in Comilla homes of "artisans, weavers, blacksmiths and baniyas…" His servant, Ramkumar Datta then found more of them in his Bankura village. He would go on regular trips, funding himself with sales of cheap and popular Battala pulp literature to village readers, out of the proceeds of which he would buy up manuscripts. While Calcutta University set up a special manuscript library out of such collections in 1910, the Asiatic Society bought about four hundred handwritten books. Abanindranath Tagore, the famous artist of the Bengal School, was an avid buyer, attracted by their illuminated wooden covers and so was Chittaranjan Das, the leading nationalist and Swarajist politician. He later donated two thousand works to the Bangiya Sahitya Parishad Library.[37]

I examined a copy of the first section of the *CB*—the *Adikhanda*—in the Calcutta University collection. Made of countrymade, heavy, *tulat* paper that would be stained with an arsenic solution, each page was about 14" X 4.75" in size. The heaviness of the paper probably protected it from ageing. Each page contains not more than ten to twelve lines. A copy of the *CCM* that I saw had pages that were very similar in size—13.5" X 4.5". It contained even fewer lines—about nine to ten on each page. Both were made up of loose sheets, pressed between wooden slats. They were bound up in red cloth and tied with string. Even opening the book would thus be a long and complicated procedure, and the pages would have to be taken out one by one, read and replaced—just the way Rashsundari had done. Each page would have very little written on it, so reading would be enormously time-consuming and cumbersome. Each section of a book could only be copied down on several different books. Both the manuscripts that I saw were late 17th century ones. Both had been located in Bankura.[38]

The staining with sulphate of arsenic gave these manuscripts a long life.[39] Yet the fact that each book would be divided into many manuscript texts or *punthis* would mean a major storage problem. Individual houses would not be able to contain very many of them, and public recitations would have been their major mode of transmission. Much of Vaishnav doctrine was orally disseminated at a fairly high level of comprehension and conceptualisation. Ritual occasions within households or local congregations organised public recitations and commentaries—*katha* and *path*—as well as devotional music where singing would often be interrupted to read aloud a doctrinal point and then the song would be resumed to explain it. Texts were, therefore, ubiquitous, penetrating even oral and musical performances. The *BP,* for instance, would be recited over a month continuously, with readings in Sanskrit every morning and explanations and Bengali commentaries every evening.[40] This way, an unlearned listener gained what had been, termed in another context as "phonetic competence"—an overall understanding over whole blocs of Sanskrit passages. At the same time, she would also acquire "linguistic competence" over each word that was read out and explained in Bengali.[41]

I would suggest that this notion of dual competency may be stretched from the realm of words to that of concepts. The simultaneous exposure to Sanskrit and to Bengali, to chaste and erudite as well as to familiar, colloquial words, created a phonetic grasp over complex conceptual statements as well as a literal linguistic competence over each idea from vernacular expositions. Popular religious songs and literature often move with effortless ease into knotted theological problems.

There was, then, an ubiquity of sacred texts that established a visible, powerful bond between reading and piety. Snatches of recitations would penetrate into women's quarters. At the same time, the notion of a shared culture cannot be pressed too far. Ordinary labouring people and women were often excluded from a systematic cultivation of religious interest, even from its oral traditions, by lack of leisure and by rules of seclusion. Rashsundari has written about the pain of that exclusion. Women who were interested in a more complete understanding, were simultaneously stimulated and frustrated by occasional but imperfect access to religious discourses.

Excited by such desires and fears, Rashsundari worked out a double-edged stance vis-à-vis her *sansar* and her identity. She underlined her submission and her unqualified success here. At the same time, she took care to indicate that a deeper truth lay veiled behind this apparent reality, this partial truth, this *maya* that was her *sansar*. By evoking this contrast, she wrested for herself an interior space which was her faith. She prised open both *sansar* and faith to accommodate a new figure: the serious yet domesticated woman *bhakt* who creates her autonomous religious understanding all by herself, a faith that is carefully insulated from all that the woman's *sansar* had on offer. And also a faith that can only be expressed through the forbidden activity of writing a book.

Notes

1. Surendranarh Dasgupta, *A History of Indian Philosophy*, Vol 4, Cambridge University Press, Cambridge, 1961, pp. 2–6.

2. R.C. Zaehner, *Hindu Scriptures* (1967; Rupa edition, Calcutta, 1992); F. Max Mueller, ed, *The Sacred Books of the East*. Vol xxv, translated by Bubler (Cambridge University Press, 1886; Delhi reprint, 1964); Kenneth. W. Morgan, ed, *The Religion of the Hindus* (Delhi, 1987); also, especially Satish Chandra Chatterji, *Hindu Religious Thought* (n.a); U. Bhattacharyya, *Bharat Darshansar* (Calcutta, 1949); Sukumari Bhattacharji, *Literature in the Vedic Age,* vol 2 (Calcutta, 1986).

3. Zaehner, op cit; Bhattacharyya, op cit; Friedhelm Hardy, *Bhakti: The Early History of Krshna Devotion in South India,* Delhi, 1983.

4. Satish Chandra Chatterji, op cit; U. Bhattacharyya, op cit; Anantanand Rambachan, "Where Words Can Set Free; The

Liberating Potency of Vedic Words in the Hermeneutics of Sankara" in J.R. Timm, ed, *Texts in Context: Traditional Hermeneutics in South Asia,* State University of New York Press, 1992.

5. S.K. De, *Early History of the Vaisnava Faith and Movement in Bengal,* Calcutta, 1961, pp. 3–6.

6. See Mikhail Bakhtin, *Dialogic Imagination,* ed. H. Holquist, Texas, 1981, p. 103.

7. Freidelm Hardy, op cit, Thomas J. Hopkins, "The Social Teachings of Bhagabat Puran" and J.A.B. van Buitenen, "The Archaism of the Bhagabat Purana" in Milton Singer, ed, *Krishna: Myths, Rites and Attitudes,* University of Hawaii Press, 1966.

8. *Chaitanya Caritamrita,* op cit, p. 616.

9. S.K. De, *Early History of the Vaisnava Faith and Movement in Bengal, 1486–1900,* Calcutta, 1985; Hitesh Ranjan Sanyal, *Bangla Kinaner Itihas,* Calcutta, 1989; Sukumar Sen, *Bangla Sahityer Itihas,* op cit.

10. I owe this information to Prof. Pradip Sinha.

11. Bankimchandra Chattopadhyaya, *Krishnacharitra, Bankim Rachanabali,* Vol 2, Sahitya Sansad, Calcutta, 1954, pp 468–75.

12. Hiteshranjan Sanyal, *Bangla Kinaner Itihas,* op cit; *CB,* op cit, p. 249.

13. Hiteshranjan Sanyal, op cit; Ramakanta Chakravarti, *Vaisnavism in Bengal,* Sanskrit Pustak Bhandar, Calcutta, 1985.

14. On an important distinction between Hindu religious belief and social organization, see Maya Burger: "The Hindu Model of Social Organization and the Bhakti Movement: The Example of Vallabha's Sampradaya" in R.S. McGregor, ed, *Devotional Literature in South Asia: Current Research 1983–1988;* Cambridge University Press, Cambridge, 1992.

15. Saryendranath Basu, *Siddha Mahatma Balakdnser Jibani,* Calcutta, 1913.

16. See *CB,* op cit, where this term is continuously used to refer to brahman opponents at Nabadwip.

17. "The ideology of obedience has a particular pointedness for women which it lacks for men because it coincides with their prescribed roles." See Lyndal Roper, "Feminine Piety in 15th Century Rome: Santa Francesca Romana" in Obelkovich, Roper and Samuel, eds, *Disciplines of Faith: Studies in Religion, Politics and Patriarchy,* Routledge & Kegan Paul, London 1987.

18. Ramakanta Chakravarti, op cit, pp 174–83.

19. See Sashibhushan Dasgupta, *Bharater Shakti Sadhama O Shakta Sahitya,* Calcutta, 1957, pp. 74–149.

20. These were composed in profusion by major lyricists like Kamalakanta Bhattacharyya and Ramprasad Sen in the 18th century. See Prabhatkumar Goswami, ed, *Hajar Bachharer Bangla Gan,* Saraswat Library, Calcutta, 1969, pp 231–37. Also Asit Kumar Bandyopadhyay, *Bangla Sahityer Itihas.*

21. David Kimsley, *Hindu Goddesses: Visions of the Divine Feminine in the Hindu Religious Tradition,* University of California Press, 1986, pp. 116–30.

22. For a selection of songs, see *Hajar Bachharer Bangla Gan,* op cit; also see Rachel Mc.Dermott, "Bengali Songs to Kali" in Donald Lopez, ed, *Religions in India in Practice,* Princeton Readings in Religion, Princeton University Press, 1955, pp. 55–56. Her account, however, has a rather uncomplicated image of the goddess as the perceived nurturant figure. Also Jogendranath Gupta, op cit.

23. Sudhir Chakravarti, *Sahebdhani Sampraday O Tahader Gan,* Calcutta, 1985; Manindramohan Basu, *The Pint Chaitanya Sahajiya Cults of Bengal,* nd, Calcutta reprint, 1980; Sakti Nath Jha, *"Cari Candra Bhed: Use of the Four Moons"* in Rajat Kama Ray, ed, *Mind, Body and Society: Lift and Mentality in Colonial Bengal,* Oxford University Press, Calcutta, 1995.

24. Sudhir Chakravarti, *Sahebdhani Sampraday O Tahader Can,* Calcutta, 1985, pp. 23–37.

25. Sudhit Chakravarti, *Sahebdhani Sampraday O Tahader Can,* op cit, pp. 27–40.

26. Sudhir Chakravarti, *Sahebdhani Sampraday,* op cit; Sudhir Chakravarti, *Bratya Lokayata Lalan,* Pustak Bipani, Calcutta, 1992; Debendranath De, *Kartabhaja Dharmer Itibritta,* Calcutta, 1990.

27. Ramakanta Chakravarti, ibid, pp. 385–401.

28. Sekhar Bandyopadhyay, "Popular Religion and Social Mobility in Colonial Bengal: The Matua Sect and the Namasudras" in Rajat Ray, ed, *Mind, Body and Society,* op cit., pp. 152–92.

29. Sumit Sarkar, *Renaissance and Kaliyuga: Time, Myth and History in Colonial Bengal—Writing Social History,* Chapter 6, Oxford University Press, New Delhi, 1997, pp. 186–215.

30. Sarkar, "Kaliyug, Chakri and Bhakti", ibid., pp. 282–353.

31. Sarkar, ibid; also "The Pattern and Activity of Early Nationalist Activity in Bengal" in his *A Critique of Colonial India,* Papyrus, Calcutta, 1985, pp. 37–57.

32. Asit Bandyopadhyay, *Bangla Sahityer Itibritta,* Vol 2, third edition, Modern Book Agency, Calcutta, 1983, pp 306–69. See also Bimanbehari Majumdar, op cit.

33. *CB,* op cit, p. 3.

34. Asit Bandyopadhyay, ibid.

35. I owe this piece of information to Subhadra Ganguly. She, however, has found that copiers received only daily meals and very little remuneration by that stage. Clearly, this was due to the competition from print, although the very orthodox still objected to putting sacred words through the polluting print medium, and preferred to read holy books in manuscript.

36. Hiteshranjan Sanyal, op cit, p. 234.

37. Sen, Introduction to *The Descriptive Catalogue of Bengali Manuscripts,* Vol 3, University of Calcutta publication, 1928.

38. Ibid, pp 414, 396. Dates, 1696 and 1681 A.D. respectively.

39. J.C. Ghosh, *Bengali Literature,* Oxford University Press, London, 1948, pp. 29–31.

40. W.J. Wilkins, *Modern Hinduism: Being an Account of the Religion*

and Life of the Hindoos in North India, 1887, New Delhi reprint, 1987.

41. See Paul Singer, "Book of the Hours and the Reading Habits of the Later Middle Ages" in Roger Chartier, ed, *The Culture of Print: Power and the Uses of Print in Early Modern Europe,* Cambridge, 1989.

4

Strishiksha, or Education for Women

I
"Must We Live in Chains?"

In her own way, Rashsundari had a great deal to say about
what had emerged as a central theme in 19th century reform
in Bengal: on women's education, on the strictures against it in
orthodox families, on its growing availability in her later years.
She does not, however, refer to the debates among reformists
and the orthodoxy as such, even when her own observations
come close to the reformist position. Here she stands apart
from the 19th-century Maharashtrian widow Tarabai, who
declares her differences from the reformist agenda even when
she wants education for women.[1] She also stands apart from
the polemical writings of a Bengali predecessor, Kailashbashini
Debi, who wrote a whole book on the educational deprivation
of Hindu women.[2] Rashsundari refuses to insert herself
openly within an ongoing debate on reform although she was
undoubtedly a partisan.

The refusal could not have flowed from her ignorance
of the issues. In 1865, a little while before her book was
finished, as many as seven schools had been set up for girls

in the district of Pabna, her birthplace. Bamasundari Debi, a well-known woman teacher, was active in teaching married women in their homes. Faridpur, too, had come to acquire seven schools by the 1860s. An association of local notables—the Faridpur Suhrid Sabha—was behind the initiative, and in all likelihood, funds would have come from the district landlords—from men of her own class, and, quite possibly, from her own circle of acquaintances. Around 1867–68, the Faridpur school had employed another well-known woman teacher, Bhagabati Debi, trained by the teachers' training (Normal) school at Dacca, at the considerable salary of Rs. 20 a month.[3] Such information had no reason not to reach her, and her eulogies about changing times could well have been inspired by such news.[4]

At the time of the publication of her book, she was no longer a timid young wife, insulated from information about public events and debates, but had become an elderly matron whose learning was known and welcomed within her family. Rashsundari could not have failed to understand that what she had to say on women's education plugged into a lively, even acrimonious public debate. In fact, Jyotirindranath's preface to her book dwells on the controversies. With Rashsundari, however, all reflections needed to be shown as entirely rooted in her own experiences and understanding: that understanding, moreover, must be stripped bare of all external influence except divine interventions.

Yet, she does approximate a tone of polemical anger and zeal on this question that is surprisingly close to the more explicit reformist advocacies. The 19th-century debate on *strishiksha* or women's education was something whose terms included far wider social problems and perspectives than the matter of education alone. Rammohan Roy, in an early

writing against widow immolation, was one of the first people
to question some of the fundamental grounds and implications
of the norm that prohibited education for women. He linked
it up with an entire structure of regulations that had actively
denied moral and intellectual facilities to women and had
then naturalised the results of the deprivation by describing
the results as the cause: women's minds were too inferior—so
said the conservative opponents of reform—to accommodate
serious thinking. Rammohan separated and reversed cause and
effect. It is interesting that Mary Wollstonecraft had similarly
related differences in women's intellectual achievements
to a difference in opportunities and not to innate nature.
Rammohan might not have read her book, but he could have
been conversant with the controversies that it had provoked.
Later Bengali women, however, made the same point on their
own, although in their case, there could be no direct influence
at all.[5]

Rammohun wrote in 1818: "When did you ever test the
intelligence of women that you can so easily designate them
as foolish creatures? ...You witheld education and knowledge
from them, so how do you decide that they are incapable
of learning?"[6] This was written at a time when the first
moves were afoot to provide for women's education. In each
subsequent decade, with the inauguration of new suggestions
for *strishiksha*—whether by missionaries in the 1820s, by
the iconoclastic Young Bengal reformers in the 1830s, or by
Vidyasagar and sober Brahmo reformers in the 40s and 50s—
the debate gathered new strength and new bitterness. Invariably,
the arguments would roll into and interrogate—or defend—
the fundamentals of an entire order of upper-caste patriarchal
injunctions. We find, therefore, yet another relationship with
the world of *vidhi-nishedha* that would, through concrete and

partial demands of reform, set up some cracks within the ruling social order. Actually, in the historical context of the early 19th century, the most minimalist plans for education would open up quite a considerable excess beyond *sansar* and its demands—a potential that would steadily diminish for middle-class women as, very gradually, *strishiksha* became normalised. Its transformative implications for poor people and poor women, however, still retain some of the older valencies in a country where bare literacy remains a scarce resource.

Reformers rarely claimed to do more than loosen up older disciplines a little; they would, in fact, flaunt their limited charter as highly-controlled and soberly responsible measures. The orthodoxy, however, saw in each venture a definitive beginning of the end. Through the fiery contentions over *strishiksha,* we shall probe the nature of the fears, as a way of measuring exactly what the reforms could challenge and change.

Around the time that Rashsundari's book went to press, a vital and new dimension had been added to the debate. Women themselves had started writing about the question of their education, and the print medium had incorporated these in the public sphere of debates and arguments. One of the first printed pieces on the matter came from a girl of nine. Proponents of *strishiksha,* connected with the reformist newspaper *Sambad Prabhakar,* published a news item on 26 Baisakh, 1256 (May, 1849). They had visited the young girl at her home and had set a test for her. They also vouched for the fact that she had composed the answer in front of them. She was asked to write a poem on the theme:

> "Girls of this land are not educated
> How are they inferior to men?"

The little girl composed a poem in reply within an hour.
It was a highly finished piece, written in a rather erudite style,
and the verses rhymed perfectly.

> "Women are kept like animals since they do not get
> education
> People call them the weaker sex and they are not respected
> Since men cannot be born without women
> Why are women not cared for?
> Men treat them with contempt just because they are women
> They do not accept that women, too, have inner qualities."[7]

The paper reported this at considerable length, for it was a
major event. It was proof positive—and proof, badly needed—
in a debate where they had tried to argue that education, if
impartially distributed, would fetch the same results from a
girl as from a boy.

Kailashbashini Debi soon came out with an acid critique
of Hindu gender norms.[8] From 1863, Umeshchandra Datta, a
close associate of the Brahmo reformer Keshab Chandra Sen,
had started publishing the *Bamabodhini Patrika* or the journal
for the education of women. The first journal devoted to a
discussion of gender issues, it invited writings from women,
produced material which might help women to educate
themselves in slow stages, and it also generated arguments for
women's education and social reform. Its editor was a young
man in his early twenties, who could not pursue a medical
training because of his poverty. He later published a collection
of women's writings in 1872—*Bama Rachanabali*—and a
book to argue about the necessity of female education—
Strilokganer Vidyashikshar Abashyakata.[9] From the sixties, then,
along with reformist advocacies of *strishiksha,* there is a print
forum that welcomed women's opinion on the matter. The

new vernacular prose allowed a few women—as yet unable to acquire an English or a classical education—to express their thoughts in books, tracts, articles and in letters in *Bamabodhini*. Being closer to their everyday speech, the prose of the journal allowed them a more immediate understanding of what they read and what they needed to write. Women's own writings at this point were, indeed, quite chaste and drew quite a lot from a Sanskrit-based or *tadbhaba* vocabulary.

A tone of deep and pervasive anger was reflected by a number of letters that reached the editor of *Bamabodhini Patrika* from district towns, including one from "Shrimati Bibi Taherannechha", a Muslim woman from Boda Balika Bidyalay. It was written in extremely chaste, Sanskritised Bengali and referred extensively to ancient Hindu women of learning.[10] Uma Chakravarti has exposed the largely mythicised nature of the notion of the learned ancient Hindu woman. The myth, however, had a wide range of contestatory possibilities, and reform-minded women, even Muslim ones, needed the appeal of a mythicised ancient golden age whose glory included the spread of knowledge among women.[11] It was also, perhaps, a more revealing sign of those times, that 19th-century Hindu men preferred to construct a myth about the intellectually strong woman rather than one about the docile, servile wife.

Shrimati Soudamini Debi from Bakarganj wrote in 1865: "Why have men kept us in such a low state? Are we not the children of the Great Father? ...How much longer do we stay chained to our homes?"[12] Shrimati Kamini Debi wrote from Khaipara in 1867: "It is no exaggeration to say that our women live lives that are no better than that of animals."[13] An anonymous woman wrote in 1868 from Konnagar: "Our father! Must we live in chains all our lives, even though we are your daughters? Alas! Were we born in this land only to perform low tasks? ... Why must we live all our lives like caged birds within the home?"[14]

The words, sentiments, and particularly the motif of the caged bird and the prison-like home, are familiar themes in *Amar Jiban*. We might infer two things from the similarity, and both could be partly true. Rashsundari could have read some of this before she finalised her autobiography. She does not refer to any modern reading matter at all, but the fact that she claims to have read only some sacred texts might have been a tactical move to underline her general obedience and traditional virtue. In any case, she probably would have read some new prose in order to compose a prose text, inspiration for which could not have come from the sacred verses alone. By the 1860s, when the first version of *AJ* was being composed, a Bengali journalism had already come of age, and the new postal system had developed well enough to carry newspapers and periodicals into even remote village homes.

At the same time, the availability of the new journal for women and women's writing at just about the time when she wrote her book, might indicate something else. It might take us toward an emergent structure of feelings among upper-caste, rigidly secluded women whose families would be well-off enough to educate them if they had wanted to do so. It would be a desire for a new form of female identity that would reorient domesticity as well as disalign women somewhat from the domestic confines that they insistently described as a prison and a cage. Of course, a lot of these letters might actually have been penned by men, writing under a feminine pseudonym to carry credibility for their suggestions at a time when few women could come up with written and printable matter. But when we compare them with the few pieces of actual women's writings, we find little discrepancy.

AJ, as an authenticated piece of a woman's writing, not only intervenes in the debate at its initial stage, although without seeming to do so. The fact that its author was someone who was not connected with reformist circles at all, went a long way to give it status as an autonomous female argument that could not have been mimicking male reformism. Historically, its appearance coincided with a stage in the debate when, for the first time, women could express their opinion within the public sphere of the press and print culture. Rashsundari's very distance from the centre of that sphere—reformist circles in Calcutta—and her silence and implied ignorance of the public nature and import of the issue, made her book appear as even more the authentic and spontaneously, even innocently, produced article.

II
What Men Feared about *Strishiksha*

Whereas on her loss of the natal home, she uses the first person singular consistently, on the subject of education Rashsundari generalises, talking about all Bengali women in past and present times—a rare departure for her. She does not usually write in the discursive mode on social matters but translates her general concerns into deeply personal experiences of pain. While talking about women and education, she refers to two distinct phases: the first covers the early years of her childhood and the first years in her new home when she had to keep her thirst for knowledge a secret. The second was a somewhat altered context in the late sixties, when the first part of her book was nearing an end.

Even in her mother's home, where she had picked up some letters from listening to her brothers' reading, no one was told about it. After her marriage, when she was fourteen—around the mid 1820s—she began to long to read, but her fears were great about letting anyone know of this desire. Already, male guardians were complaining about "the Queen's rule" and about how that had encouraged a subversive spread of education among women. Both her desire and the male fears were obviously produced by some beginnings that had already been made to educate women by the early twenties.

Rashsundari, however, is a little confused about different moments of time here. Actually, Victoria's rule commenced a decade after she had turned fourteen and was pining to read. She was, then, conflating the historical moment of the twenties when the debate about *Strishiksha* had just begun, with a situation of the early and mid-thirties when Victoria's reign had commenced, a few tentative efforts had already been made towards institutionalised primary education for women and very much more was being urged by Christian missionaries and liberal reformers. This would be, in fact, closer to the time when she was twenty-five, and was actually teaching herself to read in secret. Rashsundari's account carries a vivid sense of the male fears that were whipped up to produce a hardening of orthodox lines at two slightly different junctures.

Women's literacy was virtually an unknown quantity when the 19th century opened. Ward's Report of 1803 mentioned that nearly all Bengali villages had primary schools or *pathshalas* but they seemed to have catered to boys alone.[15] Adam's Report described a roughly similar picture in the mid-thirties but, again, pre-colonial educational facilities—well organised as they were for those times—seemed to have offered nothing to girls. It was not simply a question of omission. Girls were expressly forbidden to read in literate, even well-educated households. Customary injunction had it that literate girls were fated to be widowed. In his Second Report on the State of Education in Bengal, Adam wrote in 1836:

> A superstitious feeling is alleged to exist in the majority of Hindu families, principally cherished by the women and not discouraged by the men, that a girl taught to write and read will soon become a widow... and the belief is also generally entertained in native society that intrigue is facilitated by a knowledge of letters on the part of females... when a sister... is observed imitating her brother's attempt at penmanship, she is expressly forbidden to do so. These... feelings prevail extensively ... both amongst Hindus who are devoted to the pursuits of religion, and those who are engaged in the business of the world.[16]

No mere Orientalist sneer, this, since the description resembles, in every particular, Rashsundari's own experiences. Adam's Report was prepared between 1835 and 1838, around the time when a twenty-five-year-old Rashsundari was struggling to read in the most fearful secrecy.

In his Report, Adam refers to two separate orders of fear that choked off women's education. One was the fear of sexual intrigues, since a literate woman could write and make secret assignations of an illicit nature. In the early part of the century, Shibnath Shastri, the Brahmo reformer, was taught at home by an exceptional mother who was fairly well-educated. When he went to attend the village school and told his teacher that he was being supervised by his mother, the teacher sent a letter of assignation to this entirely unfamiliar woman through her unsuspecting son, secure in the certain conviction of her immorality.[17]

The other kind of fear was about the impending threat of widowhood for the educated woman. In one of the first tracts on *strishiksha*, Gourmohan Vidyalankar mentioned the widespread belief that the gods punished the woman who forgot her appointed place by daring to read and write, with widowhood.[18] Far later in the century, the same fear is again mentioned in the pages of the *Ramabodhini Patrika* in 1863.[19]

We should look at the fears closely, for they indicate what and how much the most minimalist notions of *strishiksha,* advocated by the most moderate of reformers, would need to overcome. There are two separate dyads at work here—the educated woman and the widow, and the immoral woman and the educated one. They can be run into each other to make up a single, triangulated structure. The two base terms—the widow and the immoral woman—may be merged together to constitute the apex term—the educated woman, who now comes to represent both the base terms. The base terms can be united on the basis of a characteristic impulse of the educated woman which encompasses the states of both the widow and the immoral woman—she, like the two other prototypes, is not defined entirely by her husband's presence. The educated woman, therefore, shares with the immoral one, an extra marital desire. It makes no difference that in her case, it is a desire for learning—she is not supposed to possess a desire for anything that does not come through, or is not related to her husband. By this act of desiring something else, she has then terminated her need for the husband. The husband, therefore, dies a physical death, leaving her as a widow, since this is a logical culmination of her refusal to be defined solely through her conjugal status. The immoral and the educated women have both symbolically cancelled out the husband: widowhood is a physical embodiment of the consequences. In a farce written in 1897, the connection between adultery and widowhood is transferred from the realm of divine retribution to that of the active agency of the woman. In a play, whose title may be translated as *Educate the Woman, and You are Digging Your Own Grave,* the educated woman first turns to adultery, and then murders her husband. The distance between the three categories is completely closed off, and a new fear is offered about a new category of the evil woman: the educated woman as potential husband-killer.[20]

Education, then, is a double repudiation of the husband. It is, therefore, both immorality and non-conjugality. If we extend the connection a little further, beyond the figure of the husband, we find that the new educated woman is meant to be the opposite term of the domesticated/caste good wife of old times. If the signification is widened out a little more, then education equals the end of the patriarchal marriage system. We thus have here a fundamental kind of binary opposition between two entire ways of being, two gender systems. This puts a weight on the meaning of women's education—and on social reform in this sphere—that is significantly in excess of the strict programmatic content of 19th century *strishiksha*. There is a continual over-production and leakage of meaning that inexorably encompasses the future of Hindu domesticity. Reform, therefore, may appear partial and limited in intent, but to its adversaries—as we shall see—it was necessarily laden with momentous consequences.

III
On the Educated Woman

Very often, Indian reforms, especially those related to education for women, are seen as a simple function of mimicry, of aspirations towards Victorian gentility, for an emulation of companionate marriage.[21] This argument shoves the reformed and the educated woman under a doubled servitude—to her husband's new needs for a more sympathetic wife, and to western, Victorian standards of patriarchy. I think we need to emphasise very strongly, however, that the normative and moral horizons between the two cultural systems were so very different and distant that plain mimicry was plainly out of the question. Even if the basic digits of self-fashioning look superficially similar—a little education, closeness to the husband's interests, intelligent housekeeping, educating infants—the processes through which all this would be achieved were so vastly divergent that seemingly similar conclusions would lead up to entirely different experiences and norms. The Victorian lady did not have to hide her literacy, she was not married off in her infancy, her husband could not be formally polygamous and the widow was not customarily barred from remarriage. Nor did she live in virtual seclusion. The reforms that Victorian feminists struggled for were not basic education, end to widow-immolation, legalising widow-remarriage, de-legalising infant marriage. For the 19th-century Bengali Hindu woman, moreover, even the minimalist idea of these reforms would be possible to conceive of only after a very hard struggle against ruling *vidhi-nishedha,* after a radical break with her own inherited sensibilities. It would come about through a process that was inevitably painful and crisis-ridden. It is a historical fact of immense significance that women articulated an early yet strong sense about non-gendered, inalienable, equal human *rights,* first of all in the sphere of education; in contrast, abolition of widow immolation, legalising widow remarriage, a higher age of consent and marriage were rights that male reformers initiated. I think that such misrecognition of historical developments arises when we confine ourselves to assessments of finished literary products as the sole gauge for sensibilities of the day: we need to look closely at the concrete historical processes that went into their making to uncover more hidden breaks, ruptures and challenges that the formal texts do not make evident.

It was to cancel out the association between education on the one hand, and widowhood and immorality on the other, that the first women writers carefully underlined the fact that their education was initiated by the husbands. Kailashbashini Debi narrated in her preface, how her husband insisted that she learnt to read and write at night, indicating the appearance of a new kind of conjugal intimacy that, too, had to be secretly performed in the privacy of the bedroom.[22] The reformists assumed that the husband would be the teacher, thus trying to overturn the chain of associations that we had looked at earlier. Far from being a transgressive desire that the adulterous woman nurtured to turn away from and cancel out the husband's presence, this was something initiated by the husband himself: education was thus integrated with conjugality, a change that transformed the scope of conjugality itself. In this sense, Rashsundari's was a daring departure, since clearly, she had acquired her education without her husband's knowledge or approval.

The only exceptions to the prohibition seemed to have been the rich landlord families. According to Adam, girls of many such families were educated since, in case of widowhood, they were expected to manage the family properties. He also mentions that more than half the landlords at Nattore in Rajshahi were widows. Of them, "Ranees" Suryamani Dasi and Kamalmani Dasi were known to have a good command over Bengali writing and accounts.[23] Kailashbashini Debi also mentions the accent on arithmetic and accounts in educating girls from these families.[24] Much later, as a senior matron, Rashsundari put her education to practical use by writing a plea, in her husband's absence, on behalf of some of their tenants who were being mishandled by a neighbouring Muslim zamindar. Yet, not all landlords' daughters could have been educated since Rashsundari herself belonged to such a household and nobody tried to teach her anything. Again, according to Adam, even in zamindari households, the teaching was done in secret.[25] It seems that the literate daughter was a social liability that even the wealthiest and most influential families could not declare in public. Secrecy, with its association of hidden desire and transgression, was, indeed, a dominant motif for the entire activity. Rashsundari, therefore, was not an exception.

The other known category of women who were literate were those from mendicant Vaishnav orders—the *boshtomis* from popular, often low class and caste devotional sects, who made an income from teaching women from upper-caste households. In the Jorasanko Tagore family, for instance, a *"ma gosain"* was hired to teach the women.[26] Adam commends the fact that "the authors and leaders of this sect had the sagacity to perceive the importance of the vernacular dialect as a means of gaining access to the multitude, and in consequence, their works…form a larger portion of the current popular literature than those of any other sect…the subject matter of these works cannot be said to be of a very improving character…" The subject matter, obviously, would relate to the illicit love between Krishna and Radha. Perhaps, for that reason, not every affluent household would use them to teach their girls. On the contrary, the *magosains* were held to be dangerously immoral themselves. "As a sect they rank precisely the lowest in point of general morality and especially in respect of the virtue of the woman." Adam mentions that the example of these literate and immoral women might have produced fears about the literate woman in general.[27] For most respectable upper-caste families, the association between *boshtomis* and literacy itself would act as a counter-model and inhibit the extension of education among their women, since *boshtom* orders were looked down upon and were suspected of all kinds of sexual peccadillos. Rashsundari's families were devout Vaishnavs as well as highly educated, but they were strict about withholding education from women.

Once Rashsundari was bold enough to make her achievement known, she realised that there were others in her family who were hungry for words and letters. Many other women from these times had similar experiences. Sarada, the wife of the great 19th century saint Ramakrishna, sadly recollected in her old age, how she, as a young girl, was keen to read, and how her treasured first book was snatched away from her hands by an infuriated male relative who rebuked her: "Women are not meant to read. They will end up reading novels and plays."[28] It is precisely this fear of frivolous and immoral reading habits that Jyotirindranath Tagore tries to refute in the Introduction by pointing out that Rashsundari used her education to read sacred texts. It seems that the right to engage in systematic and extensive reading was a privilege reserved for the female ascetic-renouncer who had already left the household to join an ashram. Most of Ramakrishna's women disciples were invariably prolific readers, though the saint himself was illiterate.[29]

IV
Early Schools

Christian missionaries began to experiment with schools for girls from about 1819. Ward's campaign in England resulted in the establishment of the Female Juvenile Society in that year. Mrs. Cooke of the Church Missionary Society came to Calcutta in 1821, and managed to set up as many as twenty-four girls' schools in different parts of Calcutta, attended by four hundred pupils. By 1828, when Rashsundari first starts thinking of the possibility of reading, the number had gone up to thirty schools, visited by six hundred students. The numbers could have been somewhat exaggerated and certainly they declined fairly soon and quite rapidly. Some of these students would later be trained under the Normal or teachers' training school, set up under the auspices of the Ladies' Society that inaugurated the *zenana* or home-based education system. Under this scheme, trained teachers would teach, in seclusion, girls or married women from deeply respectable families, who would not send the women to schools. The scheme was coordinated by Reverend Fordyce and Mrs. Mullens. Special efforts were made by Mrs. Toogood to train teachers who would disseminate education through the vernacular medium, and the efforts bore some fruit in the first few years.[30] Very interestingly, the same Mrs. Mullens wrote a proselytising novel in Bengali—possibly the first full-length work of fiction—that showed the educated woman as the leader within the family and community of Christian converts. The new woman is located in a rural, low-income set-up, in sharp contrast to reformist literature.[31]

In December 1823, Bishop Heber visited one of Mrs. Cooke's Native Female Schools, founded under the Church Missionary Society. He praised the high levels of progress in reading, writing and sewing among the young students but he did not mention what kinds of readings were prescribed, or what kinds of students were recruited. Looking at the girls with a somewhat voyeuristic gaze, he described their faces and bodies in some detail instead: "It was very pretty to see the little swarthy children come forward to repeat their lessons… blushing even through their swarthy complexions, with their muslin veils thrown over their slim, half–naked figures…"[32]

In 1822 Gourmohan Vidyalankar wrote *Strishikshavidhyak* to serve a dual purpose. It advocated female literacy, and parts of the book were recommended as possible readings for girl students. It was written not only in vernacular prose, but in an excessively colloquial, conversational mode, in the form of dialogues between women. In later material, produced for women, we find a more chaste language being used that probably indicates that women had already been exposed to some printed matter. Vidyalankar, on the other hand, needed to make his writing as close to everyday speech as possible, since women were as yet not used to reading formal prose. In the next decade the Society claimed to have taught 500 girls in several districts, but no regular school seemed to have survived.[33] In the 1820s, Miss Cooke and the Ladies' Society for Native Female Education made some progress in Calcutta and neighbouring districts, but Adam reported in 1838, "It is only the children of the very poorest and lowest castes that attend the girls' schools and their attendance is avowedly purchased."[34] There is some indication, however, that girls of poor families were also eager to learn. Mrs. Cooke had apparently set up vernacular *pathshalas* only for boys under the School Book Society. She decided to open schools for girls when she found a little girl weeping at its doors since the teacher would not let her in, despite her pleas for over a month.[35]

Since schools failed to acquire a toe-hold among girls of respectable familes, Radhakanta Deb proposed that they should deliberately target their teaching at poorer girls, while the better-off should be taught at home. Missionary schools in Calcutta did remain largely confined to the depressed areas.[36] It would be very interesting to piece together a record of early missionary experiences among the poorer and the low-caste girls, to establish how the latter related to prospects of education.

Certainly, Rashsundari's childhood was not touched by these efforts. She does mention a white woman teacher—probably a missionary—who ran the village school on her home premises, but she seems to have taught only the boys and made no effort to teach Rashsundari. According to a report issued by the Serampore Baptist Mission in 1829, the institution was already running twenty-one vernacular schools in Serampore and in neighbouring areas, while it had also set up seven and eight schools at Dacca and Chittagong respectively. With the rise of high Anglicism in the next decade, the vernacular schools, run by missionaries, fell into disuse. Rashsundari's home-based school could have been an offshoot of this experiment that was founded on a scheme for vernacular education that Dr. Marshman had initiated.[37]

Since at this stage only missionaries ran schools for girls, fear of Christian proselytisation merged with the pull of custom and the deep-seated male fears that an educated woman would use her knowledge to write illicit love letters. Prasannakumar Tagore, a prominent Calcutta notable, warned in 1831 against infiltration of Hindu homes by missionaries through their daughters.[38]

A distinction must be made here between two levels within the debate on education. While the orthodox hardliners opposed the very idea of education itself, the proponents of *strishiksha* were uncertain about whether school-based or home-based education would serve the best purpose. Again, the division between the hardliners and the reformists on this issue did not always correspond to the larger orthodox-liberal opposition. Radhakanta Deb, who led the agitation in favour of widow-immolation, was, nonetheless, a pioneer on behalf of *strishiksha*. Since schools were a public space away from homes, it was unthinkable for most respectable families that their daughters could travel daily beyond their homes. To allay such fears, missionaries had turned to *zenana* education—teaching women within the safe confines of their homes. That, of course, would have aggravated fears of Christian penetration into Hindu homes. Radhakanta Deb offered his blamelessly orthodox palace precincts as the examination hall for students under the Female Juvenile Society in 1822.[39] Obviously, he, unlike most of his orthodox friends, saw in a partially educated woman a source of better and more informed female consent that needed to be generated for somewhat beseiged Hindu patriarchal norms.

Bishop Heber narrates a very interesting meeting with Radhakanta Deb at a party that was also attended by several European ladies. "Hurree Mohan Thakoor", an orthodox Hindu dignitary, remarked that these parties were so much more interesting than any others, for the presence of women lent them much grace. Heber informed him that ancient "Hindoos" also enjoyed such occasions and it was only Muslim rule that put an end to the public appearance of women. "Radhakanta Deb observed… 'it is true that we did not use to shut up our women till the times of the Mussulmans. But before we could give them the same liberty as the Europeans, they must be better educated.'"[40]

The meeting encapsulates a historical exchange. At first glance, the import seems obvious enough; the Orientalist-missionary passes on a historical self-description as well as a future agenda to the orthodox Hindu and the moment of liberal education, as of communalised historiography, originates from this exchange. Orientalist sahib, Hindu orthodoxy, liberal reform, Hindu nationalism blend into one another, all fulfilling an originary Orientalist agenda of cultural conquest. If we look closely, however, the moment unfolds more complicated meanings. Instead of assimilating and regurgitating a given statement, Radhakanta shows no surprise at it, he does not indicate that this information is freshly received wisdom. Rather, his quick response could indicate that he himself might have been already thinking on such lines. On the other hand, he immediately makes distinctions within the transmitted message and selects what he can use. He endorses the supposed information about public mobility of ancient Hindu women but he is not prepared to restore the privilege as of now, however attractive it might appear to his friend Harimohan Thakur. He puts it into an explanatory frame that would serve his present purposes better and links it up with *strishiksha* within domesticity. He thus draws up his own map of social relations and resettles the boundaries offered by Heber. What is interesting is the desire that unites the European and the Hindu: a desire for interesting and public social occasions where women's presence was essential, even if the Hindu must, for the present, be content with the presence of European ladies alone. A new sense of an ideal sociability is seen to be emerging, even if as a distant, imagined possibility. Again, in Radhakanta's immediate reply to Heber, the point of real interest would seem to be a replication of the western promise to the Indian intelligentsia: rights would be available to it only after proper education. By transferring it to Indian women, Radhakanta is repeating what was, perhaps, a larger perceived function of the Indian woman. She is, to the colonised Indian man, what he is to the sahib, and, by being that, she offers to him the vicarious pleasure of being a surrogate sahib within the family. This is, however, the tone that Radhakanta uses, a man who combines his pleas for the continued burning of Hindu widows with the hope of giving Hindu women a little literacy at home while they lived. We must note that he talks not of witheld freedom, of inflicted blindness, of Hindu male guilt as Rammohan does. He talks of Muslim culpability, of intelligent and responsible Hindu male decision-making.

If sections of the orthodoxy were prepared to loosen up the restrictions on this one particular sphere of the woman's existence, the radical, iconoclastic rebels of the next decade, the Young Bengal or Derozian students, bitterly denounced the prohibitions against education in the pages of their journal, *Gyananveshan*. They enlarged the conception of education by linking it up with a plea against child marriage, so that girls would have access to uninterrupted learning before they were given away to "strangers" and to unfamiliar homes where their future growth would be beyond the control of their earlier guardians: a fate that Rashsundari had written so eloquently about. This was one of the first systematic arguments for *strishiksha* that was consolidated into a coherent position and statement in Maheshchandra Deb's early but cogent statement on the Hindu gender system: his *Sketch of the Condition of Hindoo Women* came out in 1839.[41] Since the young Derozians had struck terror in Calcutta Hindu society with their open and somewhat exhibitionistic attacks and criticisms of Hindu conventions, their advocacy of *strishiksha* came to look like a part of their reckless rebellion and defiance against Hinduism itself. The fearful comments on education that Rashsundari heard in the mid-thirties could be partly related to the association between *strishiksha* and Derozian iconoclasm.

These few, yet immensely risky ventures framed the context within which Rashsundari acquired her education. The meagreness of the efforts against as yet undented custom explains how a daughter of an affluent, leisured class with developed traditions of reading within the home and the Vaishnav community, who herself was yearning to learn, could have been deprived of literacy and why her learning needed to be a secret to the world. The male fears that she refers to in her work, were shaped by the strength of dominant custom that begins to apprehend a breach in its rule. It is interesting that as the century advances, we hear less about the prospect of widowhood and far more about the innate immorality of educated women. Rashsundari, in fact, plays a *double entendre* on the association when she describes her desire to read as a longing for a forbidden pleasure.

Rashsundari refers to some anxious speculations among her male guardians, somewhat harshly and rudely worded, about the evil effects of having a female queen. Subjection under a woman monarch was an unprecedented political experience for Bengalis and the immediate reaction seems to have been anxieties about major tribulations in social life, a world turned the wrong side up. Living under the rule of a woman seemed to fulfil old prophecies about the onset of the last and most evil age of all—kaliyug, when women and low caste shudras would lord it over upper-caste men. The sign that accompanied and embodied the new order was, for them, the contemporary movement for educating women.

So far, reformers had been able to do little on that score. It is extremely significant that they, too, were beseiged by some of the fears that assailed the orthodox about giving the woman access to something unconnected with pure domesticity. They took care to prove that the two were, in fact, deeply connected. Sumit Sarkar has pointed out how an altered conjugal situation would have inspired reformers, excommunicated by kin groups and society, to overcome their isolation within a shrunken world of human contact, to privilege the woman's question over other kinds of reform. They needed to recreate women with whom they could communicate and share.[42] The entire concept of the mother as the best teacher for the child at home was, again, a reformist way of domesticating the education of women. Tract after behaviour tract and manual set out to prove that the educated woman managed her home better, was more chaste and modest in her ways, and was a more pleasant and efficient cook, nurse and companion. Reformers were also worried about certain unwelcome fallouts from her literacy—mostly, the "pernicious" habit of reading useless novels about romantic love and illicit passion that the new Battala publishers were churning out in great numbers at cheap rates and were peddling from door to door, to take them within reach of women readers. Fears of learning about immoral ways jostled with fears of wasting money and time, of neglecting housework. To counter this, reformers produced improving reading matter in the form of cheap behaviour manuals and moral tales in large quantities, founded journals full of "useful" things to learn for the educated housewife and drew up rigorous work schedules (for her) to teach her about the management of clock-oriented time.[43] Jyotirindranath's preface to Rashsundari's book triumphantly uses it to demonstrate that this woman expended her education not in reading novels but for devotional works.

However instrumentalist and tame their approach and

resolutions seemed to be (this in itself is an inadequate basis for judging reformist intentions and desires since bold proposals often need to wear a tame and modest face to disarm orthodox suspicion), the very act of seizing upon the written word was a departure that was full of transgressive meanings and possibilities. No matter what would be given to women by way of reading, there was no foolproof way of containing the consequences once a new capability was created. And this was no ordinary capability. The 19th-century upper-middle class and upper-caste man defined his masculine worth primarily, even exclusively, in terms of his mastery over the written word. If masculinity required, above all, a self-differentiation from the feminine, then recreating feminine subjectivity as literate, as capable of acquiring knowledge, was a dangerous gift.

In colonial Bengal, education was the only resource that could fit out the middle-class man with a self-image of transformative enterprise. It was the only avenue to some power, to profitable professions, to self-esteem under colonial conditions. By the middle decades of the century, industries, trade and business were virtually closed to those Bengalis who had some capital to invest, but who were disheartened by the series of failures of Bengali enterprises. The higher reaches of the army and the administration were, similarly, closed to Indians. Parasitic landlordism was the only field for profitable investment but rentiership was hardly a sign of masculine vigour and creative enterprise. If to be masculine was to be different from the woman/Other, then a monopoly over education would be the supreme marker of that necessary difference—particularly, for a group of men who were regularly chastised by the colonial masters for effeminacy. The sharing of this supreme capability would then allow the surfacing of the repressed feature that would fatally destabilise culturally-ordered sexual difference. In the next decades, as we shall see, women's education would evoke deep and awful fears about sexual emasculation.

Women's writings, on the other hand, argue that men had conspired to keep them away from some precious resource by positing a basic difference in matters of intellect. There is a pervasive sense of something that they had lost, something that had been cruelly withheld from them, some inflicted wound that only formal knowledge could heal. Rammohan Roy, once again, made perhaps the first major, systematic statement on the matter. He identified it as the gift of true religious knowledge and he charged brahmans for concealing it from ordinary people.[44] Absence of education was taken by him and by 19th-century women writers, as the basic lack that differentiated male and female capabilities. Unlike the penis envy, postulated by Freudian analysis, however, this was a lack that could be redeemed. Rashsundari speaks of a similar blindness that had been inflicted by the concealment of the sacred truth which can only be gained through learning. In *Bamabodhini,* a bridge is built between sacred and secular knowledge, and a case is made out for women's access to both: secular knowledge of the world is translated as knowledge of God's handiwork, and, therefore, divine in origin.[45] The metaphor of the lost inner eye, or the essential blindness that persists even when the physical eyes function, because these eyes cannot see the world properly without knowledge, pervades the writings of Rashsundari as well as the more open advocacies of education among the women who published tracts and letters.

V

The First Secular School

Christian missionaries, the great liberal reformer Ishwarchandra Vidyasagar and the radical iconoclasts of the Young Bengal group had made women's education a central plank in their reform proposals. J.E.D. Bethune, Law Member in the Governor-General's Council, gave it a new direction. He had decided by the 1840s that unless the Hindu elites were encouraged to send daughters to school, efforts would be exhausted among reformist families alone. To achieve this, he paid strange prices. He foreswore religious instruction in his Calcutta Female School, founded in 1849, and he promised to recruit students only from high-caste families. The opening of the school was a major event. It was inaugurated with a musical procession through the streets that was joined by prominent reformist figures. The school bus carried the Sanskrit shloka from the *Mahanirvantantra: "Kanyapyeba palaniya shikshaniyatiyatnatah"* (Daughters should also be nurtured and educated with great care). The school met for two hours in the morning. An elderly brahman pandit taught Bengali while an European lady taught embroidery.[46] It seemed safe and blameless enough.

The scope of the early colonial interventions was narrow primarily because the government would not part with adequate funds to build a broad social base for women's education. Efforts thus needed to be concentrated at the top, hoping for a downward percolation to follow. In the case of Bengal, that percolation remained illusory. At the same time, the effects of concentrating efforts on social elites were also costly in a different way, for they were directed at upper-caste girls, conventionally barred from all education. As soon as the school was founded, it faced a wall of implacable outrage.

The school bus attracted much public abuse on the streets and the young girls had to travel in the midst of open and aggressive jeering.[47] Influential leaders of the Calcutta Hindu society enrolled their daughters to pave the way for the lesser folk, and so did some reform-minded brahman pandits: Raja Dakshinaranjan, Madanmohan Tarkalankar, Shambhunath Pandit, Ramgopal Ghosh. Tarkalankar's two daughters—Kundamala and Bhubanmala—were the first students to be admitted, and he had to face enormous social ostracism as a consequence.[48] The more representative sections of landholders and Calcutta notables organised campaigns of social boycott to coerce supporters of the school into submission. The Landholders' Association expelled Rasiklal Sen from its ranks since he had sent his daughter to school. Sen was no longer invited to the ritual ceremonies at the homes of other members. The reformist paper *Sambad Prabhakar* reported as late as 1856 that the Dharma Sabha was sending agents to intimidate parents who wanted to send their daughters to school.[49]

A good measure of salaciousness and scandal-mongering were used with deadly effect to constitute deterrents to school-going. Doubts were cast on the purity of the lineages of those whose daughters were going to school—an aspersion that would lead to outcasting and to difficulties by way of arranging marriages for their children. Obscene mockery and abuse abounded, functioning as warnings. The journal *Chandrika O Prabhakar* was fairly smacking its lips: "If respectable Hindu gentlemen want to turn their wives into prostitutes, who can prevent that? Not us, …on the contrary, we want to visit these schools… at night and put the girl students to test." Goaded beyond politeness, the reformist *Sambad Prabhakar* replied to the aged editor in kind: a somewhat unusual departure for reformers who were otherwise careful to use a rather sanitised language, and who had acquired a reputation for prudishness.

> The editor is an ancient man, we regard him as our grandfather... But Time has not eroded his sense of humour, though it has left its marks on his body... We had mistakenly thought that Grandpa has probably forgotten the calls of youth... However, the very word 'girl' has produced such a delighted surge of youth in him that we are now fairly sure that he has lost nothing of his virility...[50]

The word for virility here is *veerya* which is used both for valour and for semen.

Other conservatives warned about sexual abuse, both at school and on the way to school, expressing powerfully a fear about daily, regular movement in public, about claiming the streets, however carefully the school bus might screen the girls from sight. *Samacharchanetrika* cited Shastric injunctions against school-going and warned against male teachers, however old or pious—for men and women, if thrown together, will inevitably turn to sinful ways. It also sounded dire warnings, composed of real dystopic anxieties about public movement as well as of lubricious fantasisings, of dangers from male lust on the way.

> If young girls are sent off to schools, they might be deflowered since lust-stricken men would never let them alone but would surely rape them... do tigers spare goats? If rich people send bodyguards to protect their daughters from such dangers, then the guards themselves will deflower the girls, the protectors will ravish them...[51]

Fears, at this point, seem to be more about school-going as a non-domestic activity that breaks down the seclusion of women, rather than against education as such, although the obsessive sexual innuendos revive the old associations between education and immoral assignations through letters.

VI
The Spread of Schools

After Bethune's death in 1851, Governor General Dalhousie undertook the funding of the school and the government formally took over its management after Dalhousie's retirement. Iswarchandra Vidyasagar, who had been closely associated with the school since its inception, remained the Honorary Secretary. Now began a phase when the government seemed to move for the first time, and, as we shall see, very briefly, into the matter of women's education. Wood's Educational Despatch of 1854 had made an explicit reference to this as an area of government responsibility and from 1857, Lt. Governor Halliday began to draw Vidyasagar into a scheme of expansion of government-aided schools for girls. As member of the Education Council, Halliday had already submitted a Minute and his views on a broad-based education system drew heavily on Vidyasagar's "Note on Vernacular Education". In 1853, Vidyasagar had started a free school in his home village Birsingha in Midnapore which included a girl's wing. Between November 1857 and May 1858, he set up about thirty-five schools, with a population of nearly 1,300 girls, in Hooghly, Burdwan, Midnapore and Nadia districts in south west Bengal where he functioned as Assistant Inspector of Schools.[52]

What seems striking is the gap between government aid and interest, and missionary urging and investment. While missionaries had been experimenting with several plans for educating girls since the early twenties, the government made its first formal commitment only in the early fifties. At that point, it chose to work through the agency of the established reformer and educationist Vidyasagar, the Inspector General of Schools, rather than of the missionaries, though they, too, had a long experience in the field of education. Vidyasagar was then left free to work on his own for a brief while. From the beginning, one feature was constant: such schools would not allow for Christian proselytisation. Will it be true to argue, then, that the colonial government had a more hegemonic vision of westernisation that went beyond conversion, that sought to control the Indian woman's mind more securely through a westernist education through reformist agencies? Do we find that Vidyasagar's pedagogical ambitions and generous hopes for mass literacy and education that would, for the first time, also include women, were an unconscious tool for completing the hegemony of the West? If so, is the history of women's education exhausted in that description, as it is annexed and subordinated to this grand master-narrative?

Such arguments are familiar enough and they have an attractive political edge turned against the imperial agenda while seeming to broaden its scope convincingly beyond mere governance or economic motives.[53] They also challenge earlier historical frameworks by inverting the relationship between education as a strategy for imperial political control and education as an instrument of cultural hegemony which now is taken to be the real historical endeavour of the Occident in the Orient. The whole argument will then need to prove a constancy of government effort and investment in one direction alone, towards women's education and reform of orthodox lifestyle, to wean them away from past traditions and align them to more westernist values. One would need to move away from Macaulay's own times both backwards and forwards and prove that his intention was true of colonialism throughout its history: that intention being that the government was committed to an Anglicist, elite-based education geared towards cultural conquest through which a middle class of "brown sahibs"—and, in this case, "memsahibs" as well—would be produced who would only feebly mime their western masters.

In my other work on social reform I have tried to show that this particular design for hegemony was atypical, temporary, undercut by other strategic plans for power and other social perspectives that felt more at home with orthodox Hindu patriarchy than with the early western feminism of the 19th century.[54] The moment of the combined efforts of Vidyasagar and Halliday would seem to disprove my thesis. Let us, then, turn to the fuller history of that collaboration.

Before the Bengal Government had assumed any responsibility for aiding girls' schools, three applications from local people had come to the Inspector General of Schools for funding for three schools—two in Hooghly and one in Burdwan. Initiative, then, lay with Indians themselves. Those letters formed the basis on which investment plans were made. They gave Vidyasagar an opportunity to move out into the districts, rather than concentrate his efforts in Calcutta. His first school was in Jaugram village in Burdwan and the subsequent ones were in the districts as well.[55]

It also seems to be his decision to opt for schools, rather than for home-based education for girls. Implicitly, then, his decision was grounded on a conviction that women needed—for however short a time—an extra-domestic identity, which would move them physically into the public domain. Schools institutionalised women's education as a public, non-domestic activity that would take out girls every day beyond the family and attach them to an extra-familial space, identity and collectivity. They would also, for the first time, generate ties and acquaintances among teachers and peer groups that they would form in their capacity as individuals and which would not be tied to their familial and kinship connections. At schools, too, they would be known under their own proper names: Rashsundari has commented in her book that she was deprived even of a name of her own. This, then, was a kind of muddying up of the other strand in the reformist agenda: that education would be home-based, undertaken by male guardians, a familial activity. Now it takes the form of going away from the home, outside the family, however briefly. There is also a conferral of an identity that might be granted under the family's consent, but that nonetheless was public/non-domestic, as well as individuating.

The fanning out beyond Calcutta seems to go back to the early missionary ventures which had also founded village schools in the twenties. The mission schools, however, were openly tied to proselytisation which required large social and geographical catchment areas from among rural low castes. Government schools, on the other hand, foreswore proselytisation, and Vidyasagar combined his reformism with orthodox brahmanical habits in personal life. In fact, so far as girls' schools were concerned, he relied on a filtration effect that would work best if the notion became widespread among girls of higher social echelons. There was some truth in this observation. Indeed, among low caste Namasudra peasants, the upper caste example inspired many aspiring improvers to seek social advancement by emulating the reformers, thus turning away from an older model which had made them insist on greater seclusion for their women, in imitation of brahmans.[56] Schools were, therefore, founded among high caste clusters in localities like Kulingram in Burdwan.[57] So, with women's education, Vidyasagar came to develop a more slanted vision than what he had about mass level education in general: he seemed to restrict his own thrust here to the upper-caste/middle-class sections outside Calcutta, and thus develop a broader geographical spread, a horizontal expansion, within the same social base.

The choice of places, then, seems to be dictated by neither missionary calculations nor by any previous governmental patterns of investment. It ties in with Vidyasagar's own inclination towards spreading elementary education beyond metropolitan elite reformist enclaves. On 7 September, 1853, Vidyasagar wrote to the Education Council: "What we require is to extend the benefit of education to the mass of the people. Let us establish a number of vernacular schools, let us prepare a series of vernacular class books on useful and instructive subjects..."[58] Women of upper castes, governed by brahmanical orthodoxy, were a part of the Indian masses who had been systematically excluded from elementary education. And here, traditional prohibitions had been fostered by Macaulay who had ruled against the spread of vernacular and elementary education as suggested by Adam, in favour of a more elitist and Anglicist education for the middle classes. Vidyasagar's plans to invest in vernacular, elementary education at non-elite levels militates, then, against Macaulay's vision. It is not the lure of the great English literary tradition but vernacular literacy that emerges as the preferred field of investment. Is mass education then the new strategy of colonial—westernist—Enlightenment mode of domination?

Vidyasagar's moment of success, we must remember, was over before it began. Tied up with the revolt of 1857, and no doubt regretting the possibility that reform might have added its bit to the causes of the Uprising, the Government reneged on its pledges. In May 1858, it refused to sanction larger funds that the new schools would require. The schools were kept going on voluntary contributions. In December 1858, after protracted and bitter negotiations, it agreed to honour the expenses of the schools already in existence, but flatly declared that it would make no further commitment to the cause of women's education. That seemed to be that, and Vidyasagar's plans for steady expansion were well and truly doomed. Shortly afterwards, he retired, and there was nothing more that he would be required to do for government plans for women's education. When in the 1860s, Miss Carpenter submitted her plans for teacher training institutions for adult Hindu women, Vidyasagar refused to have anything to do with them. In his letter of 1 September, 1867 to William Grey, Lt. Governor of Bengal, he pointed out why he thought the scheme was impractical and counter-productive. More than that, he sounded deeply tired, disenchanted and cynical about official motivation and intervention.[59] Women's education was once again left to Indian private enterprise and to reformist and missionary effort. Colonial investment neither stirred it into being, nor helped it significantly. In any case, even with Indian reformers, the educated woman was a middle-class, upper-caste person, albeit from the mofussil.

In the mid-80s, the situation was changed somewhat after the publication of the Hunter Commission recommendations for larger grants-in-aid for girls' schools.[60] Even that would be conditioned by initial Indian private outlay. So, far from women's minds being a major site for the construction of a westernist modernity for whose actualisation colonial governments existed, women's education was the first casualty that the colonial government easily and immediately incurred, when faced with a funds crunch and a political crisis. We need to seek the impulse for *strishiksha* more in the social understanding of Indian reformers and, above all, of women themselves.

While schools continued to increase in a limping and uncertain manner, the *Bamabodhini Patrika* also planned a home-based education, graded along five classes. In a syllabus chalked out for 1869, for instance, we find the first two years were devoted to Bengali grammar, tales and poems and some arithmetic. From the third year, there is also the history of Bengal through questions and answers, geography, hygeine, embroidery and moral readers. In the fourth and fifth years, there is more advanced Bengali literature like Vidyasagar's *Sitar Banabas,* history of England, map of India, geography and science. It seems that science was to be read out of specially designed textbooks for women that were published in a series called *Narishiksha. Narishiksha* also included moral lessons, biographical material, nature studies, hygeine and poems. It was brought out by the Bamabodhini Sabha, and the first part cost four annas while the second part sold for twelve annas. For other subjects, separate books were prescribed, like Jadugopal Chattopadhyay's *Bharatbarsher Sankhipta Itihas.* These textbooks were written for both sexes.[61] Most of the textbooks seem to have been illustrated. Far too many of them, however, had been prescribed, and some help from male guardians was necessary to follow the courses systematically. So much required investment in terms of both time and money would have only been possible in the most advanced reformist families of some affluence.

The emphasis seems to be on reading and writing perfect Bengali, a notion of tales from various cultures as entertainment, some improving moral matter, and a practical course on hygiene. Apart from that, there is quite a bit on elementary natural sciences, some very rudimentary facts about history, and a fair amount of geography, as also several courses on arithmetic. It seems, on the whole, non-gendered and not particularly geared to domestic needs. What is being offered to women is a sense of the world around them.

VII
The Meanings of Knowledge

All the material that went into *strishiksha* was in Bengali. In an early piece in *Bamabodhini* on the necessity of education, the proponent argues that the recent production of Bengali textbooks has paved the way for women's learning, for all its branches are now accessible in the vernacular. The piece also commends the appearance of print: "So many good Bengali books are now very cheaply published."[62] Learning was no longer confined to foreign or classical languages which had lost their monopoly.[63] There was, indeed, an earlier system of vernacular education at elementary and primary levels in the *pathshalas*. That education, however, was strictly practical and instrumental, geared to accounts, book-keeping, arithmetic and spelling and letter-writing.[64] The new concept of education that appeals to women, on the other hand, is the notion of formal knowledge without which, they feel, they no longer see their way around in the world. Vernacular prose and printed books made that kind of knowledge available for them. In fact, the very desire for education could have been largely produced by the availability of books written in their mother-tongue, in their known prose. Knowledge, freed from the ivory tower of unfamiliar classical or foreign tongues, suddenly ceased to be esoteric. It was even something that they could produce themselves by manipulating a language that they knew how to use.

Without a vernacularisation of education, the development of prose and print, such a conviction could not have taken root. In a piece published in *Bamabodhini* in 1865, a mother tells her daughter:

> Thanks to the mercy of the Lord, you are born in very beautiful times. You see the spread of knowledge everywhere these days... So far, ignorant and cruel men had deprived them (women) from such a rare and pleasurable gem that is education... Still they serve them faithfully like servants.[65]

Rashsundari praises her own times in identical words.

Why is knowledge so beautiful? We have already seen that its primary justification is that it reveals sacred truth which is the true inner eye, real seeing. This looks like a piece of religious piety that is entirely blameless and safe. The way the 19th-century woman used it, however, made it problematic and transgressive for the orthodoxy in three ways. First, no Hindu tradition would insist that religion is to be reached primarily through the path of knowledge, so far as the householder is concerned. Vaishnavism, being a proselytising religion, did generate a lot of Bengali sacred literature and thus helped mass education. Yet, it criticised the path of knowledge, counterposing against the arrogant learning of the brahman *pashandi* or sinner, the simple devotion of the lesser folk. Its democratising impulse, then, tended to ground itself on a short-circuiting of knowledge, rather than on its dissemination. In more orthodox traditions, for the woman and the shudra particularly, knowledge is emphatically *not* the way to *dharma*. It is, indeed, antithetical to the *vidhi-nishedha* that regulate their *sansar*.[66] Nor is sacred truth to be confused with modern learning or with temporal issues: the *tols* or brahmanical institutions of higher learning did not have courses on history, geography, natural sciences.[67] On the other hand, if secular learning was to be included in the courses anywhere, it was supposed to yield immediate practical, usable value. The *pathshalas* taught some arithmetic and writing even to peasant boys so that they understood the documents they needed to sign, to write letters and to keep accounts.

Strishiksha breaks with all these assumptions. It insists that religion cannot be practised without knowledge. By an extension, religious knowledge is made to cover human history in all its facets as well as the natural, physical world, for they are all God's handiwork. There is thus a new, entirely modern sense of the world, and its relationship to the individual. The first issue of *Bamabodhini* declared that all varieties of human action—the arts, literature, religion, trade, commerce and industry—would come under this sanctified rubric.[68] Secondly, *strishiksha* insists that all this knowledge is essentially non-gendered—that is, in the field of true religion, women have the same paths to follow as men of their class and caste. Thirdly, it refuses to link up knowledge with any immediately practical results. There is not yet a demand that education for women can be a means of livelihood—even though the *Bamabodhini* does mention that "these days, several women are writing good books and they make a profit with that."[69] Rashsundari herself would be an early example of that earning capacity, though she is silent about this aspect of her book. However, that, in itself, would not be a major argument since that sort of income would be limited and uncertain. In any case, no reformer had as yet ventured to forward a case for economic self-sufficiency for the upper-caste woman.

Knowledge, at this stage, then, has a more pure function for women than it has for men who, obviously, need it to get by in the world, to earn their living. In the first issue of *Bamabodhini,* a set of bold defences is formulated: learning for its own sake is desirable for it develops the faculties and opens the inner eye. It is significant that this primary function is being appropriated more for women, since men will use knowledge for practical purposes. For upper-caste men, then, education would not have held out such broad transformative hopes for a radical self-fashioning, since the purpose of education would largely be similar to what they would have expected from Persian learning in older times. Secondly, it is stated that this will give confidence to women to use their own judgement and thereby reduce their dependence on men: a bold reason, indeed, and one that bears out all the orthodox fears and anxieties. Thirdly, it will generate self-respect, for without that they accept the low esteem that men have reserved for them.[70] Not economic independence, but independence from men's opinion, regard, intellectual support. We find echoes of all these arguments in *AJ,* most especially, the argument for non-reliance, for self-sufficiency. In contrast to this non-instrumentalist approach to pure knowledge, male education stressed its instrumentalist function, its role in acquisition of power and profits.

In an educational tract for women, written in the form of a dialogue between mother and daughter, the mother tells the daughter that without education, she would have to rely on men all her life. As a result, men will convince her that she would find fulfilment in cooking, and caring for them. In another piece, women are urged to harbour sisterly feelings—*bhaginibhav*—for all women. However, there was an obverse side to all this. The new kind of home that is to emerge out of this was to be a recovery of the happy Hindu homes of old times. Even Keshub Chandra Sen, the noted Brahmo reformer, set up the Victoria College to train good Hindu women.[71] In the later decades of the century, growing Hindu revivalism was thus able to inflect the agenda even of sections of liberal reform and to appropriate reformist projects to some extent, for community purposes.

VIII
Late 19th Century Leaps and Their Limits

After the first part of *AJ* came out, Rashsundari lived to see more efforts for more comprehensive schemes for *strishiksha*. The second part of the autobiography concludes on a very optimistic vein in this respect. Certain new thrusts were developed from the 1870s, as the supervision of education was transferred from central to provincial levels.[72] One was the expansion of higher educational facilities for girls, and the other was some provision for the education for adult women through boarding schools—a step that accentuated the move away from familial confines. There is more of English medium education at higher levels, as girls now reach up to university courses. On the other hand, there is also a movement towards breaching the bastion of male knowledge—the arduous medical degrees and training that, a decade earlier, had been considered polluting and dangerous even for upper-caste men. Finally, schooling had spread far enough to become an option even for girls from the most orthodox of families who tried to combine it with a rigorous training in Hindu rites and domestic skills. As *strishiksha* strained upwards, there was comparatively far too little that was done to broaden the base at elementary or primary levels, outside towns and cities, among low-caste or poor people.

The Brahmo reformer Keshubchandra Sen set up a boarding school for grown up women under the auspices of the Bharat Sanskar Sabha in 1871. The curriculum consisted of regular courses in English, Bengali, geography, maths, science—a curriculum that was both non-gendered and secular. In 1876 the Banga Mahila Vidyalaya began to provide facilities for the University Entrance Examinations. It is noticeable that it was an English-medium school and most of the teachers were English women—a departure that became inevitable since these schools needed to keep in step with boys' schools. The growing equality with male educational institutions meant a turning away from a broader base among illiterate poor women. In 1878, with some government help, it amalgamated with the Bethune School to form the Bethune English School. In the same year, Dacca started a similar school.[73]

In 1878, a giant step was taken when two Bengali girls—Kadambini Bose and Chandramukhi Bose—passed the Degree examination and became eligible for graduate courses. This was something that would not be possible for English girls for the next few decades since English universities refused them access to formal university degrees. It is remarkable that this was allowed in Calcutta which had a much thinner ground-level basis for women's literacy and primary and secondary education than Britain had, and which was governed by a colonial ruling class that drew its highest recruits from the conservative landed English gentry. It speaks of the force of indigenous reformism that made such combined, uneven development possible. It also speaks of the fact that the colonial government would not see the educated Indian woman as a threat to itself or its male monopoly on offices which the white woman graduate in England could become. The first two Indian graduates had been private students. From 1888, the Bethune School started graduate courses and developed a college wing.[74]

In 1882, Abala Das and a Christian girl, Ellen D'Abrew,

were refused admission by the Calcutta Medical School, and had to seek entry into the more liberal Madras Medical College. That started off a public agitation for change, and the Lt. Governor was persuaded to change the rules to enable girls' admission the next year. Kadambini Bose was the first woman to receive a full medical degree in 1888.[75] The Medical College also offered certificate courses in midwifery which were rather more popular than the full medical training.[76]

The conservatives at last conceded the unavoidability of girls' education, and even of schooling. In 1893, Mataji Tapaswini, a woman ascetic with the most unimpeachable credentials in Hindu piety, opened a girls' school in Calcutta, appropriately named the Mahakali Pathshala. It offered courses in Sanskrit, Bengali, very rudimentary arithmetic, cooking and midwifery. It also taught the girls the proper Hindu female rites and a hefty prize was awarded for offering the most impeccably performed *puja*. It is significant that however loaded the syllabus was with Hindu domesticity, it needed to be taught at school, confirming the wider acceptability of the non-domestic principle that underwrote the activity of schooling itself.[77]

By the beginning of the last decade of the century, according to an educational report, we have one out of sixty girls "fit for education" going to school, as against one out of four such boys. Fitness was, obviously, decided according to economic ability, which would immediately exclude very large categories. This was admittedly a miniscule proportion although the report registered a threefold increase in the last ten years. While there were five English-medium high schools, and three English medium primary ones, there were 24 middle Bengali schools, 273 upper primary ones and 1,932 lower primary ones. There was also one college that offered courses for graduate degrees. The stream of students was thin and it petered out quite rapidly at the higher reaches. Out of a total expenditure of Rs. 3,51,087 on *strishiksha,* the Government paid up about Rs. 1,26,520. Education was primarily supported by private bodies, mostly of enlightened landholders who formed reformist associations for that purpose: Uttarpara Hitakari Sabha, Madhya Bangla Sammilani, Jessore-Khulna Sammilani, Taki Hitakari Sabha, Faridpur Suhridsabha. The preponderance of district associations, and the primacy of efforts from Eastern Bengal are worth noting.[78] The Government made a contribution of Rs. 2,876 for the provision of zenana or home-based education through teachers trained at Normal cchools, and the scheme covered about 5,662 students. A far larger number would be taught at home by fathers, husbands, and increasingly, mothers.[79]

IX
End-of-the-Century Blues

Predictably, this shift produced deep, mournful dirges, end-of-the-century blues from the emergent revivalist-nationalists. Their vision of autonomous and authentic Hindu nationhood was firmly tied to an unalloyed, pure, fully-preserved structure of Hindu domestic norms. A shift in its coordinates—especially if inspired by liberalism and reformism conveyed by an alien system of power-knowledge—would be *the* ultimate surrender to colonisation. *Strishiksha,* that women themselves saw as a means of liberating themselves from older, domestic, regulatory norms, was catastrophic for cultural nationalism.[80]

At the same time, I do not see that the real issue at stake here is the construction of nation or tradition, that gender is merely the site on which the structure is raised.[81] Gender

can hardly be a marginal concern that is left behind once the
debates take off on the so-called crucial themes of tradition
etc. What would be of more real concern to any system of
male privileges than movements to alter customary patterns
of life?

We began this exercise with a close look at the structure
of early traditional fears that had prohibited *strishiksha* with a
battery of interdictions. When we look at the altered situation
at the close of the century, we find a somewhat different order
of fears about the horrible sign of modernity—the educated
woman. There is, above all, the terror of inversion—the threat
of man turned into woman, the woman rendered male. It is
portrayed in terms of physical, biological alteration of male and
female species. Women are unable to reproduce, their breasts
are flattened out, their milk has dried up. The *Vedavyas* cited
"scientific" data to warn that even the umbilical cord is crippled
by education. Reproduction withers away. It is interesting
how earlier fears about widowhood are replayed on the new
register of loss of motherhood, now that nationalism has come
to valorise the mother-figure above the older preoccupation
with the wife. Kedarnath Mandal's play *Behadda Behaya*
(1894) pushes the masculinised, educated female body into
the wrestling arena: as a result of her education, it seems, the
woman has sprouted muscles strong enough for wrestling.[82]

And, of course, the educated woman will develop masculine
traits of character, as well as claim masculine privileges and ways.
Satire was an excellent mode of commenting upon inversion.
Even though *strishiksha* was enabled by vernacularisation of
education, in Radhabinode Haldar's *Pash kara Maag,* she will
only speak a strange mother-tongue where English words
and phrases freely jostle with Bengali.[83] She dominates her
henpecked husband who has been rendered meek, nervous

and submissive by *strishiksha:* for it makes women out of men. In Kalighat paintings and wood-cuts, he is dragged along as a tamed, chained animal by his modern wife, he neglects his mother when his wife commands him to do so. Printed cartoons lampooned the husband and the wife who have changed places with *strishiksha*. In the cartoons in *Basantak,* in the 1870s, we see the wife absorbed in a book. In the next room, the husband is crawling on the floor, hopelessly trying to light the hearth, nearly blinded by smoke. The wife calls out in irritation; "Why did you not close the door before all that smoke escaped into my room?" The mockery pursued the couple beyond the century. Jatin Sen's cartoon of the educated woman shows her smoking a huge cigar which is clearly a substitute penis.[84]

Inversion of physical and social functions is based on a particular economy of gender attributes. *Strishiksha* transfers something that men possessed, to women. With that transaction, masculinity and femininity change places, bodies. Subordination continues, but now the chains are put on men. It is as if education is a physical attribute, whose transference to women will physically and mentally masculinise them. Moreover, it is a scarce resource which cannot be shared but can only be shifted. If women have it, then men have to lose it. It thus stands in for male power, male physique: when grafted on women, sexual difference is neatly switched around.

We now begin to comprehend what the reformist suggestion of *strishiksha*—however tame, moderate, domesticated— actually involved. In colonial Bengal, for a non-entrepreneurial, passive land-owning and rent-receiving middle class, education was the only resource that fitted out the man with a self-image of transformative enterprise. Divorced from the higher reaches of business and industry by colonial discriminations, kept out of the army and of administration, and perpetually taunted for effeminacy by the master race, education provided a rare and precious opportunity to prove worth, gain esteem, establish initiative in the pubic realm of men. Even parasitic landlordism seemed threatened and the comforts of assured rent-income breached with late 19th century modifications in the Permanent Settlement. The middle-class, upper-caste man defined his masculine identity primarily in terms of his mastery over the written word. If masculinity required a self-differentiation from the feminine, then recreating female subjectivity as educated was a dangerous gift. It would undermine the supreme marker of the necessary difference and allow the surfacing of the repressed feature that would fatally destabilise culturally ordered sexual difference.

Fears were also about the loss of a beloved solace: that of a childlike wife whose innocence is based on ignorance. The satire was a protest against her growing up. For her adulthood, pronounced and established through her education, would yet again undermine a necessary sexual difference: the grown man can be sure of his masculinity if the woman remains a child forever.

The child-wife also preserved for the man—humiliated and beseiged by the pressures of colonisation—the precious memories of his own happier childhood, a pre-colonial past. Sumit Sarkar has pointed out the deep nostalgia for childhood and for the past that pervaded the 1870s when the intelligentsia was caught in a hiatus: after the activism of liberal reformers had run into a dead-end, and before the activism of organised nationalism came into its own.[85] The childlike wife was at once the recreated early innocence as well as a route back to that experience of blessedness. The protest against *strishiksha* was a cry for that beloved infant, a demand to repossess the childlike mind. In the 1890s, with the Age of Consent agitation, the Bengali man would make an effort to retain the childish body for himself.[86] To possess the child in the woman was to feel like a man in the colonised world.

Notes

1. See Rosalind O'Hanlon, *A Comparison Between Women and Men: Tarabai Shinde and the Critique of Gender Relations in Colonial India,* Oxford University Press, Madras, 1994, Introduction. The Bengali texts that I discuss here, however, precede Shinde's writing by almost two decades.

2. See Kailashbashini Debi, *Hindu Abalaganer Bidyavhyash O Tahar Samunnati,* Calcutta, 1878.

3. *Shiksha Sankranta Bibaran,* 1867–68; Jaistha, 1868. In the collection of extracts from Bharari Ray, ed, *Sekaler Narishiksha: Bamabodhini Patrika, 1270–1329,* Women's Studies Research Centre, University of Calcutta, Calcutta, 1994 p. 65.

4. *Shiksha Sankranta Bibaran,* Bhadra, 1272 and citations from Martin's Report on Women's Education in *Bamabodhini Patrika* ibid., pp. 28–30.

5. See Keith Michael Baker, "Defining the Public Sphere in 18th Century France: Variations on a Theme by Habermas" in Craig and Calhoun, eds, *Habermas and the Public Sphere,* MPP Press, Cambridge, 1992, pp. 203–08.

6. Brajendranath Bandopadhyay and Sajanikanta Das, eds, *Rammohan Granthabali,* Vol 3, nd, p. 45.

7. Benoy Ghosh, ed, *Samayikpatre Banglar Samajchitra,* vol 2, Papyrus, Calcutta, 1978, pp. 27–28.

8. Kailashbashini Debi, *Hindu Mahilaganer Heenabastha* (Calcutta, 1863).

9. See Subodhchandra Sengupta, ed, *Sansad Bangali Chartabhidhan,* Calcutta, 1976, p. 64.

10. Letter of Phalgun, 1272 (1865), in *BP*, p. 26.

11. "Whatever Happened to the Vedic Dasi? Orientalism, Nationalism and a Script for the Past" in Kumkum Sangari and Sudesh Vaid, eds, *Recasting Women: Essays on Colonial History*, Kali for Women, Delhi, 1989.

12. Letter of Baisakh, 1272, *BP*, ibid, pp. 27–28.

13. Letter of hadra, 1274, ibid, p. 45.

14. Shrimati S-d, ibid, p. 55.

15. Ramesh Chandra Mirra, *Education, 1833–1905,* in N.K. Sinha, ed, *History of Bengal, 1757–1905,* Calcutta, 1967, p. 419.

16. Section 5, *Female Instruction* in Second Report on the State of Education in Bengal, 1836, by William Adam. Edited by Ananthnath Basu, Calcutta University, Calcutta, 1941, pp. 187-88.

17. Shibnath Shastri, *Atmacharit,* Calcutta, 1952, p. 22.

18. Vidyalankar, *Strishikshavidhayak: Arthat Puratan O Idanintan O Bideshiya Striloker Drishtanta,* Calcutta, 1822, p. 3.

19. *Striloker Bidyashikshar Abashyakata: Gyanada O Saralar Kathopakathon, BP,* 1863, 1st issue, op cit, pp. 2–3.

20. S.P. Pal, *Meeyeder Lekhapara, Apna Hate Dube Mitra,* Calcutta, 1897.

21. See Sangari and Vaid, eds, *Recasting Women: Essays in Colonial History,* op. cit., Introduction.

22. Kailashbashini Debi, op cit.

23. Adams' Second Report, op cit.

24. Kailashbashini Debi, *Hindu Abalttkider Biclyahhyash O Tahar Samunnati,* Calcutta, 1878, pp. 23–24.

25. Adam's Second Report, op cit.

26. Debendranath Tagore, *Swarachita Jiban Charit,* Calcutta, 1898, p. 5. Reprinted in *Atmakatha, Ananya.* publications, Calcutta, 1981.

27. Adam, Second Report, op cit.

28. Sarada Debi, *Atmakatha.* Compiled by Abhaya Dasgupta. Ramakrishna Mission Institute of Culture, Calcutta, 1979, p. 4.

29. See the biographical sketches of Jogin Ma and Gouri Ma in Swami Gambhiranand, *Shree Ramakrishna Bhaktamalika,* Part 11, Udbodhan Karyalay, Calcutta, 1989.

30. See N.L. Basak, *History of Vernacular Education in Bengal, 1800–1854,* Bharati Book Stall, Calcutta, 1974, pp. 144–46.

31. Mrs. Mullens, *Phulmoni O Karuna,* Kanchan Basu ed, *Dushprapya Sahitya Sangraha,* Calcutta, 1992, reprint.

32. Entry for 12 December; Mrs. Laird, ed, *Selections from Heber's Journal,* in Ballhatchet, Marshall and Pocock, ed., *The European Understanding of India: Bishop Heber in Northern India—Selections from Heber's Journal,* Cambridge University Press, 1971, pp. 49–50.

33. *Bamabodhini Patrika,* in Bharati Ray, op. cit., pp. 1–5.

34. Adams' Report, op cit, p. 453.

35. Shibnath Shastri, *Ramtanu Lahiri O Tatkalin Bangasamaj,* New Age Publishers, Calcutta, 1956.

36. Sumit Sarkar, "Vidyasagar and Brahmanical Society", in *Writing Social History,* Oxford University Press, Delhi, 1997.

37. See Basak, op cit, p. 80.

38. See Romesh Chandra Mitra, op cit, p. 453.

39. See Mitra, ibid.

40. Ballhatchet, et al, op cit, p. 68.

41. See Sumit Sarkar, "The Complexities of Young Bengal" in *A Critique of Colonial India,* Papyrus, Calcutta, 1985, p. 27.

42. Sumit Sarkar, "The Women's Question in Bengal", in *A Critique of Colonial India,* op cit.

43. On the significance of a new mode of comprehending time, see Sumit Sarkar, "Renaissance and Kaliyuga: Time, Myth and History in Colonial Bengal" in *Writing Social History,* op cit.

44. See Sumit Sarkar, "Rammohun Roy and the Break with the Past", in *A Critique of Colonial India,* op cit, p. 4.

45. *Strilokdiger Bidyashikshar Abashyakata, Bamabodhini fatrika,* first issue, 1863. See Bharati Ray, *Shekaler Narishiksha,* op cit.

46. Bharati Ray, op cit, Introduction.

47. Shibnath Shastri, *Ramtanu Lahiri,* op cit, p. 172.

48. Chandicharan Bandyopadhyay, *Vidyasagar,* third edition, Indian Press, Allahabad, 1909, p. 196.

49. *Sambad Prabhakar,* 10/2/1856, in Benoy Ghosh, *Samayikpatre Banglar Samajchitra, 2,* Papyrus, Calcutta, 1978, p. 34.

50. Benoy Ghosh, *Samayikpatre,* op cit, p. 31.

51. Cited in *Sambad Prabhakar,* 31/1/1859, Benoy Ghosh, *Samayikpatre,* op cit, p. 31.

52. On Vidyasagar and girls' schooling, see Chandicharan Bandyopadhyay, op cit. pp. 120–209; Bharati Ray, ed, *Sekaler Narishiksha,* op cit, Introduction; Romesh Mitra, op cit; Ashoke Sen. *Ishwarchandra Vidyasagar and the Elusive Milestones,* Riddhi India, Calcutta, 1977; Sumit Sarkar, *Vidyasagar and Brahmanical Society,* op cit.

53. Gauri Vishwanathan, *Masks of Conquest: Literary Study and British Rule in India.,* New York, Columbia University Press, 1989, Introduction.

54. See Tanika Sarkar, "Colonial Lawmaking and Lives/Deaths of Indian Women: Different Readings of Law and Community", in Ratna Kapur, ed, *Feminist Terrains in Legal Domains: Interdisciplinary Essays on Women and Law in India,* Kali for Women, Delhi, 1996.

55. See Ashoke Sen, *Iswarchandra Vidyasagar,* op cit.

56. Sekhar Bandyopadhyay, "Caste, Widow-remarriage and the Reform of Popular Culture in Colonial Bengal" in Bharati Ray, ed, *From the Seams of History: Essays on Indian Women,* Oxford University Press, Delhi, 1995, pp. 8–37.

57. Sumit Sarkar, "Vidyasagar and Brahmanical Society" in *Writing Social History,* op. cit., pp. 278–81.

58. Ibid.

59. Ashoke Sen, *Ishwarchandra Vidyasagar,* op cit; Sumit Sarkar, *Vidyasagar,* op cit.

60. Geraldine Forbes, *Women in Modern India,* The New Cambridge

History of India, Cambridge University Press, Cambridge, 1966, chapter 2.

61. See Bharati Ray, ed, *Sekaler Narishiksha,* op cit, pp. 71–76.

62. Ibid.

63. Op cit, *Vidya Bishayak Kathopakathan,* p. 7.

64. See Poromesh Acharya, "Indigenous Education and Brahmanical Hegemony in Bengal", and Kazi Shahidullali, "The Purpose and Impact of Government Policy on Pathshala Gurumohashoys in Nineteenth Century Bengal", in Nigel Crook, ed, *The Transmission of Knowledge in South Asia: Essays on Education, Religion, History and Politics,* Oxford University Press, Delhi, 1996, pp. 98–135.

65. Ibid, *Kanyar Prati Matar Upadesh,* pp. 12–13.

66. On the complicated relationships between women and religious learning in Reformation and Counter-Reformation France and Germany, see Natalie Zemon Davis, "City Women and Religious Change" in *Society and Culture in Early Modern France,* Duckworth, U.K., 1975, pp. 66–84; Also Lyndal Roper, *The Holy Household: Women and Morals in Reformation Angsburg,* Clarendon Press, Oxford, 1989, pp. 260–66.

67. See Dinesh Chandra Sen, op. cit.

68. Ibid.

69. *Vidyabishyak Kathopakathan, Bamabodhini,* 1863. See Bharati Ray, ed *Sekaler Narishiksha,* op cit.

70. Ibid.

71. *Narishiksha,* Part 2, "*Antahpurika O Vidyalayastha Chhatriganer Vyavaharartha*", Calcutta, 1884, pp. 135–94.

72. Usha Chakraborty, *Condition of Bengali Women Around the Second Half of the Nineteenth Century,* Calcutta, 1963, p. 48.

73. Ibid, p. 49.

74. Ibid, p. 50.

75. Ibid, p. 54.

76. *Bangadeshe Strishiksha,* Baisakh, 1892, *Bamabodhini Patrika.*

77. Usha Chakraborty, op cit, p. 52.

78. *Bangadeshe Strishiksha,* Baisakh, 1892, *Bamabodhini Patrika,* Bharati Ray, ed, op cit, pp. 227–29.

79. Ibid.

80. See Tanika Sarkar, "The Hindu Wife and the Hindu Nation: Domesticity and Nationalism in Nineteenth Century Bengal", *Studies in History,* 8,2, ns, 1993.

81. This has been the suggestion made on the earlier *sati* debates by Lata Mani. See her "Contentious Traditions: The Debate on *Sati* in Colonial India" in Sangari and Vaid, eds. *Recasting Women,* op. cit.

82. See Jayanta Goswami, *Samajchitre Unahingsha Shatabdir Bangla Prahashan,* Calcutta, 1974, pp. 908–63.

83. Ibid.

84. See Partha Mitter, *Art and Nationalism in India: 1850–1922: Occidental Orientations,* Cambridge University Press, 1994, pp. 171, 173.

85. Sumit Sarkar, "Chakri and Kaliyug", in *Writing Social History,* op. cit.

86. Tanika Sarkar, "Rhetoric against the Age of Consent and the Death of a Child Wife", *Economic and Political Weekly,* 28, 36, 4 September, 1993.

5
Women's Writings

I
Creation of New Reading Needs

Rashsundari was the first Bengali woman to write a full-scale autobiography,[1] but she was by no means the first woman writer to publish her work. For at least twenty years before *Amar Jiban* came out, there had existed a distinctive tradition of women's writings in print, many of which intersected with Rashsundari's concerns from multiple perspectives and vantage points.

At first, women could write about only a few things. They could talk about the nature and the necessity of *strishiksha,* they could describe the domestic world from their own vantage point, and they could write stories, plays and poems on intimate matters, on emotional themes, for women were acknowledged as privileged, authoritative voices in the realm of feelings and sentiments. Without a sustained level of high, formal education, they could write little else at first that would be significant, new or informative. Yet, there was a steady market for what they had to say. Rashsundari found a well-known literary figure eager to write the preface to her book. Soudamini Debi, another little-educated woman in dire financial straits, hoped to eke out a living for herself and for her desperately ailing husband, from her writing.[2] Krishnakamini Dasi, whose book of poems was probably the first publication by a Bengali woman, wrote in the preface that her unworthy offering would probably pick up a sympathetic reception "from social-minded gentlemen", precisely because she was a woman.[3]

We saw earlier how new material and social conditions had combined to produce the writing woman in the 19th century. There was yet another reason for seeking out the woman's opinion, her writings. Reforms and legislative innovations in the world of public affairs revolved very largely around conjugal norms: sati, widow remarriage, *strishiksha,* child marriage, divorce and age of consent. They hoped to change the life-world of the upper-caste Hindu woman. In the process they also rendered the upper-caste Hindu home a deeply problematic territory. Major lines of argument related to the problem of whether to see it as a prison or as a sanctuary for the woman. One outcome of our colonial modernity—where so much of the criticism of the colonial order was made in the name of the consent and the will of the subjected—was that neither reform nor orthodoxy could entirely do without referring to the will of the woman when it came to gender-based legislation. The defenders of *sati* talked about her consent as much as did the proponents of widow remarriage.[4] The age of consent debates similarly hinged on conflicting constructions of the woman's own decision.[5] Much of the public sphere of critical debates on matters of large general interest was formed out of the new newspapers and journals that were founded to discuss gender issues and reformist legislations.[6] The woman's writings, again, would be solicited and publicised on both sides of the dividing line. Of course, reformists had an added advantage, since they taught their women to read and write. Out of the four polemical tracts by women in the period between the 1850s and 1870s, only one was anti-reform.[7]

Edwin and Shirley Ardener have made a distinction between the sphere of articulation and of social and self-representation of dominant groups and that of "muted" groups who do not have access to public modes of articulation and hence cannot set general cultural standards or norms. While they need to accept the standards decided upon by dominant groups, they, nonetheless, have a sliver of existence, in certain regions of practice and belief that lie outside the cultural world created by dominant groups. The latter would view this area as a "wild zone", beyond their knowledge and hence beyond their structuring. We might extend the paradigm to argue that male discomforts about the limits of knowability would create a market for women's writing. It would be an act of voyeurism as well as an act of necessity, of overcoming gaps in knowledge, and to look upon what has so far been hidden from view.[8]

II
A Study of Two Letters

We have little evidence of what women wrote in their private capacity, apart from what they considered to be publishable material. There are, however, a few handwritten letters that Panchanan Mandal had collected from village homes of fairly ordinary people. Most of the time, women would get village boys to write their letters for them. If they knew some writing, however, love letters would be something that women would prefer to write by themselves—whether to a husband or to a lover. Mandal's collection has a few illuminating samples. In two letters written by Manmohini Dasi and Champaklatika Dasya, around the mid-century, to their beloved—from the mode of romantic address, it cannot be ascertained if it is a husband or a lover—the spelling goes a bit haywire. Apart from that, the language is controlled, polished, classically hyperbolic, following the romantic conventions of Vaishnav love lyrics and the highly rhetorical tropes of Bharatchandra, the great 18th-century poet of erotic love. It seems that both women were highly conversant with some of the upper reaches of Bengali literature. We do not know whether the familiarity came from reading them in manuscript or in printed editions, or from oral recitations, or—as could be in the case with Vaishnav lyrics—from musical renderings. Love lyrics formed a major part of the Vaishnav sacred music, *kirtans,* which were sung on all ritual occasions. In any case, both of them had appropriated fragments of that literature and its basic style with great fluency. Both had a way of breaking into verse, probably of their own making, and Champaklatika, in particular, had considerable flair for arranging her prose according to an internal metrical structure. Rashsundari's alteration between prose and verse is something that happens often and with great ease in these letters. Probably, most women were more familiar with verses which were largely orally conveyed, than with prose which required a lot of systematic reading. They were also habituated to a frequent use of verses through proverbs that rhymed and through lullabies—both of which were integral parts of women's speech, and often, of women's creation as well.[9]

Both letters are non-individuated, giving no details of the individual lover's physical or mental characteristics or about the nature of the specific relationships. Broad-stroke, conventional, stock phrases and words are used to describe his looks, his beauty, his perfidy as contrasted to the love and suffering of the letter writer. Certain lyrical gestures and feminine moods are repeated, especially those of the woman suffering from disregard or long separation.[10] A similar kind of derivative tendency is very marked in Rashsundari's hyperbolic devotional perorations, although they do sometimes veer off onto unexpected tracks. It seems that if there is a well-thumbed and appropriate poetic vocabulary that exists and that captures the basic mood of the writer, then the inclination is to repeat that rather than innovate in order to individuate one's own experiences and statements.

III
Women Authors: A New Category

Usha Chakraborty has composed a very comprehensive Author Index of Bengali women writers between 1856 and 1910. I have looked closely at the list for the period between the 1850s and 1870s—the time between Rashsundari's first venture into reading and the publication of her book. I have also done a break-up of the themes and the genres, and I have studied a few representative yet diverse texts in some detail, to situate *AJ* against different kinds of women's writings.[11]

In the period under survey, there are about sixty-five odd books by women that got published, and that were dated. There are twenty-eight volumes of poems, by far the largest single genre. There are eight plays, seven novellas, four advisory tracts, one volume of past recollections and one full-scale autobiography, which, of course, is *Amar Jiban*. The rest is a collection of reading matter on reform, especially on *strishiksha;* they include textbooks, educational material like biographies, polemic for women's improvement and education.[12]

Quite a large number of authors listed in the catalogue are
anonymous, they indicate their sex in the preface. A lot of
them do not use their family surnames which would have
indicated their caste status. Following the Bengali convention,
they affix Debi or Dasi after their first names. While Debi
was only used by upper-caste women, Dasi might indicate a
shudra caste or, equally, an upper-caste woman from a Vaishnav
family. Of those who do offer their surnames, the majority
seems to come from Kayastha or Vaidya families: both upper
castes, though non-brahman, both with a tradition of learning
behind them.[13] Although few of the authors have anything to
say about their wealth and status, their access to education and
to publishing facilities does indicate that their families were
affluent and of some social importance. Soudamini Debi alone
talks about her poverty and her need to make money through
writing. It is very difficult to know anything about their ages.
Soudamini Debi says that she is a young woman, and Haribala
Debi's father, a District Magistrate, writes in the preface to
her book that she is fifteen.[14] Quite a few of them were fairly
prolific writers, publishing from nine to eleven or twelve
books, often on a variety of themes: Ambujasundari Dasgupta,
Girindramohini Dasi, Mankumari Datta, Prasannamoyee
Debi.[15] Calcutta and its surrounding district towns had the
main clusters of publishing and printing, but quite a few came
out from the East Bengal district towns, including Pabna.[16]

Krishnakamini Dasi writes in her preface that hers is the
first book by a Bengali woman to come out in print. She did
not write any others. *Chittabilashini,* a collection of poems,
appeared in 1856. She does append a short autobiographical
note which indicates that she was born in an upper-caste
Kayastha family in the Hooghly district. It is interesting
that she offers no information on the new family that she

was married into. The primacy that she gives to the natal family and lineage goes against the social injunction that the woman's real affiliation is not to her natal family but to the matrimonial one.

In a preface, written in extremely chaste, weighty prose, Krishnakamini mentions her debt to her husband whom she refers to as *pranaballabh,* or the enchanter of her soul. Of course, women's writings had used more passionate addresses in other pre-modern Indian languages. But they were either put into the words of a third person, a character different from the author, or were addressed to God, who is an acceptable, universal object of love. For the first time, at least in Bengali, we find a standard Sanskrit endearment being uttered by the woman in public in her own persona: print, thus, plucks out private words from the domain of speech and intimate letters, both meant only for one person, and allows the woman access to an unprecedented, almost shocking boldness. It instantly violates the fundamental norm of feminine modesty, silence, invisibility in public, indeed, her non-existence in that domain. We have read in *AJ* that women were supposed to be mute even in front of most family members. A wife did not talk to her husband in the presence of other people. Print now enables her to address him in an outspokenly intimate way in front of an unknown, anonymous circle, in public. And, yet, the address feigns a counterfeit privacy and pretends to ignore the presence of others who, indeed, are the intended addressees.

Rashsundari also plays on this juxtaposition of forbidden speech, private matters and the public medium of utterance. She describes her days of going without food, and then suddenly she seems to retract the description by saying that such things cannot be mentioned in public. She thus has her say in indelible print, and also makes the required gesture of cancelling out the unmentionable. Such a play was open to everybody with the coming of print and the formation of a largely print-mediated public sphere. The range of unsayables, however, was far larger for women, hence their utterances through print set up a more complicated play. It was this access to maximised publicity within a simulated intimate mode of utterance that enabled women to discuss their most private matters so thoroughly and at such length.

Krishnakamini's language is highly classicised, on the whole, though in one or two poems she uses a few swear words, expressing a wider linguistic range than what most later women poets would use. There are fragments from Bharatchandra's *Vidyasundar,* the 18th century erotic classic, displaying a high level of erudition. The metrical structures, strictly classical, are varied, and her control over rhythm and rhyming is of a high order. There is little to distinguish it from the corpus of serious male poetic writings of her times. An unusual note, however, is struck in her poem on a citiscape ("*Dibabashaner Shobha*") when she describes the view of the city from a rooftop at sunset. A romantic view of an urban landscape is rather rare in these times, since natural beauty has always been strongly associated with rural scenes or with cultivated gardens. Making poetry out of a citiscape was a modernistic enterprise, and it is strange to find a woman doing this. Another departure lies in her celebration of everything modern, from the railways to the British Raj, with especial emphasis on the advent of *strishiksha.* The standard literary tropes for talking about the times were those of decay, moral and material, of a catastrophic new world that destroys the old order without bringing in an adequate replacement. The standard mood was that of melancholy.[17] Krishnakamini's political and literary departure coincides with Rashsundari's celebration of her own times, her age: "Blessed, blessed be this kaliyug."

There is an allegorical verse drama between the woman's virtue and her vice. The former wins the argument with a strong defence of *strishiksha* while the latter contends that it will usher in immoral letter writing and loss of chastity. Virtue insists that men and women are born from the same source, they share the same Maker, so what is desirable for one cannot be undesirable for the other. There is another verse drama on the woes of the daughters of the very pure sub-castes of *kulins* whose husbands were notoriously polygamous. The moral stricture at the end, however, strongly pleads for perfect chastity even from the ill-treated wives. The conservative concluding note of caution was a strategic necessity. The educated woman was especially concerned to establish that under no circumstances would she advocate the abandonment of female chastity, suspected, as she would be, of innately immoral traits because of her education. There is also a short skit, a dialogue between two widows who are overjoyed at the prospect of the new law on the age of consent. So, the boundaries of old chastity are reformulated even as chastity itself is upheld as a non-negotiable article of faith. For, according to all canon of traditional morality, it was unthinkable for widows to consider remarriage.[18]

Krishnakamini was a housewife from an upper-caste, well-off family and, as such, was not so different from Rashsundari, though she had a more romantic relationship with a husband who supported her venture into writing. We now take up a woman who came from a diametrically opposite social pole. Sukumari Datta (Golap) was a well-known actress associated with the Bengal theatre, and was among the first four actresses who appeared on the public stage when she acted in Madhusudan Dutt's historical play *Sharmistha* in 1873. She later developed a close relationship with Madhusudan and his children. Actresses of that generation were drawn from the ranks of prostitutes and they were given a fairly rigorous musical, dance and educational training in the better theatre companies. Sukumari, who became extremely well-known as an actress, was later encouraged by the reformers to marry Gosthabihari Datta, an actor from a respectable family. There was a tremendous furore over the episode which was mentioned as a major news item in the *Education Gazette* of 12 February 1875. Marrying a prostitute/actress meant ruining the purity of the entire lineage, and the husband, moreover, came from an upper-caste family. The marriage was enabled by a new Act, Regulation III of 1872, that had been passed under urgent pressure from the Brahmo reformers. A radical marriage proposal, it eliminated the need for parental consent and allowed intercaste and community marriages, legalised divorce and raised the age of marriage.[19] The family, to avoid dishonour, disinherited and disclaimed the son. The couple lived in dire poverty. Gostha travelled to England as a sailor in search of a living, but he died there in a practically penniless state. Sukumari gave birth to a daughter shortly afterwards. Although she decided to earn a living by writing plays, obviously her first venture did not pay enough and *Apurba Sati* seems to be the only play that she wrote. She was forced to go back to acting but her long absence from the stage had dimmed her prospects and she died in great distress. This was probably the only well-known play written by an actress.[20]

Apurba Sati Natak: Tragedy! Tragedy! Tragedy! was published by the author herself from Calcutta in 1875. It seems to have been staged as well. It is the story of the daughter of a prostitute who has acquired some education and who refuses to engage in her mother's profession. She falls in love with a penniless boy, and when the mother tells her to go to bed with a client, she threatens to kill herself. She does manage to protect her virtue, but unable to unite with her beloved, she commits suicide. The play is largely in the melodramatic mode but it is quite verbose, full of long moralising dialogues and monologues. There is a suggestive and titillating scene where the mother dresses the daughter on the stage to prepare her for her first client. This scene would not have been written by another woman author. In any case, most other contemporary women playwrights chose to deal with historical themes rather than contemporary and social ones. There is a dialogue on the necessity of womanly chastity, a familiar issue with most women writers, but there is a significant difference. The argument in its defence is a practical rather than a moral one: the immoral woman lives a life of great insecurity once her youth is gone. The play is clearly autobiographical, as well as a piece of wish-fulfilment, since the alter-ego of the author, the heroine Nalini, dies a virgin—educated, virtuous and untainted. The vastly different literary creation of an author who lived a totally different life from Krishnakamini and Rashsundari, however, does still share a central preoccupation: the absolute value of *strishiksha*. In the first scene, in the very first line the heroine exclaims:

> Education has such wonderful possibilities! … If I had not been educated from my early childhood, I would have surrendered to a life of sin! Men consider that women do not need education. Alas! Has the Father of the World made them out of such inferior stuff that they do not see the splendours of *strishiksha* because they are men![21]

She thus turns the morality argument of the orthodoxy on

its head, and she repeats the charges against orthodox men. Reform and print made strange bedfellows, unlikely champions fighting for the same cause.

Dayamayi Debi's *Patibrata Dharma Arthat Kulakaminiganer Pattr Prati Kartavyakarmer Upadesh* (The Dharma of Wifely Chastity, Or Advice to Good Wives about Their Duties to Their Husbands) was a very early tract, coming out within a few years of Kailashbashini's *Hindu Nariganer Heenabastha*. It was published by her brother after her death. This was her only publication. In a brief concluding verse, she discloses that she was born in the high Vaidya caste and that her father was a practitioner of traditional ayurvedic medicine.[22] It was a piece of writing that professed to be entirely uncritical of the Hindu domestic order. It criticised no injunction, nor did it ask for anything new for women. The only knowledge that women needed, she said, was the realisation that there is no God greater to them than their husbands. She added accounts of legendary chaste women whose devotion should act as exemplars to modern ones. She also advised them about how to serve their husbands best. She revealed that it was her husband who asked her to compose this book. So, in one sense, the trajectory is the same as Kailashbashini's, whose husband had pushed her into writing. The whole purpose of writing, however, was different. This, then, is a curious piece of a wholly modern defence of traditional patriarchy. It is interesting that times had changed so much that husbands needed to tell their wives to write and print a defence of husbandly powers; mere injunctions, issued by male authorities, no longer sufficed. Moreover, Dayamayi admits that when she first started to read, she got so carried away by its pleasures that she neglected her domestic chores for some time. She even neglected her supreme *dharma*—that of looking after her husband. "I developed such a thirst for reading poetry and prose that I began to shirk my daily household chores, I was even a bit lazy about serving my husband." No doubt, this is a warning against unwise and extreme *strishiksha*, but it does confess the heady pleasures of the first encounter with reading and writing. It also admits the fragile hold of the domestic discipline, once another world bursts upon the woman with the entry of print culture.[23] The intentions and the conclusions are different, but the experiences confirm what Rashsundari says about both domesticity and education.

The defence of the old gender order shades off from a total refusal of reform and a full-throated defence of male power in Dayamayi Debi, to a more ambiguous, carefully organised piece of polemic. Basantakumari Dasi's *Joshitvigyan* of 1875 came out from Barisal, a district town in East Bengal.[24] She seems to have been born a Ray and married to a Ghosh—both upper-caste Kayastha families. The book tries to combine the energies of defence with those of a critique—of both orthodoxy and reform—through an intelligent ordering of the polemic. For the first few sections, the book is an unambiguous rejection of new demands and changes. *Striswadhinata,* or women's freedom, in whose name the reforms are planned, is a violation of natural hierarchies. Our country itself is ruled, parents control their children, women are the weaker sex so they need male protection. Simultaneously, she subtly undercuts the orthodox position by celebrating women's self-choice in marriage in the legendary old days, and thus refuses to endorse the current insistence on non-consensual child marriage. She also says that this very sensible custom came to an end at the time of Muslim invasions. So, evocation of Hindu glory is deployed to undermine the present unequal conjugal order. But this is done at the cost of a historical slander against another religious community. She then argues that present *strishiksha* is a most unsatisfactory basis on which to grant freedom to women. Even if it was toned up, freedom itself was undesirable.

Suddenly, the polemic slides off from the straight and narrow path, and gets mixed, adulterated. Gradually, she works her way towards a new synthesis which not only comes close to, but goes beyond most reformist planks. True knowledge, she says, if properly disseminated, will surely and smoothly lead one towards freedom, without any strife. Then she goes into a celebration of the passage of time which is very reminiscent of Rashsundari's language, leading one to believe that Rashsundari might conceivably have read this work. Basantakumari would have been a well-known author in the early and mid-seventies, for she had already published five more books on varied subjects: poetry, essays, textbooks.[25]

"Time is a priceless jewel," says Basantakumari, it creates more and more conditions for freedom. Time, in most contemporary male writings, is associated with loss, with decay, with the advent of a modernity that is catastrophic. In many women's writings on the other hand, time is linear, progressive. We find that women's articulations move in a reverse trajectory from a lot of male writings in the revivalist late decades of the century. With time, people realise that women deserve education, since "they are not animals, they, too, are human beings." All their mental faculties are the same as men's, and they require the same food. The capacity for knowledge is essentially ungendered. Chastity, surely, is a must, but can the polygamous husband really deserve it? Non-consensual child marriage makes chastity both mechanical and difficult, for physical intimacy is a form of horrible coercion where mental compatibility is absent. Self-choice by adult women is the best guarantee against her adultery, and so is education.

In many ways, these are bold suggestions. Defenders of

strishiksha did not always or often raise the vision of freedom, they were careful not to raise too many spectres at the same time. Nor did they link up education with self-choice in marriage. A lot of them would not participate in the campaign against child marriage. The assertion that the husband needs to *deserve* the gift of fidelity cuts against the basis of the old conjugal system where the wife's commitment must be unconditional, and polygamy went unchallenged. Even reformers led no campaign against polygamy as such, they took up the issue of excessive polygamy for the extremely pure sub-caste of *kulins* alone. Mental compatibility was yet another problem area. I have tried to show elsewhere that reformers tended to interpret the age of consent as a physical capability where the wife can cohabit with the husband without grave physical danger to herself.[26]

Probably, it was the very boldness of Basantakumari's later suggestions that needed a mask, a cover that began the argument by polemicising against both *striswadhinata* and *strishiksha*. Yet, the boldness was not very sure of itself. For both reformers and for women polemicists, there were grey areas where the thrust of their own emancipatory argument in one area would be undercut by their more conservative choices and preferences in others. Basantakumari says that self-choice in marriage would eliminate the demand for widow remarriage, for true love for the husband would ensure that the widow would not want to remarry. She also defends caste divisions, on the ground that it stands to reason that men performing low tasks would have low natures.[27] So, criticism of aspects of traditional patriarchy was in itself multiphonal and not linear, containing within itself several trajectories that pointed in very different directions, even within the same person.

The relatively open-ended position shades off into a hard-nosed critique of the Hindu woman's condition in the next book that we shall consider: Kailashbashini Debi's *Hindu Nariganer Heenabastha,* or The Miseries of Hindu Women. The title is self-explanatory. A piece of unambiguously critical polemic, it is something of a landmark publication for being both an example of a very early piece of polemical and discursive writing by a woman, and for summing up a comprehensive critique of Hindu domestic practices and gender norms. It was published in 1863 from the press of her reform-minded husband, Durgacharan Gupta. He wrote a preface to the book where he described the bedroom lessons that he used to provide after her day's gruelling domestic chores. The book was quite lengthy for its times: it covered seventy-two pages. She wrote another polemical tract in 1865, this time more specifically on *strishiksha: Hindu Abalaganer Vidyabhyash O Tahar Samunnati,* or The Practice of Learning Among the Hindu Weaker Sex, and Its Improvement. In 1869, she published a book of poems—*Bishwashobha*—on the beauties of Nature, expressing a versatile mind.[28]

Durgacharan, along with a pandit, certifies that she wrote the book entirely by herself. The prose is so strong and clear, the arguments are so powerful and cogently mustered, that it really does take some convincing that it was composed by a woman who did not have formal education. Interestingly, this reform-minded husband ran a press that flourished on the proceeds of the *Gupta Press Panjika,* the most authoritative series of Hindu almanacs that enjoy unchallenged sway down to our times. Kailashbashini was the only woman author whose presence was registered in the writing of at least one male contemporary in a general work. In a book published in 1870, on the theme of *Patibrattya Dharma Shiksha* or Lessons in Wifely Chastity, Shibchandra Jana appends a short biography of Kailashbashini and describes her books as an affirmation of his main argument about the supreme value of wifely fidelity. He has nothing, however, to say about her dominant critical concerns.[29] The strategy is the same as in Jyotirindranath's preface to *Amar Jiban:* to publicise and render acceptable the writing and the educated woman by appropriating her arguments within the domain of traditional Hindu virtues.

Kailashbashini says that without great help and support from Bamasundari Debi, these "hands of mine, so used to holding the ladle and the spoon, would not have been willing to take up the pen."[30] Like Rashsundari, she, too, posits an opposition between domestic chores and creative labour, and hints that the former stands in the way of the latter and the two are not easily synthesised. We have seen that usually reformers took care to give just the opposite impression. I have no definite information about who Bamasundari was, but she could have been the well-known teacher who was going into Hindu homes and teaching the women in seclusion at Pabna around that time.[31] A certain Bamasundari Debi also wrote a book in English, which makes it possible that she could have come from a family of Christian converts. That book was published from Pabna, Rashsundari's birthplace, so the teacher and the author were probably the same person. It came out in 1876, according to the date published in the text. According to the *Bamabodhini Patrika,* however, it was published in 1861.[32] It was called *An Essay on the Superstitions, the Removal of Which Can Give Prosperity to Our Society.* The subject matter would have been dear to the heart of Kailashbashini who might have also read it or heard its contents in translation, if we assume that the edition that is extant is a later one, and there was an earlier one that came out in 1861, before Kailashbashini wrote her book. Kailashbashini said that she wrote for her "sisters" who were still beyond the pale of reforms. Obviously, she was trying hard to make them look upon their own condition in the worst possible light. Unlike even reformist works like *Narishiksha,* she would not make any concession towards the Hindu domestic order.[33]

She categorically states that Hindu women suffer a worse fate than do any other women. Their sufferings and deprivations begin even before birth, since would-be parents pray for sons. She makes devastating attacks on a variety of Hindu practices: *Kulin* polygamy, the ban on education for women, child marriage and patrilocality. Her polemic about the forced transplantation of little girls in strange homes finds powerful confirmation in the personal experiences of Rashsundari. She says that girls are provided with light entertainment and games, so that their minds do not grow in seriousness. Her criticism of the "illusory pleasures" in women's quarters is reminiscent of what Rashsundari says about her first years with her in-laws: she was encouraged to play but her mind grew increasingly weary of these frivolities and sought knowledge. Here is a questioning of women's culture as a domain of happiness, creativity and self-making that feminist scholars tend to celebrate a little too unproblematically. When we find that women, consigned to such pleasures, turn to the forbidden fruit of "male" pursuits of knowledge, we need to be a little more wary about happily recreating sexual difference through such celebrations.[34]

Her most telling form of criticism was to insist on the fundamentally loveless and unhappy nature of Hindu households. Thanks to the norms that she criticises, no loving relationship is possible there: "Conjugal love has all but disappeared from our country.... our homes look like mountains infested with very fierce beasts..."[35] She talks again and again of the self-destructive quarrels and distrust that are tearing all relationships apart, and that occur because women cannot develop adult minds, full-grown personalities. This is strong condemnation. In a different place, I have shown how the Hindu home was constructed as a site of deep pleasure and fulfilment by revivalist/nationalists during the Age of Consent debates. It was made into a haven where the colonised man would lick his wounds after the deprivations that he suffered in the world of work. In a collection of poems written in 1897, Srinibas Basu evoked male desires very poignantly: the woman at home was the refuge after the insults at the place of work, she was the restorer of manhood after the emasculating insults the sahib at the office flung at the man. Significantly, the poem is signed as "your *sahib*". The woman thus makes the Bengali man the omnipotent white male through her act of submission at home.[36] Kailashbashini had constructed a powerful image of lovelessness that needed to be countered with an equally powerful evocation of the loving home when the revivalist campaign against reforms was at its height.

IV
Lineaments of the Woman Author

Through a tracing out of differences in the genres and modes of women's writing, in their diverse social and personal milieus and political intentions, we reach a strong sense of continuities in experiences and in their ways of reflecting on them. It is striking that none of the great and famous women achievers—the first graduates, the doctors, the teachers—had left personal accounts or discursive reflections. Nor have women from the most prominent Brahmo or reformist families who were often very brave and helpful comrades to their husbands: wives of men like Keshubchandra, Shibnath Shastri, Dwarkanath Ganguly, "the friend of the weaker sex." It is women from lesser-known circles—housewives fully engaged with domestic chores, professional women like prostitutes-turned-actresses who suffered from low social esteem for the nature of their work—who seem more preoccupied with a public self-disclosure, self-definition: either of an individual or of a collective self. Bereft of a strong sense of vocation that could be expressed through their "normal" conjugal or professional life—it was enough of a declaration of the self if you were a graduate or a doctor or the wife of a prominent personage—these women probably needed to reflect more on what still constituted their undeniable sense of selfhood. They needed to convince themselves about it in public, as much as they needed to convince public opinion about it. Writing self-reflexively both mirrored and made that self. We shall think later about how and why such a necessity arose at these times.

If the modern Bengali woman created a new identity through her writing, it was certainly not one which placed the female body at the centre of her enterprise: either as the privileged or dominant object of discussion or as the authentic source of a female mode of writing whose conventions obey the urges of a female physicality. Anatomy was not textuality. Nor do we find the makings of a separate female language—ecstatic, esoteric or shaped by symptoms of sickness, madness, hysteria and paralysis, imparted to her by her awareness of her biological lack that the psychoanalytic understandings derived from Freud and Lacan would insist on. We do not find that her themes are those that uniquely arise out of a world of female culture.[37] Bengali men—reformers, orthodoxy and revivalists—were talking about the same things. Women, on the other hand, wrote about broad concepts like the politics of freedom and unfreedom, at home and for the nation, of other kinds of social power like caste, about the direction of Indian history, about education and reforms—as men did, too. They repeat shared poetic conventions, they are at ease with discursive prose, they are analytical as much as they are lyrical.

Is the act of writing, of participating in print culture, a colonisation of female culture and of female subjectivity by the modern Indian man who seeks to uproot her from her own world and make her his subordinate just as he himself is a colonised and subordinated mimic of Enlightenment traditions? I think that we need to ponder seriously on the felt needs of the modern woman to write in less gendered ways and to live in a less bifurcated world, her preferred move towards more universalist modes of knowledge. If we dismiss it as a sign only or necessarily of surrender, mimesis or colonisation, we will be both patronising and forgetful of the specific compulsions and problems that created this choice. We would be mimicking certain intellectual paradigms that are first made in the West rather than try and explore the authentic historical experiences of our own subjects.

The modern Bengali woman was strikingly bound by her class and her caste confines. Her writings take on many aspects of the brahmanical gender system—non-consensual child marriage, patrilocality, the widow's plight, domesticity. But the woman victim that she has in mind is entirely a person from her own circle. She has nothing to say on the lower social segments whom she would have seen toiling in the fields, being tried and often tortured in the landlord's *cutchhery* for not paying rents on time, low-caste servants who work at home for a pittance. Basantakumari, who does have a word to spare on other castes, thinks that low castes deserve their low status for their work reflects their low minds. Even if the world of men from other groups passed them by, that of low-caste maidservants would very closely intersect with their domestic sphere. Rashsundari talks of them as the first persons to be told about her reading, she mentions them as people whom she trusted and relied on. That would largely be due to the fact that for a long time they would be the only ones that the young, inhibited housewife would have been able to command. Contemporary behaviour manuals for women commented worriedly on the intimacy that upper-caste housewives cultivated with low-caste maidservants. The intimacy, cutting across class and caste, did not, however, produce concern, sympathy, awareness. The omission is in sharp contrast to the other kind of critique of brahmanical codes—that of a low-caste reformer like Jotirao Phule, for instance, who underlined their exploitative basis by talking about what upper castes do to their own women as well as of what they do to low castes.[38]

This was partly an effect of the partial nature of reformism in 19th century Bengal which was far more preoccupied with gender than with class and caste at this point.[39] It reflects the very urgency of women's concerns with their own world, now that some chinks had been opened up in its governing injunctions and regulations. More important, however, was, perhaps, the necessity of retaining some ground on which they could claim power, esteem and importance, on the basis of which they could demand change in their condition. Lower classes and castes provided that principle of difference which they would not undermine or question. We have already remarked that women, at best, were unfinished class and caste subjects. They, nonetheless, did belong to their inherited social location, however imperfectly.

Notes

1. The other early autobiographical sketch is Prasannamoyi Debi's *Purbasmriti,* Krishnagore, 1875. It is not, however, a complete autobiography, but a series of early recollections.

2. Soudamini Debi, *Matangini: Adbhut Ghatana,* Calcutta, 1888, p. 1. She claimed that she had already, published four or five books.

3. Krishnakamini Dasi, *Chittabilashini,* Calcutta, 1856. See Preface, p 1.

4. See Radha Kumar, *The History of Doing: An Illustrated Account of the Movements for Womens' Rights and Feminism in India, 1800–1990,* Kali for Women, Delhi, 1994, pp. 10–11.

5. Tanika Sarkar, "Colonial Lawmaking and Lives/Deaths of Indian Women: Different Readings of Law and Community", in Ratna Kapur, ed, *Feminist Terrains in Legal Domains: Interdisciplinary Essays on Women and Law in India,* Kali for Women, Delhi, 1996.

6. According to Rev. Long's reckoning, as many as twenty-five newspapers were founded to discuss the law on widow remarriage. See Benoy Ghosh, "The Press in Bengal" in N.K. Sinha, ed, *The History of Bengal 1757–1905,* Calcutta, 1967, p. 227.

7. This was Dayamayi Debi, *Patibrata Dharma,* Calcutta 1870. The total number of tracts had been mentioned in Usha Chakraborty, *Condition of Bengali Women Around the Second Half of the 19th Century,* Calcutta, 1963.

8. See Ardener and Ardener, "Belief and the Problem of Women" and Shirley Ardener, "Women, Culture and Society: A Theoretical Overview" in Rosaldo and Lamphere, eds, *Women, Culture and Society,* Stanford University Press, 1974.

9. Sushil Kumar De, *Bangla Prabad,* op cit.

10. Manmohini Dasi, circa 1827–76, No B 301; Champaklatika Dasya, circa 1876, B 4281. Panchanan Mandal, ed, *Chitthipatre*

Samajchitra, Viswabharati Publications, Viswabharati, 1953, pp. 14, 25.

11. Usha Chakraborty, op cit.

12. For example, see Kailashbashini Debi, *Hindu Mahilaganer Heenabastha,* Calcutta, 1863, and *Hindu Abalakuler Bidyabhyash O Tahar Samunnati,* Calcutta, 1865.

13. Usha Chakraborty, op cit.

14. Soudamini Debi, op. cit.; Haribala Debi, *Sati Sambad Ba Dakshajagna Parvati Parinay Vishayak Kavya,* Calcutta, 1889, p. 1.

15. Usha Chakraborty, op cit., pp. 145–83.

16. Ibid.

17. Tanika Sarkar, "The Hindu Wife and the Hindu Nation: Domesticity and Nationalism in Nineteenth Century Bengal" in *Studies in History,* New Series, July-December, 1992.

18. *Chittabilashini,* op cit., Calcutta, 1856.

19. See Sarkar, "Colonial Lawmaking" in Kapur, ed, *Feminist Terrains in Legal Domains,* op cit.

20. Introduction by Bijitkumar Datta in reprint by Paschim Banga Natya Akademi, Calcutta, 1992.

21. Ibid, p. i.

22. *Patibrata Dharma,* Calcutta, 1869, pp. 50–51.

23. *Patibrata Dharma,* op cit.

24. *Joshitvigyan,* Barisal, 1875.

25. See Usha Chakraborty, op cit., p. 152.

26. Tanika Sarkar, "Age of Consent Debates", op cit.

27. *Joshitvigyan,* Barisal, 1875, p. 1–45.

28. Usha Chakraborty, op. cit., p. 160.

29. Shibchandra Jana, *Patibrattya Dharma Shiksha,* Calcutta, 1870, pp. 33–34.

30. *Hindu Mahilaganer Heenabastha,* op cit., pp. 1–2.

31. See my section on *strishiksha,* above.

32. Usha Chakraborty, op cit., p. 152.

33. *Narishiksha,* op cit.

34. Ibid, pp. 28-31 and p. 67.

35. Ibid, p. 62 and 47.

36. Srinibas Basu, *Khokababu Prasange,* Calcutta, 1897.

37. For a discussion as well as a critique of some of these positions among feminist critics, especially in France and in U.S. academies, see Elaine Showalter, *The New Feminist Criticism: Essays on Women, Literature and Theory,* London, 1986.

38. Rosalind O'Hanlon, *Caste, Conflict and Ideology: Mahatma Jotirao Phule and Low Caste Protest in Nineteenth Century Western India,* op cit.

39. See Sumit Sarkar, "The Women's Question", op cit.

Amar Jiban
(My Life)

Introduction[1]

This book is written by a woman. On top of that, it is written by an old woman who is eighty-eight years of age. I started to read it, therefore, with great curiosity. I had decided to mark out all the important passages with my pencil. As I went on reading, however, I found that the whole book was getting scored over with pencil marks. The events of her life are, indeed, so surprising, and her writing carries such sincere and simple sweetness, that it is impossible to put it down before one has finished it.

Her autobiography reveals that she is, indeed, an exemplary woman. Her domestic skills match her piety and her love for God. As a child she used to be excessively full of fears. Her mother then gave her a sacred formula to help her fight them. That formula has protected her all her life like some magical amulet. Her mother had said; "Whenever you are afraid, call out to Dayamadhav."[2] Since then, in times of sorrow, distress, (fear or danger, she has always found comfort in this name. We hear a lot these days about the importance of religious education. In truth, the mother just needs to sow the seed of religious thought in the tender heart of the child in her infancy. The wonderful results that follow cannot be matched even by reading hundreds of religious texts later in life. Another characteristic of her life is her tremendous keenness for education.

She never got a chance to be educated. In those days, learning was thought to be a vice in women. She learnt to read and write with tremendous effort, all by herself. It was her religious quest that inspired her to educate herself. It was not to read plays and novels—but to read a religious manuscript, to read *Chaitanya Bhagabat,*[3] that she was so keen on learning. Her religion is not a matter of external ritual, rites and ceremonies, it is a living, spiritual religion. She sees the hand of God, she feels his mercy, she depends on him in every event of her life. Truly, she is immersed in God. It is extremely unusual to come across such an elevated, exalted religious life. In our country, we worship images of God. It is not exactly idolatry, since the image is taken to symbolise God. Its worship, therefore, lacks the narrowness of idolatry. Christians castigate Hindus for being idolaters; Hindus, however, worship images in quite a different spirit. This becomes clear from the instruction that she received from her mother:

> 'Then I asked my mother: "Ma! How could Dayamadhav hear our cries from the shrine at home?" Mother said: "He is the Great Lord, he is everywhere, so he can hear everything. He listens to everyone. The Great Lord has created all of us. Wherever and however people call out to him, he will listen. If you call out in a loud voice, he will hear you, if you call out in a small voice, he will listen. That is why he is not a mere mortal, he is the Great Lord." Then I said: "Ma! Everyone talks of the Great Lord. Does he belong to us?"[4] My mother said: "That Great Lord belongs to all, everyone calls out to him, he is the first and the only Creator. He has created everything that the world contains, he loves everyone, he is everybody's Great Lord."'

Can there be an idea of God that is more advanced than this? Every household ought to possess a copy of this book. Few books are as satisfying as this one.

20 Jaistha   **Jyotirindranath Tagore**
Ballygunge

Initial Sacred Rite

My salutations to Mother Saraswati.[5]   You are the dispenser of
strength and wisdom
All terrestrial beings obey you
Be charitable towards me.   Come and reside within my heart
I will adore you as well as I can.
I am but an insensible, weak daughter.   Lend me some grace of yours
So that my wishes are fulfilled
I shall hope and pray.   That along with your beloved husband
You will come to reside in my throat.[6]

First Composition

Account of My Life

Where are you, Lord of the universe,   Lord who fulfils all wishes
Come into my heart, grant me mine.
I am an ignorant, mean creature,   Moreover, I am but a mere woman
How will I ever learn to sing your praises?
Still, I yearn to chant your name
Out of your great mercy, bless Rashsundari.

I was born in the month of Chaitra in the year 1216, and in this year of 1303,[7] I have completed eighty-eight years of my life. I have spent such a very long time in this Bharatbarsha since I came here.

This body, this mind, this very life of mine, have taken on several different forms. I do not entirely remember what they were like at different times, nor do I recall how my days went by, or how long I lived in different places. I recount whatever little comes back to me.

I remember nothing at all about the states of my body and the moods of my mind until I was four or five. My mother knows it all. I do remember a little bit about the time when I was six or seven, and I will talk about it here. I used to play with our neighbourhood girls. They often beat me up for no reason at all. I was so full of fear that I would not cry, but my tears would flow silently. I cried partly because of the great pain, but more out of a fear that my folks would scold and abuse them if they came to know of this. I also cried because I remembered a certain conversation. My mother had told me that I should not go anywhere on my own. When I asked her why, she had said: "Child lifters are on the prowl these days, they steal any child that they can lay their hands on and they take them away in a sack." When I heard this I was terrified, my face fell. My mother hurriedly gathered me up in her arms and started to comfort me: "Don't be scared. Child lifters pick up only those wicked kids who beat up other children. What do you have to fear, they won't touch you."

Those words had stayed with me. Whenever a kid gave me a thrashing, I would recall them, I would remember that my mother had told me that child lifters take away kids who beat up others. That was why I would never cry out, I would only shed silent tears, thinking fearfully that they might be taken away by the child lifter. Nor would I ever report the beating. On the contrary, I was scared that someone might hear me cry. So it got around that it was safe to beat me, it would never be reported. Everyone took to beating me up secretly, I was terrified of all the girls.

One day a girl came to me and said: "Ask your mother to make up some snacks for us, let us go and have a dip in the Ganga". Delighted, I told my mother: "Ma, I am going off to bathe in the Ganga."

She smiled and said: "What do you want for that?" I said, "Make up a pack for me." I had no idea what such a bath meant, I only knew that it involved having some snacks on the way and walking to the river with a bundle on the head.[8]

My mother understood and she packed up some snacks and a couple of mangoes in a bundle. My happiness was beyond description. It was as if I had been given a priceless treasure. Much happier events do occur these days, but they no longer bring such pleasure. What delightful days were those! I set off with that girl and with the bundle. On the way, we sat down beside a pond and opened the pack. My companion said: "Let's make believe that you are the mother and I am your child. Take me on your lap and feed me." I asked her to sit close to me and I fed her all my food. Then she said: "Wash my hands now". That put me in a fix. I didn't know what to do, I could not fetch the water even when I got into the pond. The girl slapped me, I began to tremble in fear and my tears flowed. I hurriedly wiped my eyes and looked around, hoping that nobody had seen us.

At that point, another friend came upon us. She scolded the girl: "What kind of a person are you? You ate up her food, you had both her mangoes, and now you are beating her up and making her cry! I am going to tell her mother." She went home to report this, and then she came back and said: "I have told your mother. Let's see what she does to this girl". I burst into nervous tears. Then my travelling companion gave me another smack on the face and exclaimed: "She is like a precious mirror,[9] she bursts into tears at the drop of a hat!" My fears increased, I began to wonder as I wiped away my tears: "What has happened to me that I have become a precious mirror?" I anxiously thought that the child lifter would now come and take us both away. I did not go home because of such worries, I went back to my companion's place. Her mother asked her: "Why is her face flushed? Did you make her cry?" My friend kept laughing as her mother scolded her. When her mother went away, she said: "See, I did not cry when my mother was scolding me! Why are you such a spoilt cry baby? Will you tell your mother all about this?" I said, "No, I'll say nothing." I sat there gloomily till I was fetched back home. I found everybody laughing about me and my travelling tales. The elders decided that I shouldn't play with other girls, I would stay at home. Those days, girls were not educated as they are these days. We had a vernacular school in our own home. A memsahib taught there.[10] Next morning, my uncle took me there. I was wearing a long black skirt, with a scarf wrapped around me.[11] I would be rooted to the very spot where I would be set down, too terrified to move. I was eight years old at that time. I cannot say what I looked like, I can only repeat what others said of me:

> My complexion was most bright
> My figure matched it in beauty
> My limbs were exquisite
> People called me a golden doll.

I would talk to no one as I used to lisp, and everybody found it funny. I would be terrified if someone called out to me loudly, one had only to say something to me in a loud voice and I would burst into tears. So everybody was gentle with me. I would spend the entire day at school, I did not have to stay indoors like other girls. Those days, boys used to scratch out letters from the alphabet on the loose earth on the ground and then they would loudly recite them.[12] Since I was with them, I got to know many of these letters. It was fashionable to learn Persian those days. I even got to learn some of that. No one came to know that I had picked up anything. I would stay there all day long, coming inside only to bathe and to eat at midday, and then, in the evening, I would be fetched inside. The rest of the day was spent with the memsahib. I cannot sort out the feelings of those days, it was as if terror enveloped my mind. If anything else chanced to sprout there at all, fear would at once clamp down on it.

Second Composition

Praise, much praise to thee, my Lord, you are blessed in all the three worlds

How much praise can this single mouth utter?
Your mercy is blessed, blessed are your rules
Blessed is the illusion with which you enfold the world.
Blessed are your marvellous ways
Blessed are the stars, the sun, this earth
Blessed are the beasts, the birds, the trees.
The world is radiant with such dazzling beauty
The wind blows so gentle and cool
Hundreds of rivers flow along their divine courses
I fail to describe the fragrance the air carries
Rashsundari's birth is blessed
Your sacred name permeates her touch, her hearing.

One day, as my uncle was taking me outside, a cow doctor appeared before us, a sack in his hands. I took him to be the child lifter and I nearly died of terror. I covered my eyes and began to shake convulsively. People started to laugh and to comfort me. My uncle carried me inside and teased me: "We were nearly snatched away by the child lifter today."

I went straight to my mother and started to cry. She hugged me and said: "Why do you fear everything? There is nothing to fear, there is no child lifter, all that is nonsensical. We have our Dayamadhav, why should you fear anything? Whenever you are afraid, call out to him, and your fears will be gone." Those were encouraging words. I told myself, mother tells me that there is no child lifter, and our Dayamadhav is there for us. The thought brought some relief. Still, I would never venture out anywhere by myself, there would always be someone with me. Really, there was no child as nervous as I. Even the sight of old people struck terror into my heart, I could never be left to myself. I had an aunt who had been widowed very early, before I could be aware of it. One day, I asked her: "Auntie, where are your conch-shell bangles and your jewellery, why don't you wear them?"[13] She told me, "I am not yet married, that's why." I believed her. Since then, I thought that all the widows around me were actually unmarried women.[14] I had lost my father at the age of four, I knew nothing about that. One day, as I was sitting with the memsahib, a gentleman asked my uncle about me: "Ray Mahasay![15] Are you brightening up this place with this precious and beautiful thing? Whose daughter is she?" My uncle said: "She is Padmalochan Ray's daughter." The information worried me no end. So far I had believed that I was my mother's daughter, and, moreover, I had thought that my mother was not yet married. I brooded over this and then I asked my mother, "Ma, whose daughter am I?" She smiled, but she would not give me a reply.[16] Then I went and asked my aunt. Much to my surprise, she began to cry. I was bewildered, I could not fathom the reason for her tears. She restrained herself after a while, took me upon her lap and exclaimed: "Alas, Lord, how cruel you are to this child, depriving her of her father's love! Don't you know, child, that you are the daughter of Padmalochan Ray?" I kept quiet, but my mind was in a painful whirl. Eventually I asked: "Auntie, how am I his daughter?" She laughed at that and said: "There never was such a foolish child as this one. Listen, your father had married your mother, that's why you are his daughter."

My worries grew. Thinking hard, I asked again: "Where is he then?" Aunt said: "Child, don't bring back those old sorrows, he is dead." I was terrified at the mention of death. I told myself, mother advised me to call out to Dayamadhav if I am afraid. If the dead man comes to me, I shall call out to him. That settled my worries a bit.

I had a brother two years older than me and another one who was two years younger. When all three of us were quite small, a fire broke out one night at a neighbour's place. There was a large bare field near our house, it had no houses or trees on it. A river flows quite near the field. As the fire started raging, people began to take out all the stuff from the burning house and to dump it in the field. The three of us were also taken there. The fire was blazing fiercely, people were screaming and sobbing, bamboo poles were loudly bursting into flames. We were crying by ourselves. When the fire spread to our house and the flames were rekindled, we felt as if we, too, were going to be burnt alive. We ran away from the field, occasionally looking back to see if the fire was still raging. We were gripped with panic.

We reached the river bank where the cremation ground

was located. It was strewn with bedposts, mattresses, pillows, sheets, logs of wood and stacks of bamboo poles. The whole place was deserted. My elder brother said, "Look, this is the cremation ground, all this stuff is the bedding that comes with corpses."[17]

At the mention of corpses, I felt as if terror was sucking me in, drawing me inside its belly.

All three of us began to sob helplessly. Suddenly, I remembered: Mother had told me to call out to Dayamadhav in times of fear. I told my brothers to do that. The three of us began to chant the name of Dayamadhav loudly, weeping all the while. Nobody was there to heed us. The river was on one side of us, on the other side there was the deafening roar of blazing flames. People were screaming and crying, each crying for the other, all of them drowning out our cries. We were, in any case, far away from those people. Our terror was beyond description, we were close to dying of it, we could only stammer out that name.

There was a small settlement on the other side of the river. People had rushed out from there when they saw the fire. At one point in the river, the water level is very low, one can walk across it. They forded it there and came upon us, drawn by our sobs. One of them said, "Ah, these kids must be from the house of the Rays. The house is on fire, that's why they are crying." They picked us up and carried us home, comforting us all the way.

In the meantime, our folks could not find us. They decided that we must have died in the fire. They had flung themselves on the ground, siezed by violent grief. When these people brought us in, grief turned into great joy and they began to dance around us. Since they had thought that we had died in the fire, they had not bothered to pull any of our belongings out of the flames, so everything in the house had been burnt to ashes. But nobody had any regrets, so happy were they to get us back. Our neighbours put us up for the night. In the morning we came back to our ruined home and wandered around, gazing at the heaps of burnt objects. Even the fruit trees and the vegetables plants—with aubergines, *bel* fruits and bananas growing on them—had been roasted by the flames. Burnt pieces of poles and roofing were mixed up with pieces of pots and pans. The sight filled me with delight. I carried all that burnt stuff away and started to play with it. We have a sort of a ritual that wherever a house is burnt down, an offering of rice pudding is made to the household deity on that spot. So, we, too, got a portion of the pudding. Since at home, a daily ritual offering is also made to Dayamadhav with rice pudding, my younger brother thought it was the same thing. I was the elder sister, so I thought that I understood more than he did. I had decided that the man who had carried us home last night was surely Dayamadhav.

So I told him, "Yes, Dayamadhav does love us well. He carried us home in his own arms." My brother began to mock me: "What on earth are you saying, Elder Sister! Can Dayamadhav be a human being? Does he have a beard?" I insisted: "Mother had told me to take his name in times of fear. Last night we did just that, so he came to bring us back home." My brother said, "That wasn't Dayamadhav, that was a man." I burst into tears. My mother came to us and scolded him; "Why are you making her cry?" When he had told her everything, she began to laugh. She said to me, "Even your younger brother understands all this, don't you have any sense at all? Let me explain." She took me upon her lap and she explained.

✳

Third Composition

❋

I am a foolish creature   I don't know how to pray
My mind is poisoned with thoughts of worldly goods
I am so very weak   Death comes closer everyday
Lord, it is because I do not get to see you.
Shame and fear wrack me   Merciful One, I am in chains
I do not see a way out.
Lord, listen to your slave   Come, come into my heart
Merciful One, be kind to me.
You are the tree of mercy   You are the ocean of compassion,
teacher to the world
Look upon me with compassionate eyes.
Rashsundari is afloat   On a bottomless ocean
She does not have your feet to hold on to.

My mother said to me: "The deity who resides at the shrine at home is called Dayamadhav. The person who had carried you home from the river yesterday is a man." I asked her: "You had told me that I should call out to Dayamadhav whenever I am afraid, for he belongs to us. Last night we were so frightened, we chanted his name so often, why didn't he come himself?" My mother said: "You had cried out his name in fear. He heard you, and he sent a man to rescue you." Then I asked her: "Ma! He stays inside the shrine at home. How could he hear our cries from there?" Mother said: "He is the Great Lord, he is everywhere, so he can hear everything. He listens to everyone."

"The Great Lord has created all of us. Wherever one calls out to him, he listens. If you call out loudly, he will hear you, if you call out in a small voice, he will listen. If you utter his name in your mind, he will still hear you. That is why He is the Great Lord, he is not a mortal being." Then I said: "Ma!

Everyone talks of the Great Lord. Does he belong to us?" My mother said: "Yes, he belongs to everyone. Everybody calls out to him, he is the one and the only Creator. He has created everything in this world, he loves everybody, he is the Great Lord of us all."

So far I had no idea about the Great Lord. I only knew that everybody talks of him. My mother now explained that he is our God, he sees into our hearts. Those words gave me much strength. That day, the first seed of intelligence was planted in me for I came to know that the Great Lord and our deity are one. My mind was comforted by the thought that he listens if one utters his name even to oneself. Why should I fear anything, I can always think of him. That word of my mother will never die within me: Mother has said that the Great Lord belongs to us.

The sacred word that came from my mother went straight into my heart. I used to play with the girls till I was eight years old. The next two years I had sat with the memsahib. Ten years had passed that way. Then there was a fire at home, the school was destroyed. That meant I could no longer come out of the inner quarters. My mother's brother had lost his home, so my mother brought over his little son into our house. I was very pleased with this, all day I would carry him around in my arms and play with him. He, too, became extremely fond of me. I took over his bathing, his feeding. I would never let him cry.

A distant uncle had his home close to our place. An aunt stayed there. I spent all my days there with the little boy. There were few people in that house, only the three uncles, that aunt and some children. Auntie used to suffer from a kind of gout, but she still had do all the housework. I would always hear her groan: "I wish I could die, all this work is too much for me."

I felt so sorry for her! Even though I did not know how to

do that work, I said to her: "Why don't you rest, I'll do all your work for you." She said: "How will you do it, I have never seen you do anything. Also, your folks will scold me if I make you work." I told her: "No one will know, you show me how to do it, I'll do everything."

Then she began to instruct me and I began to follow her words. I was delighted to do her work for her. Gradually, I learnt to do everything. I would make all the preparations for her cooking, she would sit and cook, and I would watch her. Soon, I learnt to cook. I began to cook all their meals. No one at home knew anything of this. Since my aunt was so fond of me, I spent all my time with her.

Some time passed in this way. As I sat oiling her hair one morning, my own aunt came over to visit her. I went and hid inside as soon as I saw her. She asked: "Child, why do you hide?" The other aunt said, "She was oiling my hair, so she was embarrassed to see you." My aunt laughed and picked me up. She asked: "So you know some work now, who has taught you?" The other aunt said: "The child is really a good worker. I can hardly move around, my gout bothers me so. She is doing all my work. She has brought me new life." My aunt was so pleased that she carried me home in her arms and said: "Did you know, this child knows how to do all the housework! Our sister-in-law in the house over there is suffering from gout, so she does all her work, she even cooks their meals." Folks at home were most pleased about it. My mother's happiness knew no bounds. She said: "Little Mother, show us what you can do." From that day, I took over all the work at home. They did not want me to work, but I would still do it on my own, without telling anyone. This pleased them so much that I became everybody's darling. From that day, my days of play were over. I played no more, I only worked.

I learnt all about housework. For two whole years I would spend all my days at that aunt's, with the little boy at my side. We were so fond of each other. However, he died suddenly and tragically, leaving me desolate. I was twelve years old. So far, my time had passed happily. I had lived in joy among my folks, close to my mother's arms.

Clouds were gathering, nonetheless. I got married when I was twelve. I had not an inkling about what was going to happen. One day I had gone for a bath at the pond behind our house. There were a lot of people around. Someone looked at me and said: "Whoever gets this girl will be blessed, it will the crowning of all desire." Another person said: "So many people are already eager to take her away immediately, but her mother doesn't allow it." Yet another one exclaimed: "How can she hold her back, sooner or later her mother will have to give her away, otherwise why was she born a girl?"

I was stunned when I heard this, I was oppressed by a sense of dread. I went home and asked my mother: "Ma! If someone asks for me, will you give me away?" Mother said: "Hush! Who told you that? Who will I give you away to, how will I give you away?" She went into her room, wiping away her tears. When I saw that my mother was weeping, my heart nearly stopped, I was sure that my mother would give me away. Pain tore at my heart. I began to wonder, what has happened, where will she send me away?

The thought obsessed me. I brooded over it endlessly, I felt deeply depressed, I lost all joy in living. Sobs racked me day and night, I would not talk to anyone, I did not feel like eating or working. I would call out to the Great Lord in my heart. Tears never stopped. Even though my health broke down, I kept all my sorrows to myself, only the Great Lord knew what was going on in my mind. I had long heard people talk of marriage, I knew everyone got married, but I knew nothing of what it actually involved. Now everyone told me that I would soon be married off. My folks had always cared for me deeply, but now they were affectionate as never before. I was made much of.

All that started to work on me and to cheer me up. The wedding would take place, music would be played, women would ululate. It was going to be fun. Nonetheless, I kept worrying. The house began to fill up, all sorts of things started flowing in. Our kinsfolk began to arrive. At this, my fears came back, I stopped talking, I took to crying all day long. Everyone comforted me, cuddled me, but a nameless pain would not leave me for a minute.

Merriment increased at home. The day before the wedding, I looked at the red silk sari, the jewellery, the music. I forgot all my dread, I began to move about happily, wreathed in smiles. After the wedding was over, people came to my mother the next morning and asked her: "Will they leave today?" I thought all the new guests would be going away. The music started up again.

I began to move around with my mother without a worry in my head. The house became very crowded. I saw that some looked happy but others were crying. I was startled. By and by, my brothers, my uncles, my aunt came to me, hugged me close and started to weep. My tears started again, now I knew that my mother was surely going to send *me* away. I clung to her and said: "Ma! please don't send me away." The crowd around me began to weep and to comfort me. My mother put her arms around me and said: "You are my own little mother, you are my goddess of Fortune, try to understand, don't be scared, the Great Lord is with you. You'll be back soon. Everyone has to go away to their in-laws, they don't mind so much, why are you so upset? Try and be calm." By then, I was petrified, my whole body was trembling uncontrollably, I was speechless. I forced myself to speak through my tears: "Ma! Will the Great Lord come with me?" Mother said: "Of course, he will, he will be with you, do not cry." Nothing that she said took away my dread, my tears.

People had to make a great effort to snatch me away from her arms. I was seized with such violent grief at that moment! The memory still fills me with pain. Is it not a great tragedy that one has to go away to a foreign land, leaving one's mother, one's near and dear ones behind, to live under lifelong bondage? But such is the will of God, so let us praise the custom.

I clung hard to whoever came to pull me away. I cried and cried. Everyone wept at the sight. They did not bring a second palanquin for me but, very tenderly, they put me into the same one.[18] As soon as I was inside, it started to move. I was all by myself, not a single familiar face came with me. I felt that I had been plunged into a sea of danger. Helplessly, I pleaded within my heart: "Great Lord, be with me," and I cried as I said it. At the time of the annual worship of the Goddess Durga or of Shyama, when the sacrificial goat is dragged towards the altar, it cries for its mother, abandoning all hope. I was crying exactly the same way. My one thought was: Mother had told me, when you are afraid, think of the Great Lord.

As I thought, I cried, and as I cried my throat choked up. By and by, I had not even the strength to weep.

Fourth Composition

Lord of this universe   Who supports and pervades the world
Who rules over the entire Creation

I am immersed in sorrows   I have lost my mother's arms
I call out to you in great fear.
I do not see my friends   I cannot wait to see them again
My heart is convulsed with terror.
When I longed for my mother   You took me into your own arms
You filled up her place for me.
It was then that I learnt to yearn for you   To offer up all my devotion
To think of you incessantly.
You were always ready with shelter   To soothe away the tears
To grant me my desires.
You have always been there   To save me from distress
To help me cross over all dangers.
Your mercy has been incomparable   Shame on me forever
That I do not recall any of that.

Even the tears would not come any more. I began to drown in a heavy slumber. I cannot recall where we went after this.

When I woke up the next morning, I found myself on a boat, surrounded by complete strangers. There was not a single familiar face at my side. Where did I leave behind my mother, my family, all the neighbours of my village who had been so fond of me, my playmates? Where was I going, all by myself? These thoughts pierced my heart as I sobbed. The people on the boat tried to comfort me, but their affectionate words only brought back memories of my own people. My tears flowed faster, until I was nearly choking, and then, at last, they stopped, exhausted. Since I had never been on a boat before, I began to feel a little sick. All hope fled. Following my mother's words, I once again began to chant the name of the Great Lord.

Alas, what dangerous times were those! Only the One who saves us from danger would know, no one else had any idea.

Even now I sometimes think back on those days.

The bird was thrust behind the cage, the fish fell into the net.

However, that was His will, one cannot question it. I can only describe what I had felt at that time. Who knows what other girls go through, maybe not all of them suffer as much. One can hardly see what causes such suffering but the absence of my own people was, indeed, an unbearable grief.

People have fun, taming birds in a cage. I was that caged bird. I was now shut up in a cage and I won't ever be free again for the rest of my life. A few days passed on the boat. One day I heard the people say, today we'll reach home. I suddenly thought that we were returning to my own home, but, of course, I was not thinking straight, full of fears as I was. The Great Lord alone knows the thoughts that passed through my mind, words cannot describe them. An endless flow of tears were their only outward sign.

Ah, my Lord, King of this universe! Let me sing your praises a hundred times, let me thank you for your laws. Where have you brought me, away from my dearest mother, my beloved friends? That night we left the boat and went to their house. It was full of so many different kinds of people, everyone was having such fun! Not one of them was from my own land, not one face did I know. My heart was broken, I was inconsolable, my tears would not stop. People began to comfort me: "Do not cry. This is your new home, these are your new relatives, they will now belong to you, so why do you cry? Now you will have to make your home here, live your life in this place." Whatever few hopes I still had about getting back to my own people were now finally crushed. My mind was scorched with the flames of grief. Those who have gone through the same suffering will, perhaps, not use such words as comfort. The same thing happens when a mother loses her son. Quite often people come and tell her:

"Who are you crying for, he wasn't your son, he was an enemy from many previous births, otherwise he wouldn't have left you. Don't even think of that evil one!"

Do such words ever bring any consolation? That is impossible, the mind never finds any comfort in them. They only stoke our grief all the more, just as pushing bales of straw into the flames makes them blaze forth. My heart filled with terror when I listened to them. Helplessly, I recited the name of the Great Lord to myself. There was no other way left to me. My tears were inexhaustible. Then my mother-in-law came and put her arms around me and began to soothe me with her soft words. Praise be to the Lord! What a marvellous way of grafting the bark of a tree onto another.

Her arms reminded me of my mother's, her loving words made me think as if she really was Mother. But they were not at all alike. My own mother was beautiful while my mother-in-law was dark. Nor were their faces alike. Still, her arms comforted me, I could close my eyes to all fear and remember my mother. Actually, I had nothing to fear. These people fussed over me more than my own folks did. They carried me around m their arms all day, my feet never touched the ground. Still, my fears never left me for a moment, I cried and cried. I kept thinking of the Great Lord, I asked him to protect me. My Lord, the merciful one! Now I know that you are infinitely kind! But then I would think of you only because I was afraid, I knew nothing of the glories of your name. I thought of you because my mother had told me to do so. Still, I did think of you, even without understanding your greatness. And that, too, is a sign of your grace.

> Whoever calls out to you sincerely in times of trouble
> You shower your mercy on him unstintingly.

I stayed there for three months that first time, and I was like a motherless child, mourning all the time. After three months my uncle came and fetched me back. I went straight into my mother's arms and began to sob: "Ma, why did you give me away to a stranger?" My words made everyone laugh. Mother said: "Look, younger girls go through this, but they don't cry so much. Everyone has to live with their in-laws, when will you get a little wiser, when will the Great Lord send you a modicum of sense? God knows how much you used to cry there." As she was saying these things, however, I was suddenly surrounded by all my friends and playmates. Fears were now forgotten, I was filled with joy and laughter. What a day that was, it is truly beyond description. I would cry so easily and, yet, the Great Lord had also sent so much joy! Now I was completely restored to happiness and I moved around in great delight. At that point I was no longer a child, I was twelve. Those twelve years had passed in a state of ignorance. I still behaved like a child of five. Alas, I was such a fool, I was taken to be an idiot. My uncle did not send me back to the in-laws for a year. I spent that year happily with my mother.[19] But I did have to go back after a year and then I spent two years there.[20] I still cried, but I gradually got to know those people a bit, though I never spoke to anybody. All my conversations were with the Great Lord and I thought endlessly about my father's home.[21] I cried incessantly. I would even look at a bird, a cat or a dog and tell myself that they might have come from there. At my father's home, I was loved very dearly. Daughters are disciplined so sternly, mothers sometime beat them up. Let alone a beating, thank the Lord, nobody had even rebuked me, I was always made much of. When I became a bride I was again bathed in love, I lacked nothing, in fact, I got even more. My mother-in-law heaped toys on me, called in the children of that village to be with me. They sat and played and I sat and watched them. I still cried by myself, but since I had to spend all my days with them, I gradually became tamed. I was their pet bird. Memories of my childhood are but a heap of rubbish. However, I have gone and set them down.

Our merciful Father! You are always with us, you are inside the mind. Why, then, does the mind suffer so?

> Since the father is merciful
> What is there to fear?
> Since you yourself are my father
> Why do I have any fears at all?
> When we depend on your name
> No danger comes upon us.
> Wherever your name sounds
> No male or female ghosts may survive.
> The sweet nectar of your name
> Fills up the place with holiness.[22]

That household had nine maidservants. Of them, one was to help out with the household work, the others worked outside.[23] I had nothing to do at first. My mother-in-law used to cook for us all, she would not let me do anything. I sat around all day, surrounded by the children of the village. They played with me, as did those maidservants. Since I spent so much time with them, we became really close. They were like the playmates from my father's home. I no longer cried that much, though I still did, a little. I was idle all day long for nobody would let me work, there were servants and my mother-in-law was also there. I wondered what I should do. Girls were not allowed to read or write those days, so there was nothing at all that I could do. People did not use coins then, they made their transactions with shells or cowries. I began to design a whole lot of things with those cowries: miniature chandeliers, flowers, mirrors, umbrellas, hanging shelves, drawers. I would decorate the rooms with these.

I would also cut out moulds from stones for shaping milk sweets. I used ropes of jute to construct hanging shelves. And I made a whole lot of toy animals with clay—snakes, tigers, jackals, dogs, cows, birds—human figurines, figures of various deities. One day, I made a clay snake, painted it and put it under the bed. No one had seen me make it. Suddenly, someone saw a snake and ran out to call in people from the *cutchhery*.[24] They came in with all sorts of weapons, thinking they had to kill a real snake. Some climbed up on the roof, some ran around with cudgels or with spears. I did not know that it was my clay snake that had caused all this pandemonium. I could have prevented their exertions had I known about it. It really was something to look at. It was quite terrifying, as if a real snake had spread out its fierce hood and was poised to spring! No one dared to come close to it. Finally, someone took aim from a pole that was suspended from the ceiling, and brought down a blow with a cudgel. The clay snake shattered in a thousand fragments. There was a great deal of laughter about the whole episode and at last I got to hear of it. I knew what had really happened but I was too embarrassed to say anything. After that I gave up toymaking and went back to my idleness. But something in my mind kept telling me: "You are wasting your time, nothing worthwhile is happening to you. All this pleasure is mere foolishness."

Some time passed this way. Soon my mother-in-law lost her sight from enteric fever and she could do no work. She could not even look after herself, I had to nurse her. Moreover, all the household chores fell on my shoulders. I was worried out of my wits. I had never been allowed to work before. Also, this household was quite a large organism. There was the household deity, and tending to him was a daily chore since his meals had to be ritually cooked.[25] There was a perpetual flow of guests and they had to be fed separately. Our own meals were on a large scale. Though I had no brothers-in-law, there was still a number of servants and maidservants. I had to cook for twenty-five to twenty-six people twice a day. On top of all this, my blind mother-in-law had to be cared for. I had only one maidservant to help me out, and she, too, was absent at that time. I was all by myself. Hurled into this ocean of responsibilities, I felt myself to be completely inadequate. I called out to the Great Lord helplessly: "Lord, I can't possibly cope with all this on my own. It can only be done if you mercifully see me through." With this prayer on my lips, I started on my life of labour. God helped me to do all that, I became such an expert worker that singlehandedly I managed all the cooking twice a day. Women were not educated in those days. They had to do all the work at home. If they had a single moment of leisure, they were expected to tend to the head of the household. That meant they had to stand at his side meekly and humbly. People used to insist that women were only meant for domestic chores. Newly-wedded girls had to be especially hard-working and quiet. They had to work from behind a long veil and then they would get to be known as good wives. Our clothes used to be so coarse, not like the fine cloth of today. I had to cover my face with that, my veil had to reach down to my chest, and, dressed in this way, I did all the work. I spoke to no one, I could hardly see anyone beyond my veil. My eyes were covered, like the eyes of the oil presser's bullock. I had to look down, all I could see were my own toes. This was how young married women were supposed to work. And I worked that way, too.

✳

Fifth Composition

*

Lord of us all   Great Lord of the world
The One without beginning or end
Let my heart   Adore that treasure
He is the Original Cause behind all things.
My heart sinks   In the ocean of worldy goods
It is immersed in bottomless greed
It cannot escape   Ah, what folly is this.
He is cast out of the heart, forgotten.
Why have you forgotten him?   Do you not know
That he is like the sun in the sky?
Do you not know yet   That this world of wealth and kin
Is but mere illusion?
You think your family belongs to you   And you care for them
You cherish them from the day they are born
But they all have to depart   For the House of Death
And then you are all on your own.
In vain do you care   And nourish your wealth
You will have to leave that behind
My heart, do ponder on this   You came alone into this world
And so will you depart alone from here.
You have to go   And meet that Being
Who brought you into this world
Why do you forget it   When you are in the world
Why are you ensnared in illusion?
My own mind   I plead ardently with you
Do not travel along this false road
Dwell on him alone   He who is closer than all others
He who is the Great Lord.
He is the real treasure   And you may attain that
Only if you are empowered by knowledge
Take shelter at his feet   That will release you from fear

You will overcome the terror of death itself.
You want to cross over   This sea of Life
Why, then, do you forget?
That Kind Friend of the poor   He alone is your help on the way
Never forget this truth.

I would start working at dawn, and I would still be at it until well beyond midnight. I had no rest in between. The Great Lord, however, mercifully made me see it as my own responsibility, so I never resented it. Thus he willed, and thus I took over the entire housework upon myself. I was only fourteen years old at that time. I came to nurture a great longing: I would learn to read and I would read a religious manuscript. I was unlucky, in those days women were not educated. People would say: Ah, it seems the kali age[26] is, indeed, upon us! Now women will take over men's jobs. This had never happened all this while, but now it is going to come! In our days we were spared this; now the man is but a passive thing, the woman is the public figure. This is the age of a female monarch. What else do we have to put up with? The way things are going, soon gentlefolk will lose their caste. Perhaps these wretched females will get together and start educating themselves!

Clusters of people would sit together and carry on in this vein. Such talk terrified me. Let alone express my wishes openly, I was so scared that someone may stumble upon them that even if I came across a piece of paper, I would not glance at it, in case people suspected that I was trying to read it. In my heart, however, I was forever praying: "My Lord! Teach me to read, I'll read religious manuscripts." God, who befriends the poor! I used to think of you at that time only because of this need. I used to pray: "Great Lord! You have brought me so far, from my birthplace Potajia to this Ramdia village. It takes three days to travel this distance. You have taken me away from all my friends and relatives, now Ramdia is my own place. How strange is this! Once I knew nothing about working and my mother used to be so delighted whenever I made the slightest attempt at it. Now that I have been enslaved, I have learnt to do so much work. So all these people have come to like me." So would I speak to myself, and, behind my veil, I would cry and cry, but nobody would see my tears. Friend of the poor, you alone have been their witness. Ah, my Great Lord, my father! Ah, the heart of my heart, life of my life! Ah, you gem of mercy, ocean of compassion! I am afloat forever on your mercy. You have stayed with me in my days of trouble and in my days of success. You know my every feeling, nothing ever escapes you.

I left my father's village of Potajia when I was twelve. Since then I have been in Ramdia. The people of this household have been very kind to me, they are good people. Their affection made me forget all pain.

All the servants and maidservants of this household, all the neighbours in this village loved me so well that I was convinced that the Great Lord has spoken to them. I was also convinced that these people loved me more than they loved their own folk. Not once has anyone rebuked me. Truly, people of this land are good people. I have lived here so long, I still live here, they (not to speak of my own family) sincerely love me. Not even unwittingly have they been rude to me. This has been so until now, but who knows what is going to come later. Who knows how much longer I have to stay here. Who knows what I'll have to face in my last days, how they will look upon me then! Only the Great Lord can tell.

My Lord! Father of the world, who pervades this world! Infinite is your glory. You alone know your deeds, we'll be fools even to wonder about them. I was twelve when I came

to Ramdia. For the next six years I was like the young bride.
Even my mind had remained immature. It was like this until
I was eighteen. But it was rather a nice mind that I had.[27] I
never thought of worldly affairs, my one thought was how to
do all my work and how to please everyone. Nonetheless, it is
deplorable that I was not allowed to educate myself because
I was a woman. How very lucky are girls of this generation!
These days many try to educate their daughters. Whatever
others may say, I think this is a most positive development.

Let me give some details about my children. When I was
eighteen, I had a son. He was called Bepinbehari. At twenty-
one, I had a second son, he was Pulinbehari. At twenty-three,
I had a daughter, she was Ramsundari. At twenty-five, another
son was born, he was Pyarilal. I had a son again at twenty-
eight, he was Radhanath. At thirty, another son was born, he
was called Dwarakanath. At thirty-two, yet another son came,
he was Chandranath. At thirty-four, I had another son, that
was Kishorilal. After that, I miscarried a son in the sixth month
of my pregnancy. At thirty-seven, I had another son, he was
Pratapchandra. At thirty-nine, I had another daughter, she was
Shyamsundari. When I was forty-one, I gave birth to my last
son Mukundalal. I had my first child when I was eighteen and
my last child was born at forty-one. The Great Lord alone
knows how those twenty-three years went by. No one else
knows anything about that. There were eight maidservants
attached to the household at that time, but they all worked
at outdoor jobs. I had no one to help me with the domestic
chores. I did the entire work all by myself, as I had been doing
it before, but now I had all these children to bring up as well.
I never knew any rest, nor could I look after myself. Let alone
other things, often I could not even manage to get two square
meals a day. There were days when I missed having even a

single meal, such was the pressure of work. Anyway, let us not
talk of all that. It's not worth mentioning, I am ashamed even
to bring it up. Nevertheless, it is necessary to briefly describe a
day or two. I would get up in the morning while the children
still slept and I would start working. I had to cook the rice
before they got up. After I had fed them, I would finish off
other chores and then prepare for the ritual meal that was
daily offered up to the domestic deity. Then I would prepare
and cook lunch for the entire household. It was quite a lot
of food! It would be about ten to twelve seers of rice for
the evening meal alone. In the meantime, *karta*[28] must have
his rice as soon as he had finished his bath. He did not relish
anything else for breakfast. So, his rice had to be cooked early
and separately. Then I cooked for everyone else. I would be
cooking lunch until three or four in the afternoon.

One day, I had just finished off all this work and was about
to sit down to my own lunch, when a guest arrived. He was a
Namasudra by caste.[29] He would not cook for himself so late
in the day even when he was given all the provisions, but he
asked for some cooked rice. It was too late to cook anything,
so I just had to give him my own food. I told myself that I
would eat at night after I had cooked dinner. I did all the
afternoon chores and after I had put the children to bed, I
began to cook dinner. I was nearly dying of hunger by then.
I was alone in the kitchen and it was full of various kinds of
foodstuff. I could have eaten some of that, who would tell
me not to? In fact, folks would have been glad if I had taken
something. But I never used to serve myself any other kind of
food except rice. That is why, I never got to eat a whole lot of
things. I also thought that if I took something, people would
get to know that I had no lunch that day and there would be
a lot of fuss. Also, if they found that their mother was eating,

the children would come and create pandemonium in the kitchen and that would bother others. Let me not waste time with this. So I started cooking dinner. After it was over, I had to wait till late in the night. The *cutchhery* work went on and on, and *karta* had not yet come inside, so I sat and waited. I served the others and finished off all other chores and then I waited with his meal. I was worried that since he was coming so late, the children would start to wake up while he ate. And once that happened, I would have no time to eat. And that is exactly what happened. As soon as *karta* came inside, the baby woke up and started to cry. I served *karta,* and I took the baby into the kitchen. I told myself that he would drop off to sleep by the time his father had finished eating, and then I could eat while he slept on my lap. But before *karta* had finished his meal, another child got up and began to cry. I brought him in as well and thought that I would eat with both the sons on my lap. But before I could get started, a storm broke out and the lamp was blown out. The kids were frightened in the dark, so they began to howl. I was so very hungry that had I been alone, I would have eaten in the dark. But there were only two maids, and they were meant to do outdoor jobs. I could not leave my sons outside in the dark by themselves. Also, whenever they cried at night, *karta* used to wake up and shout: "Why are they crying?" For all these reasons it was better to go without food. So I left my plate of rice in the kitchen and went away. The boys went off to sleep once the storm had abated. By that time it was very late and I was too tired to get up and eat, so I went without any food that whole day. The next day, again, I did all the usual chores and went over early to cook. No one knew that I had gone without food. I had decided that I would eat as soon as all the others had eaten. But someone was looking after the baby, he needed to be fed. After I gave him his share, I took the baby upon my lap and sat down to eat. But as soon as I sat down, the baby crapped on my lap. He also peed so profusely on the rice that it was practically washed away.

I began to laugh to see the Great Lord try me so. I told no one that I had gone without food for two days, I kept it to myself. It would have been most shameful to refer to my eating in public.[30] No one ever came to know of these things, but quite often I had to go without food for whole days. Thank the Lord that I was not a sickly creature. Had I been so, what would have happened to my children? Lord of the world! Who can measure your boundless compassion! What deep concern you have shown to this daughter who is in your bondage! The very thought makes me dizzy, it is overwhelming! I am your ignorant daughter, I know nothing of your glory. This slave of yours used to chant your name those days only because her mother had asked her to do so. But it has blessed my very birth, my whole life has been blessed, I feel gratified.

My compassionate Father! I am a miserable creature, I know you not. Had you not been with me at that time, if this body of mine had been invaded by sickness, what on earth would have I done? Who would have looked after my children, what would I have done with myself? I would have been cast out on a sea of sorrows. So I thank you a hundred times! Preserver of the poor! Out of your kindness, you have shown me how much a mother suffers to bring up even a single child. I had not known before how great is the burden of pain for the mother who raises a child. One can only know it through one's own difficulties and experiences, I got to understand it so thoroughly because I suffered so much myself. Every human being should know of this but very few actually do. I had a very loving mother of my own, but I never got a chance to look after her—this will be a great sorrow forever. A mother is such a precious gift, but even when I came to realise it, my knowledge was useless to me. My mother had suffered so much for me, but I was of no use to her, I did nothing for her. She always missed me bitterly, she tried hard to get me to visit her. But I have been locked up in a prison ever since I came here. I could never be allowed to visit her because the household chores here would suffer. If ever I had to go to her on some ceremonial occasion, I was like a prisoner let out on parole, I had to be back within a couple of days. At least ten to fifteen people, two guards, two maidservants accompanied me on the boat ride. I had to come and go according to the letter of the contract.[31] I could only visit her on ritual ceremonies. My mother longed so to see me when she was on her deathbed. I am such a miserable sinner that I made her suffer even in her last moments. I, too, tried desperately to pay her a last visit, but I had no luck, it was not to be. This is not an ordinary grief! Alas, my Lord! Why did you create me as a human being? It is a rare fortune to be born a human being among all the lower creatures of this world. I was born one, and yet I lived to be such a sinner! Why was I born a woman? Shame on my life! Who in all this world is as loving as the mother? It is hardly an exaggeration to call her the representative of the Great Lord. I did have this priceless treasure in my mother, but I could not look after her. Is there anything in the world to match this sorrow? Had I been her son, I would fly like a bird to reach her side when I got news of her end. What was I to do, I was behind bars, I was shut up in a cage.

✳

Sixth Composition

Born in the land of Bharat   Immersed in dreams of false desires
I have wasted my time carelessly.
How will I escape this   Where are you, Lord, who sustains the world
Have mercy upon me I am a wretched creature.
Lord, You pervade the world   You are the apocalyptic end
Who can have perfect knowledge of you?
How will I describe   That Five faced God,[32] had I even five mouths
Even Infinity itself cannot reach the end of him.
The Agams and the Nigams[33]   The Vedas and the Koran[34]
Try to understand your truth
How can they know you   And comprehend your designs
Who can have perfect knowledge of you?
In all the three worlds   Who is there to understand you
Unless you choose to reveal yourself?
What power do I have   Which will lead me to you
I am but a helpless woman.
You inhabit everything   As the essence of all things
That alone is my hope
I throw myself upon your feet   Whether you take me across or
you don't
Is going to be the measure of your glory.

I was immersed in a life of labour, I hardly knew how time
went by. Little by little, a desire took shape in my mind and I
came to be possessed by a single wish: I will learn to read, and
I will read a sacred text. I began to resent my own thoughts.
What is wrong with me? Women do not read, how will I do
it, and why does this bother me so! I didn't know what to do.
It isn't as if all our ways were evil those days, but this certainly
was. Everyone got together to deprive women of education. It
must be said that women of those times were most unfortunate,

they were hardly any better than beasts of burden. However, it is useless to reproach others about this, that was what fate had decreed for me. Really, how cross those old housewives would be if they saw a woman with as much as a piece of paper in her hands. So, how was I to learn anything? But my heart would not accept this, it was forever yearning. I began to ponder: as a child I had learnt something at that school at home from the other students who used to recite the letters loudly. Would I remember any of that? Slowly, with great effort, I managed to recall the thirty-four letters, the vowels and the spellings. That, again, was something that I could recite but not write. What was I to do? Truly, if no one teaches you, you can't learn a thing. Moreover, I was a woman, and a married one at that. I'd die if someone was to rebuke me. Nor was I supposed to talk to others, so my fears kept me nearly mute. I prayed all the time: Lord of this world! If you teach me yourself, I shall certainly learn. Who else will teach me if you don't? These thoughts were always with me. Many days passed thus.

Then I had a dream: I was reading the manuscript of *Chaitanya Bhagabat*. When I woke up, an unearthly joy possessed my body and heart. I kept closing my eyes even when I was fully awake, I kept going back to the memory of the dream. It was as if I had been given a priceless jewel. As my body and mind filled with delight, I began to wonder: "Isn't it strange? I have never seen this book before, I wouldn't even recognise it. Yet I was reading it in my dreams. I can read nothing at all, let alone something like this, it is impossible. Even then, I am blessed that I was at least able to read it in my dream. Since I am always praying to God to teach me to read, he has allowed me to do so in my dream, for he never actually did teach me. This is, indeed, a great blessing, thank the Lord for blessing my birth, for fulfilling my deepest desire." I was so happy.

I began to think, "This house has many books, maybe *Chaitanya Bhagabat* is also there." But what difference could that make to me? I didn't know how to read, I couldn't even identify the book. So I resumed my prayers: "Lord of the poor! Lead me to the book that I saw in my dream. You have to do this, who else can bring *Chaitanya Bhagabat* to me?" Thus I spoke to the Great Lord.

What a miraculous proof I had of the wonderful mercy of the Compassionate One! As I was brooding, he heard my wish and he set about granting it immediately. My eldest son was eight years old at the time. As I sat cooking in the kitchen, I heard *karta* say to him: "Bepin, I have left my *CB* here. When I ask for it, bring it in." He left the book there and went away.

I heard all this from the kitchen with great delight. I rushed over to look at the book. Thanking the Lord for listening to my prayer, I opened it and felt it all over. Manuscripts were very different from the printed books of these days. They used to be pressed between wooden slats which were colourfully illuminated.[35] Since I didn't read at all, I memorised the illumination in order to identify the book.

When the book had been taken inside, I secretly took out a page and hid it carefully. It was a job hiding it, for nobody must find it in my hands. That would lead to severe rebukes and I would never be able to put up with that. It was not at all easy to do something that is forbidden and then to face the consequences. Times were very different then, and I was an exceptionally nervous person. Such days! One was entirely in bondage and my fears were great. That page was a headache. Where could I hide it that nobody would come across it? Eventually, I decided that it must be a place where I would always be present but which nobody else visited much. What else could it be but the kitchen? I hid it under the hearth.

But there was never any time to look at it. I finished cooking very late in the night. After that was over, the children started waking up, one after the other. And then it was pandemonium! One says, Ma, I need to pee, another says, Ma, I am hungry, and yet another says, Ma, take me on your lap, while someone else wakes up and starts bawling. I had to look after them all. After that it got even later, I couldn't fight off sleep any more, there was no time to study the page. I could see no way out of it. How can one learn without a teacher? I could silently say a few letters to myself, but I could not write them. It is impossible to master the word[36] without knowing how to write.[37] I saw no way of reading that page, however hard I thought about it. Moreover, the fear of exposure was always there.

Helplessly, I prayed to the Lord: "Great Lord, do help me to read this, who else is there to teach me?" Thus I prayed all the time but I would also despair at times. Even if someone did teach me the letters, where was the time to pursue that? Why cherish an impossible dream? At other times, I would hope again. Since the Great Lord himself has planted this hope in me, he will not thwart it. So I held on to the page. Even though I hardly had the time to glance at it, I would occasionally keep it in my left hand while I was cooking, and sometimes I would steal a look at it from under the veil. The letters, however, remained inscrutable.

My eldest son was practising his letters on palm leaves at that time. I hid one of them as well. At times, I went over that, trying to match letters from that page with the letters that I remembered. I also tried to match the words with those that I would hear in the course of my days. But after a quick look at them, I would hide them under the hearth once more. I spent quite a bit of time in this fashion.

Ah, what a sad thing it was! Such misery, only because one was a woman! We were in any case imprisoned like thieves, and on top of that, reading was yet another crime. It is good to see women having an easier time of it now. Even if someone has a daughter these days, he educates her carefully. We suffered so much just to learn to read. Whatever little I learnt was entirely because God was kind to me.

The man who was my master was a good person. But it is most difficult to abandon the custom of the land. That is why I suffered so. However, why dwell on past misfortunes! Those days, people were convinced that it is sinful to educate women. Why blame them alone, even now there are those who go up in smoke at the thought. It is useless to blame them either. Time is a priceless treasure. Those times and these are so different, if we compare them, we won't be able to count the changes that have happened. If people from those times were to see the ways of today, they would die of grief and horror. Actually, we happily accept whatever the Great Lord decrees at a particular time. Women would then wear coarse clothes, heavy ornaments, an armful of conchshell bangles, their foreheads would be smeared with vermillion paste. It didn't seem so bad then. We ourselves didn't dress quite like that, but even so, I shudder to think of what we had to wear then.

Anyway, the Great Lord had taken care of me all that while, I was happy and contented. I can only say that whatever he does is providential. As a child, I had been made to sit in that schoolroom, and that now helped me a lot. I could match the letters I remembered with those on the palm leaf and on the page. I read to myself, in silence.[38] All day, I would try to go through this in my mind. With tremendous care and effort and over a long stretch of time, I learnt somehow to limp and stammer across *CB*. Those days, we did not see printed letters, the handwritten letters on the manuscripts were immensely difficult to read. My reading was so painfully acquired! Even after such effort, I didn't know how to write. It takes a lot to be able to write—paper, pen, ink, inkpot. I would need to spread them all around me and then sit down to write. I was a woman, and on top of that, a married one. They are not meant to read and write. The authorities have decreed that this is a cardinal sin for women. How could I have tried to write in that situation? I was so scared of rebukes. So I killed my desire for writing and I would only read, and that, too, in secret. Even that had so far been beyond my wildest dreams. It is almost an impossible achievement, it was possible in my case only because the Great Lord himself guided me with his own hands. The fact that I could read at last was enough for me, I didn't think of writing.

✳

Seventh Composition

✳

Where are you, compassionate friend of the poor?
Look upon the sorrows of this miserable woman, take pity on her.
Merciful father, whose kindness is bottomless like the ocean
Help me across this sea of sorrows.
My heart is poisoned with the greed for possessions
I have forgotten you, what is going to happen to me?
I am an orphan, who will comfort me?
Who else will know my pain but you?
My sins are countless
I know not how I shall go across this life.
I can see that your mercy is incomparable, endless
I hope, therefore, that I shall strike shore.

Alas, I then remember within me
I do not know how to call you with a sincere heart.
Anxieties sieze me
Lord, You overwhelm me utterly.
I watch this endless ocean with despair
Saviour, save me in this moment of danger.
Father, who else can I call out to?
Who else has the power to save me?
Merciful one, your very name bespeaks your compassion
Why, then, am I so desperate?
I am devoid of intelligence and strength, I can hardly speak
Come and show yourself to me, come as the raft on the waves.
Lord, I cannot, I cannot bear this delay
Look at Rashsundari's pain, reveal your compassion.

Father! King of kings, Emperor over all! How can I be sorrowful, being the daughter of a great king? Is it at all possible? But Father! Just as a child suffers when her parents are far away, so I, too, suffer constantly for I do not see you.

I learnt to read in this way when I was twenty-five. I had spent twenty-five years in this manner. In the meantime, my childhood was irretrievably gone. The body had abandoned the garb of the child and had decked itself out for youth. The mind, too, had changed and had entered the realm of wordly duties. Ah me! What a wonder! No traces of my childhood were left!

At this point, my mother-in-law passed away and the entire responsibility of the rudderless household fell on my shoulders. It was a time of great difficulties. I had four children by then, and now I was to direct the household. Past conditions changed entirely, even the appelation that had been given to me—the new bride—was transformed. Some would address me as Mother, some would call me Mother-Mistress, some said

Daughter-in-Law, some others would call me Sister-in-law, or Mistress of the Household or Mother of the Household.[39] Thus I acquired a lot of new names. I was made over into a new person, my childlike ways disappeared. My body and my mind also entered upon a new state. It was as if I had become someone else. My uncertainties began to disappear, I gained new strength and confidence. I acquired a lot of property as well—I had my children, my servants and maidservants, my tenants and retainers. I began to tell myself, I have become a full-fledged householder now, isn't it strange? To most people, I have become the Mistress of the Household. Let us see what follows now.

I had three sisters-in-law. As they were widowed, they came to me.[40] They were very fond of me, they cared for me deeply. I, too, adored them as if they were some sort of deities. Even though they were my husband's younger sisters, and, hence, junior to me in kinship status,[41] I—always a nervous person— feared them and served them humbly. So they, too, showered their affections on me. It is rare, indeed, to be on such terms with sisters-in-laws. Even after I had four or five children, I wouldn't dare to meet their eyes when I spoke to them. Though I was responsible for the household, I sought their opinion at every step. They were nice people in every way.

I was twelve when I left my father's house to come to my in-laws. Even when I was twenty-five, and my mind had changed a lot, I remained a bit childish. But it rarely came out in the open. When I was eight or nine, people used to tease me: Your mother hasn't been married yet. And I would believe them! When I was twenty-five, my intelligence at last began to send down a few roots, but that, too, was kept a secret, nobody could sense it.

There was a horse in the house, it was called Jayahari. One

day, my eldest son was sat upon it and was brought inside so that I could see him. I could hear folks say that this horse belongs to *karta* and some of them called out to me: Come and see, your son is riding a horse. Since I had heard that this was *karta's* horse, I began to wonder: how can I go out and stand before it? It must be shameful if *karta's* horse gets to see me.[42] So I hid myself inside. Even though people kept calling me outside, I simply peeped out once or twice.

Heaps of paddy used to be piled up on the inner courtyard of that house.[43] That horse used to come and nibble at them every day. Now I began to hide myself from his view.

Once, after I had served a meal to my children and had gone into another room, that horse came and started nibbling at the paddy. I was in a fix. The children had just started their meal, they were calling out to me, some had begun to cry. And that horse kept on nibbling, there was no sign of its departure. I didn't know what to do, I kept dithering. I couldn't let myself be seen by *karta's* horse! My eldest son came to look for me and he tried to reassure me: "Ma, there's nothing to fear, that's the horse Jayahari, it won't do anything to you." Then I began to laugh at myself: Shame on me, am I really a human being? It isn't as if I am afraid of the horse, I avoid it because I am shy. But this is just a horse, not a person, how does it matter if it sees me? If people come to know of this, they will think that I am mad, they'll laugh at me. Actually, no one knew that I was shy of the horse, they thought that I was scared of it. I was too ashamed of myself to explain the real reason to them. But I gave up running away from the horse. In fact, those days we feared everything while these days younger people don't fear anyone. On the contrary, it is the older people who are wary of them. Anyway, how very foolish I was! Other people may legitimately laugh at me, I do so myself when I now recall all that.

So far, I had always done all my work from behind the veil which reached down to my chest. But now I found that the ways of the new bride won't do any more, the work suffers. I now began to talk to the maidservants a little bit. And I spoke to my sisters-in-law in a clearer voice.[44] I did all the household work by myself, and at moments of leisure, I'd read the *CB* in secret. Only the maidservants got to know of this. Some of the village women used to be with me all day, they, too, came to know. Some time passed in this way.

As more and more children began to arrive in a row, my status as the mistress of the household was consolidated. We often find that people pray to the Great Lord for wealth but I swear that I never longed for that. The Lord of the world was nonetheless kind to me, he gave me a bit of all that wordly people need. There was no room for any regret. I had my share of all that brings pleasure to householders, thank the Lord— sons and daughters, servants and maids, loyal tenants, relatives and kinsmen, status and honour, pleasure and enjoyment.

Folks say that numerous children are a source of pain for the mother. It is true. Obviously, not all of them are the same. Some are ignorant, some are immoral, some turn out to be ugly or foolish and some ruin their patrimony and engage in undesirable pursuits. People criticise them and their parents suffer so much that they lose the will to live. Since people love their children with all their hearts, their evil ways or their bad reputation bring them such pain that they are beyond comfort. Truly, children can make their parents suffer as nothing else can. If they turn out bad, they make you suffer when they live as much as when they die. And the mother suffers more than the father. The Great Lord, however, was generous to me, never did I have to suffer from this. All my children were good-looking, morally pure, educated, generous, kind, pious

and righteous. Their nature was such that they never brought
me any pain. But one mustn't boast, God destroys the boastful.
No one knows what fate has decreed for one.

Lanka was destroyed for it was too arrogant.[45] The Kauravas
were ruined for they were too proud.[46]

Bali was captured for excessive charity.[47] Excess is always
evil.

✻

Eighth Composition

✻

You are the Lord of this life   You are the beginning and the end
You see into our innermost soul
If the heart is deceitful   You punish it instantly
You alone are its judge.
There is none else   Apart from you
Who knows our hidden pain
How much more can I say   Lord, you know it all
Do not say otherwise.

Lord, the saviour of sinners! Merciful friend of the poor!
You dwell in my heart, you know my every emotion, nothing
escapes you.

You are the life of the world, the essence of the world
Lord, blessed be thy name.

If I have concealed any wrong that I might have done, do
expose me. Remind me of all that I have managed to forget.
I have never tried to deceive anybody by word or by deed.
Even if I had done so inadvertently, do reform me, let me not
err against your rules. My Father, the Great Lord! You know
every thought that appears in my mind, there is nothing left
for me to reveal.

I am but an ass, I know not how to write
It is only your grace that helps me to compose a few things.
Whatever I utter, whatever I think
Lord, all of it is in the hope of reaching you.

I had ten or twelve children. Had they turned out bad, had people spoken ill of them, I would have suffered horribly. By God's grace, I never needed to face that. On the contrary, people praise them abundantly, to my delight. So do their ways reassure me. I will now disclose all that this body and this mind had to go through at that time. People talk of the ocean of life. It is an ocean, no doubt, but if we compare its waves to those of a real sea, perhaps the waves of the sea of life would appear just as formidable. Nonetheless, the Lord has preserved me in great tranquility in the midst of those mighty waves. Even at times of grave crisis, I retained that serenity. Adversity failed to destroy that.

It was no ordinary crisis that I faced, it was no less a calamity than losing some of my sons. When I had to face that, it seemed as if waves of pain were tossing me up and down. My mind has generally been full of cheer. For the last twenty-eight years, my physical and mental states did not vary much. When I was forty, my eldest son Bepin was married off, and a new bride entered my home. My joy knew no bounds, my whole body was filled with delight. I became a mother-in-law. Now I was a senior person.[48] Out of these forty years, I had spent twelve at my father's home. After that I was subjected and subordinated and I spent twenty-eight years as a young wife. Those years did not see much change in me. Now, gradually, I began to age. Everything about me was changing. I thought to myself: What wonders the Great Lord works! Even though I was not really old at that time, so much had changed. Reviewing them, I reached a solemn realisation. Earlier, I was forever fearful. Who planted such fears in me and who helped me to overcome them? Earlier, I could never venture out of the rooms alone at night, I needed at least two people to be with me and even then I would be nervous. Nowadays, I am still the same person with the same mind. Where did I get access to courage and strength? I could not understand it at all. How amazing! Who has made me fearless? Now I fear nothing, but what is it that has made me so? I never confide my desires to any living soul, yet all that I wish for does happen—who makes it so? There is yet another wonder: where did I get all this from—this house, these children and servants, such wealth, so much property over which I preside as the Revered Mistress of the Household? Who has appointed me to look after all this? It is entirely wonderful! The mind is dazzled by all this! What can I say about the One who makes all this happen, I can only thank him over and over again. Merciful father! Where are you? Do reveal yourself to your miserable daughter, fulfil her longing, bless her existence!

Why am I chained to this world? Who has ensnared me in this web of illusion? My heart has abandoned itself to greed—to desires for wealth and property. Yet, that isn't fair, someone is making it so. It is that one who causes everything to happen—he is the one who binds us to this enchantment. My mind was filled with such arguments. It became distracted and restless.

I longed to listen to recitations of sacred texts, to sacred music. But times were strange! Those days, women were not at all free. They could take no initiative themselves, they lived in subjection, like caged birds. What were my feelings at that time?

I had such strange feelings
As if a midget longed to reach out to the moon.

It was as if my mind had sprouted six arms. Two of them served the whole household, so that none should be unhappy. Two others were clutching my sons close to my heart. But the other two thrust themselves up to reach out to the moon. Really, my own mind amazes me! Look, the moon is millions of miles away from us. Can one ever hold it in one's hands? The very desire is absurd. Just as when babies cry for the moon and the mother distracts them by singing songs, asking the moon to come down to the child, so I, too, tried to distract myself like a child. I longed to listen to sacred texts and songs. But how to do it? All these things took place at the outer quarters of the house, they couldn't be heard from the inner quarters.[49] The outer courtyard was quite far off from the inner parts and I could never go there. What was to be done? My heart would not be calmed, it yearned to hear the sacred texts.

I did read a little, but where was the time for it? Moreover, I was so scared of rebukes and criticism! My mind would not accept this, and yet there was no way out. After much thought I decided that I would read out from the manuscript when my three sisters-in-law would be busy with their daily ritual worship in the morning. If they were to catch me at it, I'd have had it. I chose a deserted spot, sat down with the village women who were always with me, and began the reading.[50] One of them was detailed to keep a watch and to warn us if someone came that way. I would read out only in small bits, and even then I would be seized with terror so very often. Truly, my fears were my worst enemy. I was always afraid, I feared everything. My companions, however, were good people. Sometimes, when they asked me to sing, I would even do so just for them.[51] Many years have passed since then. There are still some people from those times who say that it is evil to teach women to read. They say: "Do women need to earn money? These days women are crazy about education. We used to think that women need to observe the proprieties, do their work at home, cook and serve the food. We had lived in saner times. These days there is a craze for education. We are not educated, aren't we human beings, then? Did we not live full lives?" Thus they grumble among themselves. Clearly, the only use that they can see for education is that of earning money. Such talk frightened me enormously, but I didn't stop my secret reading.

After some time, I began to talk more frankly with my sisters-in-law. It made them happy and it brought us much closer. Soon they came to know that I could read books. They were delighted and began to say: "How marvellous that you can read! We didn't know that all this while!" I began to teach two of them but they soon had to stop, they could not pick up much. I was much adored because I could read. I needed to read in secret no longer, I obliged my sisters-in-law by reading out to them. How wonderful it was that the Great Lord at last granted me my deep desires! My joy knew no bounds, the work at home felt light as feather. The Great Lord had granted me an old wish. Sometime I would sing together with my women neighbours. So the days passed happily. I cared very little about wordly concerns, my heart was filled with a sacred love.

Evidently, people have to put up with much anguish in this life. Even though no one had deliberately hurt me, yet bitter suffering came my way. Ah, my Lord! Nothing can be worse than the death of sons. I had borne twelve children. Ten of them were sons, and two were daughters. Let me talk about those who died. The second son Beharilal died at the time of his Rice Eating ceremony.[52] Pyarelal died when he was twenty-one. He was studying at Behrampur College and he died over there. Radhanath died when he was thirteen. Chandranath died when he was only three. Mukundalal, the youngest one, died when he was four. My eldest daughter gave birth to a son when she was seventeen, and she died thirteen days later, while she was still at the lying-in-room. The son also died there. I miscarried a son in the sixth month of pregnancy. My eldest son Bepinbehari had two sons. Both have died, at the ages of three and four.

Sorrow overwhelms me when I think of these deaths. So many have died—two sons of my son, one son of my daughter, six sons of mine and one daughter. Now I have four sons and one daughter left. The Lord alone knows what awaits me. He measures out possessions and dangers equally for the householder. Some may think only of the inevitable pain and dwell obsessively on that. On the other hand, there are those who go through terrible misfortunes, but who make little of that.

Folks say that losing a son is like being struck by a weapon.[53] But when we think about it, we find that the comparison does not hold. A man may even die of a bad physical injury. If it is a light one, then the wound may hurt for some time. But the pain goes away once the wound dries up. The pain of bereavement, however, lives as long as we live. Even if with great effort, we manage to conceal it and attain some semblance of outward normalcy, the pain simply digs itself in and burns up the heart. Bereavement is the worst pain of all. It can drive one mad. One is hardly human, one longs for death. Death escapes us, however, and that pain is worse than death.

✳

Ninth Composition

✳

My Lord, the ocean of mercy   Friend of the destitute
Saviour, who saves us all from danger
I call out to you from the bottom of my heart   Do you not hear me?
Why are you deaf to my pleas?
I am your creature   Do look towards me once
Lord, I am dying!
You know my heart   Why are you false to me?
How much more should I plead?
Even a cruel and evil person   Will respond to such appeals
While your mercy is as bottomless as the sea
I am a woman, I am subjected   I am also so very weak
Do not be uncharitable to me.
There are innumerable sinners   All over this world
All will be saved at your feet
Will you abandon this helpless woman   And save the rest of the world
Goddess, let me see how you can do it!
You are the Lord of the universe   The shelter of wrongdoers
You are called the saviour of sinners
You will not avoid Rashsundari   It is beyond you
You are bound to take her into your safe custody.

It is impossible to make sense of what the Great Lord does!
He alone knows what he will do! I remember perfectly well
that after I had learnt to feed myself, no one ever had to feed
me. However, on 27 Bhadra, in 1280,[54] I was reduced to that
infantile state. My food was ready, I was about to start on it,
when suddenly I cut open the index finger on my right hand.
Blood spurted out, so I couldn't eat by myself, someone else
had to feed me. Since we can't even be sure of the fact that we
will eat by ourselves if we wish it so, it is certain that we can't
take a step without God's help. What do we boast of, then?

Clearly, everything else is false, he alone is real. Why, then, do people say, my body, my house, my home! It is all false. Human beings don't ever stop erring.

Enough of that, let me get on with my story. Even though the loss of my sons continued to haunt me, I was not completely crushed. Even before I had learnt to use my intelligence, my mother had imparted to me the sacred name of the Merciful One. That was the great panacea, it has seeped into my bones. Whenever my body and mind succumb to the deadening poison of worldly greed, that marvellous medicine in my bones grows like the sacred Vishalyakarani tree[55] and cures my malaise, and fills me with joy. The poison is drained out and all the inner evil is routed. The Vishalyakarani is invincible. A whiff of that marvel is enough to destroy all our evil inclinations, to relieve us of all poisonous maladies, to bathe us in nectar. Alas! People suffer so much because they know it not. This is so very sad! We are born with eyes, yet we are blind! People think that the Vishalyakarani is situated on the top of the Gandhamadan Hill, it is impossible to procure it. How wrong we are! The seeds of that medicinal plant have already been sown in our heart, yet we know nothing about it. That is why we wallow in sorrows. It is our evil fate that even though our hearts are full of such priceless gems, yet we, wretched beings that we are, fail to discover that and therefore live in poverty. The very thought pierces the heart. If I did not possess this great inheritance from my mother, I do not know how I would have come through. Anyway, thanks to the mercy of the Merciful One, I am always filled with the joy of divine love. I am blessed! Our great Father! Preserver of the wretched, Merciful One! We see but we do not realise that you shower your mercy upon us all the time. You work such wonders with our bodies! We inhabit these bodies, we look upon them constantly. But we never fully know what is going on within. Lord! We cannot even know a fragment of your wonders, and we desire to know you! There is none so ignorant as he who wants to grasp your essence! But we are convinced that you love your devotees. You have said so yourself: "My devotees are my parents, they are my prayers, their hearts are my place of rest." Whoever calls out to you sincerely, you go to him, you become his unchained captive. You are the original cause of all my action. You know all my feelings, nothing escapes you. I was yearning to read books, and you worked your wonders so that I got to read all the books in that house.

I am amazed when I think of this. I knew nothing, it is a marvel that I learnt to read at all. It is only his glory that worked this miracle, that fulfils all desires. For better or for worse, the Great Lord did grant me my wish. I was dying to read, and I read enough to satisfy myself. I gradually finished all the books that the house possessed—*Chaitanya Bhagabat, Chaitanya Charitamrita,* eighteen chapters of Jaimini's *Bharat, Gobinda Lilamrita, Bidagdha Madhab, Premabhakti Chandrika, Balmiki Puran.*[56] However, we had only the introductory chapter (Adi parva) of *Balmiki Puran,* not all the seven chapters.

God has made us so that if we get even a fraction of anything, we immediately hunger for all of it. Our minds have this innate tendency. I was eager to read the seven chapters, once I had finished with the Introduction. Ours is a mere village, however, and I could not acquire it despite a lot of effort. My mind gave me no rest. My fifth son Dwarikanath was then a college student in Calcutta. If I could write him a letter, my troubles would be over. But I did not know how to write. Almost everyone knew now that I could read even though they did not know what it had cost me to learn. When they heard that I could read, they were pleased. I was very lucky. I used to be so scared, but then I realised that no one minded at all, they were happy about it. Had I just asked for the book, they would surely have got it for me. But I always found it difficult to ask anyone for anything. It is only now that I can occasionally ask my children for a few things.

Anyway, I was longing to read the book. In the meantime, that son came home from Calcutta in the holidays. I said to him: "Dwari! There are so many books in your home, but there isn't a complete set with seven chapters. I would love to have a copy." Dwari said: "Ma! I'll send you one as soon as I get back to Calcutta." I was so keen on the book that I felt quite ill with longing. The mind, too, suffered a lot.

After a few days, that book reached us. I was very excited as I opened it. It was a book in very small print. I couldn't read it at all.[57] I was incredibly sad. Tearfully, I reproached the Lord. I said to him: "Lord of the poor! You have brought this book to me at last, but it is useless to me. I can't read it even though I got it after such effort." My tears soaked my breast.

I felt ashamed of myself after a while. If someone were to ask me the reason for my tears, what would I say? I did not know how to read at all, who taught me? He gave me so much when he taught me to read. If he wills it so, I'll surely read this book as well.

I checked my tears and concentrated on the book. With God's help, I could soon read the print well enough. I had thought that it would be impossible to read a printed book. Then I found out that print is better than the handwritten manuscripts of old times. Since I had very little education, it was easier for me to read print. I learnt to read a bit of everything. But I still could not write and this caused me much pain. I used to cry before the Great Lord: "Lord! In a way you have kept me in reasonable comfort, I have a little of all that wordly people desire. But I suffer so because I cannot write. Teach me to write." I spent many days crying and praying over it, but I never did hope that I would be able to write. God willed it and out of the blue, my seventh son Kishorilal asked me: "Ma! Why do you never reply to our letters?" I said: "I can read, so I read your letters. But I can't write, so I do not reply to them." He said: "I can't have that. How do I stay away from home unless my mother writes to me? You have to write to me." He left ink, inkstand, paper and pen with me before he left for Calcutta. I was in a quandary. I could read a bit but I didn't know how to write at all. Even if I were to scribble a few letters with great effort, the household chores kept me too busy to have the time for it. But my son had sworn me to it. I did not know what to do.

While I worried about it, *Karta* suddenly contracted enteric fever. It affected his eyes. He went to Krishnanagar—Goari for treatment. I had to go with him. My fifth son Dwarakanath was working at Kanthalpota and we stayed with him. I had much less to do here. I learnt to write a little during that bit of leisure.

My learning didn't come easily, it cost me a great deal. I still marvel about it. It was as if the Great Lord guided me with his own hands. Otherwise it would have been impossible. I am fortunate indeed that I did learn a few letters. Perhaps, had I not known even this much, I would have been dependent on others. I am satisfied with what the Lord has given me. And that is not all. Even after he has given me so much, he stays with me and protects me in good fortune and in adversity. Alas! He is such a dear friend, a true companion of the heart, yet I hardly think of him, I am such a sinner! Shame on my greed, shame on my human existence, shame on my wretched life! Why do I carry this sinful body any longer? My life is meaningless.

�֍

Tenth Composition

✖

My careless mind   You forget yourself
What made you forget?
Immersed in wordly goods   That sweet Kashr[58]
Is burning in its own sins.
If it falls down   What is going to happen
Can you tell me that?
The play is over   Time is over, too
Pick up your merchandise, let's go.
Into this market-place of the world   You came to trade
You came here for that
But hordes of bandits   Surround you on all sides
Who knows what is going to happen!
Your debt needs to be honoured   After all this while
You need to settle your accounts.
Beware, beware   Be alert all the while
So that you are not cheated.
The day is done   While you haggled over prices
And while you pored over the purchases
Rashsundari thinks   Whatever little you have left
Take it back to your own home.

Ah me! What miracles the Lord of the universe works! When I reflect upon my own body and mind, I am overwhelmed and bewildered. In this one life of mine, my body and mind have gone through several phases. It is not easy to spell out how they were before, what they are like now, and what they are moving towards at this moment. It is all the more difficult because I cannot regulate these changes. But let me try and say a few things.

I have no memories at all about these things upto the time when I was five or six. Perhaps, I was still not self-conscious or sensible.

When I was seven or eight, I was a little more intelligent. That, however, had little effect. My mind was still passive and the body was extremely delicate and weak. Others looked after my needs, I could take no initiative on my own. Some time passed in this way.

I was married off when I was twelve. After that I lost the unbounded love that I had enjoyed at my father's house. I have become completely subordinated. My childishness was totally stripped away, I became the new bride. All my ornaments were new, I was dressed differently and I learnt the ways of the new bride.[59] For six more years I was the new bride.

In the meantime, the Great Lord had decked out my body as one fits out a boat, with every necessary article. What a wonder that is! It is nothing short of a miracle. So many things happen to my body, and I know nothing of their causes.[60] Ah! Is this some sort of magic, or do I dream? Truly, if only we think of our own bodies, we come to believe in the Great Lord, we do not have to go any further. He is visible easily and vividly to our eyes. Our great father, that merciful ocean of compassion, is not far away from us, he is very close to us.

When the waves of this wordly existence were rough on the boat journey of my body, he, who saves us from all danger, was there to reassure me. Whatever I did, I knew that he was with me. I had my first child when I was eighteen. I bore twelve children.

Gradually, I joined the ranks of old women, but I remained attached to my household. For the next few years I was a keen householder. Slowly, detachment began to set in. My body began to sag. I was in my late fifties now. I had three daughters-in-law and my youngest daughter had also become a mother. I was so happy with a full life, with such a large contingent of children, daughters-in-law, relatives and neighbours. Great Lord! Who can fathom your designs! You will do whatever you want to do.

> You bite as the snake, you cure like the snake doctor
> You give your verdict like the judge, you punish like the policeman.

I was born in 1216 and when this book was published in 1275, I was fifty-nine years old. Now, I am eighty-eight years old. Suddenly, everything has been transformed—my body, my mind, my dress and habits. Everything has became the opposite of its old state. People say that there are changes in each life. I found out that this was, indeed, true.

> No one can change the decree of Fate
> Be it Brahma, Vishnu or Maheswhar.[61]

Whatever the Great Lord wills, must be done. My long boat journey was in vain, the boat sank in sight of the coast.

> Having your head tonsured is worse than death.[62]

The Great Lord had done that to me. On the 21st of Magh, on the day of Shiva Chaturdashi, in 1275, my *Karta* passed away at two thirty in the afternoon.[63] I had a golden crown on my head, and now the crown has fallen off. Anyway, I do not regret it. Let the Great Lord keep me in any state that he wants to. In the same year, on the first day of Agrahayan, our family priest, Gunanidhi Chakrabarty also passed away.

So long my time had passed in a rather changeless fashion.[64]

Now, at the end of my life, I am a widow. There is something that I want to say which is both shameful and sad.

> Even if a woman with a hundred sons is widowed
> She is regarded as most unfortunate by the people.

They always want to tell you that you have been widowed. Anyway, this body and mind, this life of mine have gone through such changes. Magic is wrought upon my body ceaselessly. I get to understand nothing of this. Let me praise that craftsman.

Eleventh Composition

Praise be to you, the eternal Brahman[65]
Your slave submits this to you.
I came happily into the land of Bharatbarsha
Lord, why then, do I suffer from pangs of sorrow?
My heart suffers like the snake which has lost its jewel
So often it is startled and restless.
Lord, you see into our thoughts, you love your devotees
I know that truly you are a friend of the poor.
I have sinned a thousand times
Ocean of mercy, forgive me out of your own goodness.
What can I tell you, Lord, you know it all
I never desired wordly goods.
I do not hanker after sons, friends or wealth
My only desire is to attain your feet.
The world is false, only the path of right action is real
Let Rash be successful there.

My merciful father! Protector of the world who is immanent in the world! Great Lord! Lord of the poor, the sea of mercy, do save your poor daughter from her sins. Friend of the wretched, saviour of sinners, show some charity towards your daughter, your slave. Strength of the weak, wealth of the poor, Mother who saves us from danger! Take your weak child across the sea of life. I cannot live without you. Oh, eye of my eye, you who ravish my eyes! Do not go beyond my eyes, let my eyes be forever immersed in your great beauty. Lord of my heart and mind! Come, be at one with my heart. Let my heart not be absent from you for even a moment. Life of my life! My life's delight! Come, be enthroned in my heart, let my heart be afloat on a sea of love, let it be enfolded in your sweetness. My body still belongs to its frame, but it no longer is as it used to be. I could use it then for anything I wished to do. Now the boat no longer sets sail. Let me describe its present state briefly.

> The frail body can hardly move
> Straight lips are getting twisted at places.
> The skin sags, the hair is greying
> The teeth have melted away from the mouth.
> How can I describe my movements?
> I assume a more hideous shape by the day.

Anyway, it is difficult now to support this body of mine. It is decaying fast. The Great Lord had decked out my body once with a lot of decorations. Now he is taking them off one by one. Now I can see him, the life of my life. He sits at ease in my heart. Maybe, he is going to depart, once he has collected all his dues. However, I now think of something else, something that is strange. I came into Bharatbarsha such a long time back, and I am still here. When I look back on everything, I find that no one has ever said anything unpleasant to me. I have always had nice things said to me. No acquaintance or friend, no neighbour or villager that I can think of, has ever said a word in rebuke that I can recall. I thank the Great Lord for this. He has always been entirely merciful in everything towards me. It is as if he told all these people to be kind to me. This has made me very happy all these years. Now, however, I am a widow. Now I have altered my old ways, I have almost renounced the household. But the Lord works such wonders! What amazing things have happened through this body of mine. He alone knows what is going to come next.

Now I am the only senior member of this household. All the rest are in the next world. My time is up, but no one knows when one .has to leave for the next world. That is a problem. Had we known the date of our death beforehand, we would have escaped many misfortunes. But the Great Lord has planted the tree of hope in the human heart, it is most tenacious. That hope drives us through life. I live my life in the hope of the eternal fruit.[67] But, you who owns the fruit, who can tell what kind of fruit you will award to me at the end! Maybe, my last days will be full of bitter words. The very thought numbs me. Lord, the saviour of sinners! Let not that name of yours be in vain. You will never quench my hopes since you raised them yourself. You will have to fulfil them. I am firmly convinced that you decide our fate even before you create us. I think this is fairly evident. You do not rest even after you have sent us fully prepared into the world. You are with us in life and in death. At every instant you protect us. Why should we worry when we have such proof of your compassion? You will never go back on your promise. Moreover, you are the Lord of the wretched, the wealth of the poor, the boat in times of need and the strength of the weak. Your many names express your qualities. You will not go against your name in my case, a low creature even though I am. Lord, who pervades the world, who is all powerful! There is nothing beyond you. You have created everything in all the worlds. Your wishes regulate the world. If you so wish, one glance from you can destroy Creation. But, that is impossible, you will never do that. Even if we sin a thousand times, even if we commit despicable deeds, you will never cast us away from your arms. You will be wherever we are.

✻

Thirteenth Composition[68]

✻

Account of a Dream

Whenever we look closely into all that the Great Lord has created, we get a feeling that it is but a dream. Truly, people dream of the strangest things. When they wake up, however, all is gone. Likewise, all that you had in this world vanishes before your very eyes, so that, later, it feels as if it all had been a dream. There are two kinds of dreams: one that you see when you are awake, and one that you see in your sleep. Jagannath Mishra dreamt one night that his son Nemaichand had shaved off his head and had left Nabadwip. He broke into loud lamentations, calling out, Nemai, Namai. Whatever he had dreamt of came true.[69]

Dasarath, the king of the Surya dynasty, passed away when his son Bharat was visiting his uncle. He died because Ramchandra, along with Lakshman and Sita, had been exiled to the forests. All this had actually happened, Dasarath was, indeed, dead, and the people of Ayodhya were mourning him. Bharat, at his uncle's place, dreamt of this very thing, and woke up, crying. How strange! Whatever had happened in his dream at night was confirmed in the morning.

Once I, too, had an equally strange dream which I'll set down carefully. My son Pyarilal was twenty-one, and he was studying in a college in Behrampore. I dreamt one night that my Pyarilal was very weak and ill. He was, in fact, at death's door. I dreamt that I was standing at his side. After a while he died before my eyes. He was set down on the ground and his body was covered with a cloth. I was standing there, watching all this. In the dream, I lost all control over myself, I started shaking convulsively. I flung myself down upon the ground and burst into sobs. Then, again, I saw that Pyarilal was being taken away for cremation. I was with him, I was going round the cremation fire, crying. My heart was bursting, I wanted to throw myself into the flames, but I couldn't quite bring myself to do that. After the funeral, when the last rites had been performed, everyone went home. I saw myself on the banks of the river Ganga, crying out and sobbing loudly: "Pyarilal, Pyarilal."

After a while, I saw a little boat coming towards me along the Ganga. It had no cover at all, there was nothing on it. There was only a man who was rowing the boat, and another who was travelling in it. I looked up, sobbing, and it seemed to me the other man was my son Pyarilal. I had been crying so hard and so long that my whole body was streaked with mud. I got up hastily and gazed at the boat. It seemed that I was no longer on the bank where I had been earlier, but had gone over to the other side. The boat was coming towards me. My joy knew no bounds. My whole body was filled with strength. I stood up, crying out to him like a madwoman. When at last the boat reached the shore, I remembered the earlier scene and moaned in pain. My Pyarilal stood before me with a melancholy, downcast face, as if he was sorry to see me in such a state. I cried out, "Pyari, come to me," but he did not respond. After a long while, he spoke to me from the river in a very low and sad voice: "Ma, do you want to listen to the recitation of a religious text?" I was overjoyed to hear those words, to see that he was alive. In my dream I embraced him and said: "Yes, I do. Where is it?" He said, "Come with me," and he led the way. By and by, we approached a royal palace. There were many grand buildings, imposing courtyards, all manner of bright and beautiful things. There was also a most impressive building with a magnificent throne in the middle of it. Countless people surrounded the throne. I assumed that it was a courtroom. So far, Pyarilal had said not a word to me except that one sentence: "Ma, if you want to listen to the recitation, then come with me." Nonetheless, I was heartened to have him back with me, I followed him into the room contentedly. He left me behind at the courtyard and went up to ascend the throne. Never did he once glance back at me. It seemed to me that I stood there crying, calling out to him to come back to me.

I could see him quite well from where I stood. But Pyarilal responded neither to my calls nor to my tears.

I woke up from the dream, crying so hard that my clothes and the bedsheets were soaking wet. Even after I woke up, I felt as if I was still dreaming, I kept crying in my sleep. I could hardly speak, my heart was beating hard with dreadful anxiety. However much I tried to comfort myself, I would not be calm. I wrote down the date.

I was so upset that people sent for news from Behrampore. All that I had seen in my dream had actually happened. Pyarilal had passed away on that day, at that time and in that manner. The strangeness of it! What I had dreamt of in my sleep, what I could not make myself speak about once I woke up—so horrible had the dream been—had all come to pass.

[*I have omitted some passages on similar experiences, including a second sight that enabled her to follow the accident that happened to another son who, however, survived.*]

Anticipating Death

Most people in this world are terrified of death. If we carefully consider the matter, however, there is nothing so fearful about it. It is out of ignorance that people fear it so. I have seen for myself that dying is not really terrible. I will never forget about that.

Once I was very ill and weak with high fever. I was, in fact, close to death. I was lying on a bed. Suddenly, my body and mind went numb, I could neither move nor speak. I tried to get down but, however hard I tried, I couldn't move at all. I was not unconscious, my mind was fully alert, but my tongue was unable to utter my thoughts. All my children were quite small at that time, only the elder two were somewhat grown-up. They were sitting beside me and were sobbing wildly. I wondered, why can't I respond to them, I can hear them! But my tongue would not move. I was in a room that faced south. All of a sudden, everything seemed to turn red, and a little later, I could see nothing at all, everything went dark. As I tried to open my eyes fully, everyone cried out, she is going. They carried me outside.[70] I could not understand what was going on. I could see them all. I could even see that I had been brought outside. As I was being taken out, my head rolled out of their clasp and a man rushed over to hold it up. I was perfectly aware of all this. I was put down on the courtyard. It was amazing! Here I was, a corpse, but I could see it all. Loud lamentations broke out all around me. My eldest son sat beside me, his head thrust into his knees, crying and hitting himself on the head. His aunt clung to him and wept. The second son threw himself down on the ground and sobbed. The other children were also crying, but they were small, other people had taken them in their arms. *Karta* of the household sat at the door and asked: "Is she gone? So be it then." A whole crowd had collected at the courtyard, everyone was crying. We had a *gomosta*[71] called Thakur Harimohan Sikdar. He had never been inside the house, I had never seen him before. He sat next to me now, checking to see if I was still breathing, feeling my hand, my chest, and crying: "Alas! Our mother has left us." *Karta* was calling out his name. I could see that he was weeping profusely.

It was so strange! I could see everything, I could even see my own corpse. My eyes were closed, but I saw it all so clearly. I felt sorry for them, I wanted to comfort them, but I could do nothing. I could not understand how this was so. Some time passed in this way. I had no idea about what was going on.

At last my consciousness returned. It was as if I woke up from sleep. Strength returned to my body, I could move my limbs, I could speak again. I found that I was lying on the ground. Then I said: "Why have you brought me here?" People were thrilled at this. They lied to comfort me: "It was so hot inside, so we brought you out in the fresh air." They took me inside. How could I see all of this after I was dead? I have always found this astonishing, but I feel embarrassed about discussing it with other people. They might think that all of this has been made up. But I am telling you the truth, I am only saying what actually had happened to me.

❊

Fourteenth Composition

✳

[The verses at the beginning are omitted.]

Seeing A Ghost With My Own Eyes

People say that there are no ghosts, there can be no such things! I used to agree with them. However, ghosts do, indeed, exist. Once I saw something that might well have been a ghost.

I was about to set off for a bath one afternoon. There is a garden at the southern corner of our house. A very old tamarind tree stands there. I had just reached it on my way to the bath. There is a thorn tree (Babla) in front, and one of its branches was leaning on one side. That entire place is rather bare, there is only a little shrubbery. It was broad daylight. As I looked at the thorn tree, I saw that a dog was lying on top of the leaning branch. Its tummy was resting on the branch. It looked exactly like a human figure. Its limbs were hanging down from both sides of the tree. It seemed as if some bright conch-shell bangles were shining on them. I was amazed at the sight. I gazed at it and wondered: "It is incredible. Why should a dog lie on a tree in the first place, and, on top of that, why should it wear bangles? Has anyone seen or heard of such a thing before?" I stared at it for over an hour, I saw the whole thing perfectly clearly. I thought: "If only the others had seen this as well!" I looked behind just once to see if there was anyone else there, and, as soon as I turned back towards the dog, I saw that it had vanished. I looked for it all around the tree, but I couldn't find it again. There was, indeed, no other bird or beast in sight. It was broad daylight, I could see everything so clearly. Such a large dog just disappeared, and not a leaf had stirred! When I couldn't find it at all, I went back into the house and told everybody about this. Some said it was a ghost, some said it was nothing, it was some sort of an optical illusion. Some others said, it couldn't be anything but a ghost. I know that I had seen a ghost. But people find it hard to believe since it was in the middle of the day.[72]

Anyway, I have written about what I have seen. This is a partial account of the sixty years of my life.

My name is Mother. I had a name when I was in my father's house. That name has disappeared long back. Now I am the mother of Bepin Behari Sarkar, Dwarka Nath Sarkar, Kishori Lal Sarkar, Pratap Chandra Sarkar and Shyamasundari. Now I am everybody's mother.[73]

This is the account of my life upto this point. Another account will be written at the time of my death.[74]

✤

Fifteenth Composition

❇

I do not so much long to see Shantipur, Nabadwip or Ganga
But it is for Vrindaban that I yearn.[75]
My mind had long desired
To travel around in the name of pilgrimage journeys.
What are Gaya and Kashi[76] like, what is Vrindaban like
Why do people settle down in these holy places for the rest
of their lives.
The Vedas say that Vrindaban is as sacred as Golak[77]
Why, then, do people stay anywhere else at all?
The city of Baranas is, indeed, a second Kailash[78]
The ascetic Ramat Dandi lives there.
I have always longed to see Annapurna[79]
I wanted to gaze at Lord Digambar.[80]
At Gaya one can see the holy footprints of the Lord clearly
The sight would bless my body.

My heart cries out for Vrindaban
How and when shall I reach it?
When will I be so very fortunate
That my sinful body will go to the land of Vraj.[81]
That I will actually set my eyes on the face of the merciful
Lord
When great ascetics do not even reach his feet through their
meditations.
Place your hands on my head, bless me
So that Rashsundari attains the Lord of Vraj in the land of
Braja.

I have set down a few facts about my life but the account
has not a single word about *Karta*! I suppose that this leaves the
book quite incomplete. However, a catalogue of all his virtues
would be quite beyond me. It would be too large an account,
if it were to be told properly. All that I can say is that he was a
good man, the like of whom is rare in this world. He was big
and heavily built, his very appearance proclaimed him as the
head of the household. This was clear even to a stranger. He
was a very kind man. He was immensely kind to his tenants
as well as to others. He was also most generous. If a person
interrupted his meal, asking for food, he would wait until that
person had been served, and only then would he resume his
own meal. He was very adept at official business. He loved
litigation. He was a very powerful man, at any point of time
he had twenty to twenty-five court cases going. He was never
without them, he even lodged cases against important people.
He would never lose a single one, but would always return
victorious. Such was his power and his awesome voice that
whenever he chastised someone, the whole village would
tremble. He would be fighting cases with all the big zamindars.
Once or twice he even brought *fauzdari* (criminal) cases

against planter Sahibs[82] but thanks to the mercy of the Great
Lord he never lost the suits. Mir Ali Mahmud was a very big
landlord of Dakshin Bari. There were a lot of civil suits over
land and estates that the two of them were fighting between
them. In the village of Tentulia, Mir Ali owned twelve annas
of the estates [75 per cent] while they *(Karta)* owned about
four annas [25 per cent]. Apart from that, there were other
lands and properties under dispute. Cases had been going on
for over three generations. *Karta* had some land in the North.
Once he had gone there on a visit. My eldest son Bepin Behari
was only six at that time, many others were not yet born. All
of a sudden, Mir Ali ordered that *Karta's* tenants should be
harassed and thrashed and should be forced to pay him rent.
The *gomosta* who looked after such affairs was extremely ill
at that time. The folks at home said, what can we do, there
is nothing that we can do now. I was the person in charge
at home, but what do I understand of such matters? I was
not supposed to look after these things. But the women of
those tenant families came to me and began to lament about
the oppression that they had to face. I found it impossible
to ignore their suffering. My son was not yet old enough to
write a letter himself. So I composed a letter in his name and
sent it to Mir Ali through someone. He was most pleased with
the letter. He got our tenants released and he sent two senior
and responsible people to our place so that the case would be
resolved through arbitration. *Karta* was absent all this while.
I was scared because I had been responsible for such a major
decision without ascertaining his intentions. I knew nothing
about lawsuits. That suit had been dragging on all this while
and nobody had tried to resolve it in this way. It had also
been done in *Karta's* absence without his permission. Maybe
he would be furious when he came home. My heart trembled

in fear and anxiety. He came home in a few days. Those who had acted as intermediaries in the matter had no worries, but I was terrified. When he heard that I have been instrumental in resolving the generations old dispute with Mir Ali, he was most pleased with me. He was, in fact, an important man. He passed away, leaving much good work unfinished. These are a few words about *Karta's* life.

Notes

1.   The Introduction is written by Jyotirindranath Tagore, the elder brother of Rabindranath, and an important literary figure in his own right. Neither Rashsundari nor Jyotirindranath mention how he came to be asked to write it.

2.   Literally, the kind slayer of Madhu. Madhu was a demon whom the Lord Vishnu, the God who preserves Creation, had killed. Here it refers to the domestic deity.

3.   This was the first biography of the medieval Bhakti saint Shri Chaitanya who was later deified by a large section of Bengali Vaishnavs. It was written by Vrindaban Das around 1548. See Kanchan Basu, ed, *Shri Chaitanya Bhagabat,* Reflect Publishers, Calcutta, 1986.

4.   The confusion at this point arises because of Rashsundari's inability to distinguish between levels in divinity. Since the family idol is Dayamadhav, she imagines that he is a household property, and cannot see how he can belong to all.

5.   Saraswati is the Goddess of learning, wife of Brahma.

6.   This means that Saraswati should inspire her speech. Since sacred knowledge (the *Vedas*) was orally transmitted, and because in the traditional institutions of higher Sanskritic learning, teaching was largely orally dispensed, conventionally, the throat is seen as the seat of learning.

7.   This should be 1809 and 1896, according to the Gregorian

calendar. She follows the Bengali traditional calendar in putting down dates. The only dates that are given, relate to her birth and to her present age.

8. The river that flowed through her home district was actually Padma, a tributary of the sacred river Ganga. In the absence of the main river channel, people referred to it as Ganga. It is considered a pious act to walk to the sacred river for a bath. People would travel some distance to do so, and they would usually bring their own food for the journey. Rashsundari must have seen such , travellers, walking towards Ganga. She is implying here that she was too young then to realise the religious meaning of the bath.

9. It means that she is a spoilt child.

10. Since her family was rich, the village school must have met at their house. It was customary for such elementary schools or pathshalas that taught some Bengali and indigenous arithmetic, to meet at spaces provided by the rich people of the village rather than in a building of their own.

11. Even though most little girls would be wearing the sari, some initially wore a pleated long skirt with a scarf on top for the sake of modesty, before they graduated to the sari.

12. At *pathshalas*, boys were taught first to scratch out letters on the earth. At a slightly more advanced stage, they would write on plantain leaves, and then on palm leaves. Only the most advanced of them, in some places, had access to handmade paper. All the lessons were recited loudly for purposes of memorisation. Blackboards and textbooks came into use much later, and only in some places.

13. White conch-shell bangles are put on once a girl marries, it is a sign of her married status. Widows take them off and they are not allowed to wear any ornaments.

14. Neither widows nor unmarried girls wear conch-shell bangles or the vermilion mark on the forehead. However, unmarried girls wear ornaments, colourful saris, and there are hundreds

of differences in dress, diet and behaviour to mark them out from widows. Rashsundari uses the incident to underline her ignorance of wordly custom, her innocence of the basic facts of domestic life.

15. A mode of address, directed to men of high status.

16. A woman is not allowed to utter the name of her husband or of her male relatives on the husband's side.

17. Corpses are brought on new cots with new bedding on them. After the cremation, these are left behind at the ghat or river bank. Cremation always takes place at the river bank, wherever possible, preferably at the Ganga. Funeral pyres are built up of logs on which clarified butter or ghee is poured before the fire is lit. Considered an impure and polluting place, where the untouchable Chandal caste is in charge of the work, it is also a place full of oppressive associations, of many smells and sights that evoke dead bodies and burning. It is a place of dread, especially at night. The presence of mats, etc, is a reminder that a corpse had been cremated fairly recently.

18. Palanquins are carriages borne by four to eight men. It was a more comfortable mode of transport than the bullock cart, and horse-drawn carriages were rare on the country roads. Brides conventionally go away in palanquins for, closed as they are, they ensure complete privacy. Here she probably means that she was placed in the same palanquin as her husband.

19. After the wedding ceremony was over and the ritual at the groom's house had been completed, it was customary for the bride to return to her natal home and stay there until she reached her puberty.

20. This probably means that she could not visit her natal home for two whole years.

21. Father's home is the literal term for the natal home and this is what she uses even though she was fatherless.

22. Among the Vaishnav sect, recitation of the many names of the

Lord is the most important path to salvation in the modern, degenerate age of Kali.

23. This means that they would be exempted from domestic duties, but would fetch and carry things to the field, look after the cattle, fetch water, etc.

24. All landowners had an office (*cutchhery*) for accounting, receiving rent and produce, and also for trying petty, local cases informally, since they had lost their formal judicial powers with the Permanent Settlement of 1793. Nonetheless, their informal powers were considerable, and they were, most of the time, a law unto themselves.

25. The domestic deity or idol would have daily worship ritually enacted, and the arrangements usually were the wife's responsibility, even though the act of worship would be performed by an upper caste male relative or the priest. He would also be offered daily ritual meals that had to be cooked separately under conditions of great purity.

26. The last and most degenerate of ages in the Hindu four-age cycle, after which a new cycle begins all over again.

27. She is quite precise about when exactly she grew up. She had her first son when she was eighteen and, possibly, that raised her status.

28. The head of the household, in this case, her husband.

29. A low, agricultural caste.

30. For women, their eating was an activity that needed to be done away from male eyes and never to be talked about in public.

31. She means that it would be strictly stipulated beforehand about how long she could stay and she must obey that stipulation.

32. Brahma who is God the Creator, has five mouths.

33. The Puranas—sacred law books, and the Tantras—books of esoteric ritual practices.

34. Note how easily and unselfconsciously she slips in the *Koran* with Hindu religious texts.

35. Pages of the manuscripts were not sewn or tied together, but were pressed inside heavy wooden slats. Taking out a page was possible without damaging the book.

36. Here she uses the significant word, *jitakshar* which means one who has mastered the word. There is a word that is somewhat analogous in construction and that is a familiar word in religious discourses: *jitendriya* or one who has mastered the senses. She probably had that construction in mind and stretched it to substitute 'word' for 'senses'. I have not come across this word elsewhere, nor is it in the better-known dictionaries.

37. She says this because of her experience of the village school, where students were taught to write out the letters first and then to memorise them one by one. Writing was, then, the first step to reading and one would read what one wrote down. In the absence of blackboards, the teacher did not have to write out anything for the students to read, he would help them with shaping letters. Later, he would recite memorised passages which they would take down to practise writing and spelling. Nor were primers used at all in traditional *pathshalas.*

38. Silent reading was unusual. At schools, lessons were recited aloud, and manuscripts—mostly religious or philosophical— were chanted out. With printed books came the habit of silent reading, even though, to this day, lessons are usually loudly recited to help memorise them.

39. A married woman would rarely be addressed by her own name. Each relative would use the precise kinship connection and for a senior person, her status within the household would be the common mode of address.

40. It was, and still is, largely customary for widows to return to their natal homes.

41. Within the kinship network, a woman's status and seniority depends on her husband's seniority. Even if she is much younger than his brothers and sisters, if her husband is older, then she is addressed and treated as a person who is senior to them.

42.   During the day, neither the husband nor the older male relatives are meant to see the face of the wife which is covered by the sari. Rashsundari, being somewhat ignorant about the complexities of protocol, did not understand how far the prohibition was to be extended.

43.   In a landlord's family, the produce rent in paddy as well as the harvest from directly managed lands would be stored in the inner courtyard. The scattered bits of leftover corn would be used as fodder.

44.   Prohibitions wear off gradually with the birth of sons. In her case, she clung to them longer than usual. They would include speaking in whispers, especially to older persons, and, in general, keeping silent whenever possible and speaking only when asked a question.

45.   The land of the demons that Lord Ram, an incarnation of Lord Vishnu, destroyed, according to the epic *Ramayana*.

46.   The wicked cousins of the Pandavas in the epic *Mahabharata* who were defeated by the righteous Pandavas.

47.   In one of his incarnations as a midget, Lord Vishnu had approached the King Bali, known for his legendary charity, and asked for the gift of a measure of land that would be covered by three steps taken by him. Amused by the midget's demand, Bali had promised him that land. Vishnu then assumed his true dimensions: his first step covered the earth and the second covered the heavens. When he asked Bali where the third step should be taken, Bali prostrated himself and asked him to place his feet on his head. This is a translation from a Sanskrit couplet, but I am not certain if it is her own translation, or if this was then a common Bengali saying.

48.   With the entry of a new bride into the house, her new-found powers were visibly confirmed, as the restrictions on the newcomer were both a reminder of her own new freedom, and of the distance that she had travelled from the days of her youth. It also put another human being entirely under her control.

49. This refers to the sexual division of the household space in rich families where the outer parts of the house may be located in another building, separated by a courtyard from the inner quarters where the women resided and which the household men would use for rest and sleep.

50. Reading out from manuscripts, especially sacred ones, is always made audible since it is supposed to be a public act of worship. Since only a few could read, and manuscript reading was a time-consuming and cumbrous activity, its reach was meant to include many others who could not read. So far, she had engaged in silent reading, a most unusual way of reading manuscripts, for reasons of secrecy. For the first time, the secret activity and achievement was going to be proclaimed to others.

51. Respectable families did not teach their women to sing and neither did they ever hum since female singing was associated with the work of prostitutes and of public, professional singers of low castes and presumably of dubious morals.

52. *Annaprashan,* one of the ten major life-cycle rites for upper-caste Hindus. Usually performed when the child is six months old, it is a ritual feeding of the child with rice that symbolises food and wealth.

53. The word used here is *putrashok* which literally means mourning a son. There is no composite word in Bengali to signify the death of a daughter or the loss of a child of either sex. Since she refers to the death of the daughter as well, she uses the term in a generic sense.

54. September, 1873, by the Gregorian calendar.

55. The fabulous, life-giving tree mentioned in the sacred epic *Ramayana* which was located on the Gandhamadan mountain.

56. All are late medieval Bengali Vaishnav devotional texts.

57. Since she had only read the stylised calligraphy of handwritten manuscripts so far, she initially could not follow printed matter.

It was small print and the print used letters that had been standardised in such a way that it bore little relationship to the form of the letters in calligraphic writing.

58. This is Banaras, the great Saivite pilgrimage centre.

59. The dresses that a woman wears at different stages of her life are markedly different from each other. An unmarried girl would not wear a veil, would wear very simple saris and few ornaments. Her movements would be free and supple. For a long while, a new bride wears bright saris, usually with strong red borders, and a lot of ornaments, including conch shell bangles and an iron bangle on her left wrist. She also wears sindhoor, the red vermillion paste or powder on her hair parting and a vermillion circular mark on her forehead. She hardly speaks, and does so in a very low voice. Her movements are stiff, unobtrusive and muted. An elderly woman (a woman in her early thirties would count as elderly, there's a Bengali saying that at twenty a woman turns old) would wear white saris with a coloured border and her veil would be shorter and her movements relatively more free. A widow would wear speckless white and no ornaments or marks in the parting of her hair or on her forehead. Her diet is free offish and meat and other "strong" food, and she fasts once every fortnight and goes without a proper dinner. Since she is regarded as a sign of bad luck, she cannot attend a number of ritual occasions and ceremonies.

60. This is the onset of her sexually active years and the time of childbearing. She refers obliquely to her nubile body.

61. Brahma is the Lord of Creation, Vishnu preserves Creation and Shiva or Maheshwar destroys it to begin another cycle. However, despite this tripartite theogony, there is an overlay of belief in a single divinity. The two levels often coexist in religious thinking. Fate is often conceptualised as a deity who visits each infant after birth and inscribes its fate on its forehead though no one can decipher the inscription, and none can alter it.

62. Widows were expected to tonsure their heads.

63. February 1869, on a day of the annual ritual worship of Shiva.

64. Here Time refers not to physical changes which she had commented on earlier, and which had been abundant, but to social status.

65. The ultimate soul, the only reality, according to monists.

66. In fables, snakes carry a jewel on their heads. This expression commonly denotes a great loss.

67. This refers to *karmaphal*, or the fruits of karma, the notion that the deeds of one life are rewarded or punished in the next.

68. I have left out the verses here.

69. Life of Chaitanya.

70. Ritually, death should take place under the open skies. Ideally, a person should be taken to the shores of Ganga to breathe her last, but where that is not possible, the dying person is carried into the courtyard and is placed beside the sacred tulsi plant before the last rites are conducted.

71. A zamindari official, in charge of the accounts of the estate.

72. The superstition is that ghosts are abroad only at night time.

73. This is not a cosmic statement. Within a household, the senior-most woman is called 'mother' by all.

74. This probably means that since death was coming soon, that would constitute the next and last landmark in the story of her life.

75. Shantipur and Nabadwip are important pilgrimage centres in Bengal, associated with the life of Chaitanya. Vrindaban is on the banks of Yamuna, in present day Uttar Pradesh. According to Vaishnav belief, Lord Krishna spent his childhood and youth here, sporting among milkmaids and cowherds. It is the holiest of pilgrimages for Bengali Vaishnavs.

76. These are major pilgrimages in Bihar and in Uttar Pradesh in North India.

77. This is the name of the Vaishnav heaven.

78. Benaras is another name for Kashi. Kailash is supposed to be the abode of Lord Shiva.

79. The name of the great Goddess Durga, referring to her role as food giver. Here she probably has the renowned temple of Annapurna at Benaras in mind.

80. Another name of Lord Shiva.

81. A stretch of territory, lying on both sides of the Yamuna, with Vrindaban and Mathura on two sides of the river. The entire area is associated with the childhood, youth and adult life of Krishna.

82. This refers to the European indigo planters who were feared and hated by peasants and landlords alike.

Excerpts from the Second Part

First Composition

...I was born in the month of Chaitra, in the year 1216. It is now 1303.[1] I am, thanks be to God, now eighty-eight years old. I came into this Bharatbarsha and I have spent such a long time here, but I still belong to that old frame.[2] I think that there are very few of my contemporaries left in our land. It is doubtful if even one is left.

I came into this Bharatbarsha and I have spent eighty-eight years here. The Great Lord has compressed the burden of three different life spans within a single lifetime. I must admit that I am extremely fortunate in this respect....[3]

✻

Third Composition

✻

... My Lord, today I witnessed one of your miracles. Kind One, my heart is stony, but your miracle has melted down even that stone with delight...

All this is stowed away inside my mind, others know

nothing of this. That is why I will talk about it in some detail. In our past, customs were different, now people dress very differently. Anyway, I used to own a nose-ring that was shaped like the crescent moon. Three similar rings were attached to the main one.

There is a pond close to this house. I had gone for my bath there one day. I was up to my neck in the water, washing clothes, when suddenly that nose-ring got entangled with my clothes and fell off. Lots of people immediately collected to look for it. They got into the pond and hunted for the ring. It could not be found at all. I knew that it was gone forever, there was no way that I would get it back.

I was twenty-two years old at that time. I already had two sons, after which eight more sons and two daughters were born to me. Later, the pond silted up gradually, and became useless. It was filled with shrubbery and slowly it turned into a patch of wilderness.

Many years later, my fifth son Dwarkanath—the one who works at Goari Krishnagore—renovated the pond. The bed was dug up afresh, and the loose earth was piled up next to the pond. After a while, a wall was built with the earth.

Much later, part of the wall collapsed, though half of it continued to stand. It was then discovered that my lost nose-ring was lying flat on top of the broken wall.

Rain had washed away all the earth and mud that had covered it. It could be partly seen. I was standing on the steps of the pond, I could see it a bit. There was a girl from the fisherman's family, I asked her, "What is that?" She ran and got it for me.

I took it in my hand, and I realised that it was, indeed, my lost nose-ring. I was overwhelmed. I cannot describe what I felt like at that moment. My eyes filled up, I wiped away my tears and gazed at it.

My heart trembled at this sign of the miracle that the Great Lord had worked. I had seen with my own eyes that the ring had dropped off into the water when I was twenty-two. I got it back when I was eighty-two. Even after these sixty years, the ring was utterly unchanged, the golden colour hadn't rusted at all. What a wonder!

Is there anything that the Great Lord cannot do? For sixty whole years the ring had been lost in the water, I never even dreamt that I would get it back. It was not a possibility.

Where was it all these sixty years? Who brought it back to me after sixty years? It had spent sixty years in water, earth and mud, the earth had been worked over so many times. It had been taken out from the pond, many feet had stamped on it to soften it into mud, the mud went into the wall next to the pond. The ring had stayed inside the wall. With all the pulling about this way and that, it had remained just as it used to be. Had it been with me, it would have been broken and ruined by now.

... My Lord, you have shown such mercy to this wretched sinner, to Rashsundari! When I took the ring, I felt as if I was holding the moon from the heavens in my hands. Don't ever think that it was because I had got back the gold. I was happy that the Great Lord had been so kind to me. I began to think, where would I keep this, what is the best place? I will not melt it down, I'll keep it intact. But it will be for Madangopal.[4] It was too big for the nose, so it was attached to the crown on his head. It looked wonderful.

My Lord, Madangopal, you had kept the ring with great care so that you could restore it to your vassal, your daughter. You gave it back to me after sixty years. I took it and I felt that it is you who have come to me.

❊

Eighth Composition

✳

... I have spent a long time in Bharatbarsha. I am still here. How can I explain the states of my body and my mind over the years? He alone knows, for he is always there, ever present in my innermost being.

How was my body in the old days? It is a very old story, it is irrelevant now. If I were to talk about it now, the modern women will say that she is boasting. That isn't true, nobody should ever think that. Let me say a bit about how we were meant to work and how we worked in the old days: also how my body used to be then.

In the old days, women were not allowed to read. People of those times would say: "What on earth is this? A woman studying? But it is so wrong, it leads to disaster, women should not even touch pen and paper." That was the rule everywhere.

Now the Great Lord has decreed new rules, I find them most satisfying. Girls suffer from nothing these days, the rules are much better. Now, even if one has only one daughter, she is educated with great care. I find it wonderful. In those days, we were not educated, I am not an educated person. I don't even understand the significance of education, we had nothing to do with such things, we only did the household chores.

I am still in the same household where I have spent so many years. It is no mean household. Madanmohan resides here, meals are cooked to feed his image, lots of guests keep coming and going.

My mother-in-law was ill, she could not see. So I had to care for two divine images.[5]

I had no brothers-in-law, but there were three sisters-in-law. I was the only one at home.[6] At that time, the sisters-in-law were in their own homes. Our household had about twenty to twenty-five servants and maidservants, their food had to be cooked twice a day. In those days, we didn't employ Brahmin cooks.[7] All the cooking had to be done at home. Every single household chore had its own set of rules, and I observed every one of them. At the same time, I had ten sons and two daughters. The entire responsibility for bringing up the twelve of them was upon me.

About nine maidservants worked for us, but all of them did chores outside the home. There was no help inside, I had to do everything myself. The *Karta* would not have anything at all after his morning bath and worship, he only relished rice.[8] So I needed to cook rice for him in the morning.

I did all of that by myself. I would cook in the morning, then I would feed the children. I would then have my bath, and then I would make all the arrangements for Madanmohan's meal. I would also prepare everything for my mother-in-law's meal and I would keep it all ready in front of her.[9] Then I would go into the kitchen. First I would cook for *Karta,* then I would cook the rest. I did all the chores of that household. I wanted to please everybody.

Merciful Lord, you showed such mercy to this slave, you endowed me with such perfect physical health. I could do the work of ten by myself, without any sense of fatigue. Ocean of mercy, friend of the poor, Hari, you fortified me like a rock, I had no ailments at all. Now let me tell you how that body fares at this moment.

✳

Ninth Composition

The worn-out body can hardly walk
The world goes dark if I try to stand up
God is trying this body of mine
No limb moves as before
Little by little, such a state has come about
That all the ten senses are ready to depart
Gluttony, unfortunately, refuses to leave
Brother Belly is looking around with great eagerness.
My jewel of a daughter is always ready with her services
She provides me with everything that I need...

Tenth Composition

[ornament]

Theatre of Life[10]

Lord of the world, Protector of the world, source of Creation, Preservation and Destruction![11] You are the *adhikari,* the manager and proprietor of the theatre of Life. *Adhikari,* our master, your will is everything, everything follows your will. You drew me in among your actors, and you have also given me a seat among the audience. I have been there for the last eighty-eight years.

Adhikari, this is a most curious theatre. You have shown yourself in so many different roles, costumes. At first, you assumed the roles of my parents, brothers, sisters, relatives, near and dear ones. You brought them to me and then you took me away from them. Who can tell what you are going to do; who knows when the curtains will come down, which play is going to come to an end. No one else can know any of this. *Adhikari,* you took away all my dear ones, after you had brought them to me. I was filled with pain. But you soothed it away.

After a while, you dressed me up as a mother and gave me the chief role. As soon as you gave me directions, I dressed up as Mother, and came on stage to perform my role. I have been watching so many wonderful roles that people play in your theatre.

There is no end to the marvellous plays that your theatre performs. I have been made to play so many roles. You brought in beings dressed up as my sons, daughters, grandchildren. You showed them to me, and then you took away almost all of them.

Adhikari, you brought my son onto the stage, and came to me while the play was on. You said, "Take this son, take him in your arms, he is yours, I give him to you." I took him in my arms and I was filled with joy beyond measure. I have no words to describe such happiness.

Adhikari, you know well the excruciating pain that one goes through to bear a son. But it evaporates the moment one looks at the face of the child, when one holds him in one's arms. My whole being is bathed in joy when I sit with him on my lap. Joy, indeed, overflows, I think that I am now truly someone. Let alone everything else, *Adhikari,* I even forget about you.

With him in my arms, I feel I do matter, I feel as if I am holding the moon in my hands. Then I truly feel that this home, this household, all this does, indeed, belong to me. My body dances with joy, my mind keeps in step with it. I forget about my own body as a separate thing. I hold my child at my breast, I feel he is dearer to me than my own life.

Adhikari, who can describe your many qualities? Soon after this, you snatch away my son from my breast, from my arms. I do not know where you had brought him from, I do not know where you take him away. When you take him away from my arms, I wish that you had taken away my life as well, I wish to lose everything that I have along with him. What unnatural pain lashes out at such times! Nothing else compares with that. Only those who have gone through that pain know what it is like. And you know, as well. . .

One of your names is the Merciful One. It is chanted across the three worlds. I have to call you that even when you are merciless...

✳

Eleventh Composition

✳

Adhikari, you have many faces. Only you can tell what kind of a role you will play in this theatre. In the Dwapar age, you appeared as Krishnachandra in your theatre of life. You came to Mathura to be born from Devaki's womb. As soon as you were born in Kansa's prison, you manifested yourself to Devaki and Vasudev as the Four Armed God, decked out in conch-shell, weapons and the lotus flower... You were united with the cowherds and milkmaids in sweet Vrindavan, you played with the children on the banks of the Yamuna, in the forests, you grazed the cattle with them... I am but a lowly creature, moreover, I am a mere woman. How can I comprehend the wonder of your sport in the land of Vraj?[12]

✳

Twelfth Composition

✳

...When Satya, Treta and Dwapar ages were done, and when the age of Kali began, you were born to Shachi and Jagannath

Mishra at Nabadwip. Your name was entirely a different one now, and you came with the holy name of Tarakbrahma Hari on your lips. As Gourangachandra, you sang the name of Hari all over the world. That name saved many sinners, poor and miserable people, blind and sick sufferers... In this Kali age, your old dark form has been gilded, you have come to play your role in the theatre as the fair Gourchandra.[13]

Thirteenth Composition

...The earth was awash with love With the name of Tarak Brahma Hari. Blessed, blessed be this Kali age...

Fifteenth Composition

I was born in the month of Chaitra in 1216. I am eighty-five years old now, in this year of 1303. A little has been written about the states of my body and mind, about my life in the first sixty years. It is, indeed, necessary to write about the next twenty-five years as well... This is the end of the second part of the account of my life. After my death, anyone who wishes to do so from my family, may complete the last part.

After the book is published, whatever is left over from meeting the costs of printing, should be invested. As long as my sons are alive they will bear out my wishes. After them, someone from my lineage will use the money for an annual sacred feast in the honour of Madangopal...

Notes

1. According to the Gregorian calendar, she was born in 1808, and it is now 1896.
2. This means that she is still inhabiting her old body.
3. This is a most unconventional statement, since a widow is meant to consider her life a curse which a kind fate should end quickly.
4. This is the name of the family deity here. It refers to Krishna as a lover, so the idol would wear a lot of ornaments.
5. One would be Madangopal, the other would be the mother-in-law. She is indicating that she treated her mother-in-law like a divine being.
6. This means that she was the only able-bodied woman in the family who was available for all the household chores.
7. Brahmin professional cooks were in high demand because the food cooked by them would pollute no one. But this was an urban—mostly Calcutta—custom, and in the households of the rural gentry, the women of the family would do the entire cooking.
8. In East Bengal, people would often prefer a meal of rice for breakfast. Since this was for the head of the household, it had to be freshly cooked every day.
9. Very pious widows would always cook for themselves, however ill or old. But the preparations could be done by a relative or a woman from the same caste.
10. The word is *yatra*, which means journey as well as roving theatre that became a very popular art form in rural areas and small towns from the nineteenth century.
11. Hindu theogony privileges the divine triumvirate: Brahma the Creator, Vishnu the Preserver, Shiva the Destroyer. Each age goes through these three phases, after which a new cycle begins again.
12. This passage refers to the theory of incarnations of Lord Vishnu

who was born as Krishna in the third age of Dwapar, in a four-age time cycle, to rid the earth of the wicked king Kansa of Mathura. He was born to Devaki and Vasudev, the sister and brother-in-law of Kansa. Forewarned of his fate, Kansa had them imprisoned before Devaki gave birth, plotting to kill the newborn infant. On his birth, Krishna miraculously manifested his true form to his parents and got the prison gates opened for a little while. Vasudev waded across the river with the baby and left him in the care of cowherd foster parents at Vrindavan. Krishna spent an idyllic childhood and youth there, playing with cowherds, and engaging in erotic sport with the milkmaids, the descriptions of which form the staple of Bengali Baishnab contemplation and devotion (Vrajleela). Later, he went to Mathura, killed Kansa and assumed kingship, leaving his friends at Vraj or Vrindaban in a state of eternal longing.

13. This refers to the Bengali Vaishnav belief that the sixteenth century saint Nemai-Gouranga, the Krishna-maddened devotee and founder of the Chaitanya cult and sect, was actually yet another incarnation of Vishnu. This view, however, is not present among all Vaishnav orders.

6

On Re-reading the Text

Why *My Life?*

Autobiographies involve a relationship between two entities; the narrating self and the narrated self in the text. Despite their seeming convergence or identity, the gap between the two can never close entirely. The autobiographical exercise can handle the necessary simulation of identity in two ways. It can assume a style of writing where the author, through the manipulation of the first person singular, can drown her separate vantage point into the persona of the narrated self at each point of describing that life, to speak so that the temporal distance between the two selves is obliterated. The narrator may convincingly describe a past in terms of a vivid immediacy of feelings to make it come alive. She may base the authenticity of the descriptions on the fact that she *knows,* none better, how it was, and she can get back to it exactly as it was. The other way is to acknowledge the temporal split and to turn it into an advantage: to encash it as a matured and objective stance which is the sum of a lifetime of accumulated experience. The weight of accumulated experience allows for a hindsight, an excess of perceived meaning, a larger horizon of self-understanding that is not available to the narrated self at the various different phases of the lived life. It is only available to the author of the life and it is purchased at the cost of stepping out of the life, by self-objectification.

AJ prefers the latter mode of self-narration. Through a frequent and visible process of stocktaking, it underlines the authorial privilege, the surplus vision. The stylistic preference is central to Rashsundari's self-creation, for it is only as the author of the text of her life that she can command any control over it, can bend it to her will. At the same time, the split identity and the problem of consummation between the two is even more complicated in *AJ*. Here we have a triangulated relationship, for apart from the narrating and narrated selves, we have a third entity—the Supreme Lord. The second part of the book is almost entirely about the various lives of Krishna and of Chaitanya. Even in the verse colophons of the first part, Rashsundari says, again and again, that her life-events derive significance only as exemplars of God's mercy or his *leela*. It is not entirely clear if the book, then, is meant to be a life of the deity. In hagiographical writings, the author appends a short autobiographical sketch, a self-introduction, to explain the source and nature of inspiration behind the exercise. In a way, perhaps, we are being asked to regard the autobiographical elements of *AJ* as a very extended prose colophon, added on to the real text, which is essentially a hagiography or a sacred myth. Does she see that the only way of talking about herself—a non-sacred figure—would be to present her life as an event in the *leela* of Krishna or of Chaitanya, and herself as an author of the narration of that particular event?[1]

If that had been her intention, then the modernity of the enterprise would lie in the extension of a traditional genre, in filling out an older colophonic convention with quotidian details from a mundane life, in the use of prose. Modernity would, then, be more additive than transformative, an accretion and not a break. But I believe that Rashsundari cancelled out the humble self-deprecatory and pious denials of the significance of her life-events and life-text in the very title to the book itself, and it is in this initiating act of naming the book that it proclaims itself as an irretrievably and exclusively modern effort. The book calls itself—with a sort of thundering audacity—*My Life*. It makes a bold and a bald statement, presumptuous in the extreme, in a woman householder. A woman, moreover, who is not connected to a figure of religious or temporal significance, who cannot claim any miraculous powers or capacities. The life of such a woman would not be written—far less read—before the 19th century.

Even in that century, this particular autobiographical enunciation does rather stand out. Let us compare the naming to that of other 19th-century autobiographies. Debendranath Tagore's book is called *A Self-Written Account Of Life* (*Swarachita Jeeban Charit*). Saradasundari Debi called her memoirs *Tale of Myself* (*Atmakatha*). Diwan Kartikeyachandra Ray called his, *An Account of My Own Life* (*Atmajeebancharit*). Rajnarain Bose's autobiography was entitled *An Account of Myself* or *Atmacharit*.[2] Let us remember that the genre was just emerging in Bengali, and a stable term for this kind of text had not yet been established. What these other authors have in common is the accent on the act of writing, narration, textualisation—as though, that was the most important thing and the life itself was an object or a field to be used up by the exercise. In sharp, almost scandalous contrast, Rashsundari thrusts the life itself at us, she drags our attention to the fact that the book is about *her* life, not about writing.

We need also to compare her station in life with that of the other autobiographers that we have just mentioned. Debendranadi came from perhaps the best-known family in contemporary Bengal. Himself a leading religious reformer, he was the son of a towering entrepreneur and at the time of the publication of his book, his sons were among the best-known figures in the country—Rabindranath Tagore, Jyotirindranath Tagore. Saradasundari Debi was the mother of the foremost religious and social reformer, Keshubchandra Sen. Kartikeyachandra Ray ran the administration of a princely state. Rajnarain Basu was a noted nationalist and a well-known author. If they were householders and non-sacred figures, they did embody modern notions of distinction, of what makes a life noteworthy and writable. Rashsundari seems equally distanced from this category. Yet, it is a characteristic mark of modern times that it is precisely such a woman who would thrust her life at us to read.

From the mid 19th century, a definite appetite developed in Bengal for secular life-stories. At first, this was fed by English biographies of great historical characters. Spurred on by the syllabus requirements in the new schools, two Calcutta bookshops ordered, according to an 1825 notice in the *Bengal Hurkaru,* a large shipment of such books.[3] From the 1840s, noted Bengali biographers came into their own, writing the lives of contemporary great achievers in their own country: social reformers, religious leaders, literary figures, successful businessmen. Pearychand and Kishorichand Mitra, Girishchandra Ghosh, Bholanath Chandra, and others made biography a new and major genre within the new prose literature. We have already noted that syllabi for girls also laid stress on such readings. Brahmos were the first to write down the lives of important women from their sects. However, these dealt with active and achieving lives, whether of men or of women. Again, they were narrated as sources of moral and practical lessons for the readers. *AJ* would be partly enabled by the new vogue for reading about contemporary lives, but would not quite meet with the required criteria. The real wave for biographical writings came between the 1880s and the First World War and *AJ* had already appeared by then.

How does Rashsundari sustain her claim to attention? She does say that the value of her book lay in the fact that it was evidence of God's excessive mercy. Yet, what clinches above all the fact of that grace is her ability to read and write. The nature of evidence itself is ineffably a 19th-century one. It helps Rashsundari to take her place within the domain of the great secular miracle-tales of 19th century Bengal. A new realm of miracle lore had developed over accounts of attainment of wondrous mastery of education—especially by men who, in other times, would have lacked the mobility to do so. One remembers how Ishwarchandra Vidyasagar was supposed to have taught himself English numerals during a journey on foot from his village to Calcutta by studying the milestones on the way. Or, how he could only study under streetlamps at night, sitting on the road. Rashsundari mastered her letters through even greater difficulties, and the miracle, consequently, was a more striking one.

II
The Flow of the Narrative

In the first part of the book, a linear pattern of narration, of structuring the course of events, is maintained. There is a chronologically ordered progression. This is fairly stable up to her account of her learning to read and write. After that vital point has been reached, there is a somewhat abrupt jump to the moment of her widowhood and then the text is woven around multiple axes: old age, dreams, losses and her relationship to God. Again, in the earlier parts, there is a stable connection between events and the nature of her reflections on them. Events and comments form a continuous, spiralling chain, each succeeding the other, and each unit creating an alluvial soil for larger and more complex subsequent ponderings, an expanding and looping world of meaning.

The culling of meaning from events is continued beyond the point of reading and writing, but the linear thrust collapses. There is a proliferation of rumination on a whole range of things that are not necessarily connected to specific events, nor are events recounted in chronological progression. The necessary connection between events and their meaning is broken. Sequences get muddied, a sort of a general reflection on the nature of her life takes over, plucking out experiences from all corners of life to make a particular argument. Befores and afters get mixed up.

This is not necessarily caused by old age, or a faltering memory that causes recollections to be thrown up in an uncontrolled or random fashion. The failure of the archaeological impulse, of sequencing the layers of memory, denotes a shift to an altogether new order of reflection.

With the achievement of literacy, the structuring principle of her life is laid bare. Her faith, her intellectual feat, her sorrows, her achievements and her labour—all connect up, the design is made evident. The miracle has happened, her faith has conquered her limitations, and has lifted her above her life and its labours. The mystery behind the text—how a woman like her could produce it—is explained. The teleology is achieved, and the text, consequently, is emptied of the teleological function. With this function over, the later events of her life do not require a patterned replay, a sequentialised narration to trace out the divine design. Now meaning and its understanding only require amplification, addition. They are supportive evidence, they may be plucked out of any point in the life; or, even from; the lives of gods, incarnations, saints. The point they make is the same one. The autobiographical form has exhausted the need for narrating events in the order in which they happened. It now goes on to provide corroborative material, endnotes to the main text. The book assumes a protean form, verses proliferate, arguments multiply about a large range of unconnected themes.

Increasingly, the explicit addressee shifts from a secular modern readership to God—or even oneself, addressed through long and rambling monologues. The intended addressee, however, one must remember, is always the reader, approached through the print medium. At several points, Rashsundari makes it clear that she realises the public nature of the enunciation, that she is writing a book. Sometimes, she simulates a monologue form and intimate mode, laying her soul and its innermost thoughts bare where none but God is her witness. Sometimes, she addresses God directly. The manipulation of various modes of address and addressees is skilful in a genre which is not yet established, and in an author who has not written before. The variation depends on the nature of the statement she might make at a given point. Usually, she adopts the monologue form when she ponders over the implications of her transgressive desire for reading, about her rebellious statements on patrilocal uprooting. She talks to God sometimes in a confessional manner, customary in Vaishnavite piety where the devotee must humbly recall her sinfulness before she asks for grace. But, more interestingly, she also prays to him before and as she recalls her moments of great sorrow: when her son dies, when she leaves her mother, when she wants to read and cannot do so. Though couched as thanksgiving, they are fundamentally accusatory statements. The prayers tend to occur before she narrates some departure she makes from given norms, so as to take away the sting from her transgression.

She refers to her life as entirely of God's designing, but she does, nonetheless, have a clear sense of the social making of it. On certain issues, she speaks in a declamatory voice, where she describes the painful consequences of social regulations. She, clearly, is addressing a modern readership here which is already debating these matters: on women's education, about the restrictions of old times, about the relentless pressure of domestic labour, the problems of motherhood. In fact, while on the last point, she says that this is something that everybody should know about. About her grossly overworked daily routine, she says that though these are uncomfortable matters to mention, *it is necessary* to briefly describe a day or two of her life. She, therefore, is acutely conscious that she is educating her readers about gender issues, and she adopts an appropriate tone.

Her monologues are usually addressed to her heart or to her mind—a self-division that she makes very confidently. This confidence arises partly out of the Vaishnavite convention about cultivating certain emotional states, inducing certain moods within oneself through prescribed objects and modes of contemplation. The exercise obliges one to step outside the mind and the feelings, so to speak, in order to do things to them, to work on them, to refashion them. It is premised on a presumed duality within the self, where one part can reorder the other. Rashsundari accentuates it and makes it evident by continuously verbalising the ordering: my mind, why do you do so, why can't you do so, and so on. She also comments, fretfully and wonderingly, about the disobedient behaviour of one part of the mind which the other part admonishes and chides: why do you want to read when you know that is impossible, why do you grieve when you know that is inevitable?

The division brings out in the open the workings of the mind, renders it a public space where important and critical arguments are going on and momentous decisions for change are being undertaken. Whether she obeys or she disobeys, she is shown to have a mind of her own, unknown and uncontrolled by others, accountable—and that too, formally—to God alone. She rises above the commonplace by repeated evidence of the existence and the autonomy of this mind and of the significance of the battles that are going on there.

Yet another way of clarifying this is to underline and repeat the fundamentally secret workings of this mind. Everything that is of consequence happens secretly. From her infancy, she had this capacity—she would have us believe—of keeping things to herself. Nobody—not even her mother—knew about her fears about child lifters, her terror about her dead father, her worries about being given away to a stranger. None could guess how much she suffered at her affinal home, how she would starve there day after day, how oppressive was the burden of housework. Even on a trivial and humorous theme, nobody could figure out why she seemed scared about her husband's horse. And, above all, the great secret—her desire to read despite what her elders said about it, her ability to do so. The underlining of the hidden workings of the mind is a way of indicating—without ever doing so openly—the fact of disalignment, her sitting oddly with her families, her guardians, her *sansar*. Everything that was important to her happened within herself and nobody had a clue. She experienced events independently and came to decisions and formed opinions by herself, within the hidden recesses of her mind, arguing with none other than herself. Above all, she even disobeyed and went contrary to what had been laid down for her, conveyed to her as dos and donts.

The secrecy ensured the autonomy of her mind, marked it out as a space of her very own where, at least, she alone could make things happen. It also indicated her capacity for opposition. More importantly, it indicated that she—despite a lifetime's reputation as the good wife—never had a secure place, a real home anywhere else except in her own mind. At the same time, the text sets up a curious play with the self. It continuously questions the inner workings of the mind, the changes in the mental state, interior developments and growth whose sources remain obscure even to her. While this elevates the mind—the locus of the self—into an object worthy of speculation, the text aspires not so much to decipher it, to grasp the essence of the self, as to underline its perpetual surprises, its unknowability, its eternal elusiveness. That makes the self a serious object of knowledge, worthy of ceaseless perusal, in something of the same manner in which sages eternally pursue the nature of divinity.

This is a modern articulation about the inwardness of an individuated self. It is also a way of experiencing and reacting to an old condition in new words: the woman is not fully encompassed by the spaces that are allotted to her. The disjuncture itself might not have been a modern condition. Older songs, tales and lullabies—composed by women—contain important clues that point at this direction. But the possibility of its articulation, its publicising, is definitely a modern one, created by the new reforms and education, the development of vernacular prose and print, of new kinds of markets and a gender-oriented social movement. The very act of publicising sets up a spiral, where debates induce more open, profuse and radical articulations—at the end of which, with the beginning of a new century, we find women's activism, organisations and movements.

AJ addresses problems beyond those that male reformers and orthodoxy were debating. Those latter related to education for women, the abolition of sati, the legalisation of widow remarriage, a higher age of consent and the possibility of a higher age of marriage or the right to divorce. Rashsundari does talk about education at great length, but her other major concerns are very different, ones not frontally addressed by reformers; patrilocality, housework, single-handed raising of infants, the humiliations that surround widowhood. Other women also write about some of these things.

The area of disjuncture between male and female concerns is interesting. The latter problematise aspects of the patrilocal state that men so far have considered acceptable. *AJ,* however, does not encapsulate the entire modern condition within itself, constrained as it is by its time and social limits. It looks enviously at what is happening to the new woman of a different generation, it also approves of it. At the same time, it lets us know how much more its author had achieved since she had to do it all by herself. But it does not spell out an agenda for more drastic changes, does not call for collectivities, movements. It does not even refer beyond education to other debated issues: widow remarriage, age of consent, polygamy. Since she must define her primary identity, above all, as that of the good wife—an identity without which her transgression will not be shown to have gone against the grain of her very being—she cannot link herself up with open critiques and proposals for change. Delinked, her tone is what Virginia Woolf would describe as "special pleading", characteristic of much of women's writing. And which Carolyn Steedman elaborates: "To be resentful and angry in small ways is one form of resistance... However, it is not often called resistance: its more common name is complaint."[4]

III

Narrative Strategies in *Amar Jiban*

I find it highly astonishing that the complaints went unnoticed, in her own world, as well as among later readers. Jyotirindranath Tagore, in his preface to her book, extolled her sound housewifely qualities as wholly admirable and a fitting rebuttal of orthodox fears about educating the woman. Later on, the nationalist scholar Dinesh Chandra Sen saw in her the self-effacing image of feminine nurture, an icon cast in the mould of the Motherland herself.[5] A scholar of our times, Partha Chatterjee, places her writing against the backdrop of the appropriation of a traditional woman by a modern, male rationalistic enterprise, shaped, in its turn, by western power-knowledge.[6] Each of these readings unproblematically annexed a complex, highly individual endeavour to a different master-narrative, and considered that her story was concluded, exhausted of any other possibility after that. I would suggest that these linear readings could only be enabled by missing out on the various writing devices with which Rashsundari complicated her statements.

There are, indeed, formidable difficulties in reading the text since Rashsundari simultaneously occupied two very different sites: that of a conformist housewife in an orthodox family,

and that of a very early woman author, engaged in the highly
public act of writing about her own life. It is almost an act of
immodesty, of unveiling in public. The two compulsions could
be fitted together only by a novel mix of rhetorical modes
which would retain her Vaishnavite humility and womanly
modesty along with her assertion of a self-made and self-
proclaimed life. What emerged out of such constraints was a
sustained, skilful and delicate double-speak.

A multi-intentioned, polyvalent and polyseimic content
lay blandly enfolded within seemingly innocent statements,
or even within apparent contradictions. Carolyn Steedman
describes a particular syntactic device—the paratactic
chain—structuring the memoirs of a 19th-century
policeman-turned-soldier—a man with little education
and radical views. It occurs at moments of describing great
contradictions in the nature of events and it strings together a
whole lot of contradictions on a chain, linking them up with
unsynthesising "buts" without trying to make connections
between them.[7] At first, *AJ* seems to run along a paratactic
chain. God is kind but Rashsundari's life is full of woes, God
has decreed certain rules, but they lead to great suffering,
Rashsundari's life is blessed, but it had enormous problems,
all her acquaintances were wonderful in her matrimonial
home, but she remained full of secret fears.

A subtle crafting, however, can be seen at work, resolving
and endowing contradictions with meaning. A benevolent
God and an approving social milieu that confirm her in her
role are somewhat undone by a careful selection of incidents:
losing her mother's home, her thwarted desire for learning,
her labour, the death of her children. They peel off layer after
layer from the benevolence of God and of the social order.
They allow a radical questioning of both to run underground

without interrupting the narrative or introducing an aporia within it. Yet, what she says about God is no cover-up or mask. Times *have* changed for the better, women are a little less constrained and it is a new, more accommodating kind of society, which is also God's will.

In the very first colophon, she described herself as "lowly, ignorant that I am, and a woman, moreover". While such self-introductory colophons are conventionally self-deprecating, Rashsundari stretched hers to evoke very different possibilities. She bracketed herself with the very same categories that Chaitanya had especially promised to save—the lowly, the ignorant, the woman. By using near-identical terms, familiar to all Vaishnavs, she obliquely invoked the promised inversion of status, the assurance that her very lowliness would save her more surely than others. In the same sentence, she also subtly reminded us about the remarkable feat that she had accomplished by herself—the fact of writing a book in her condition. And she did all this without recourse to open self-praise or self-aggrandisement.

She, similarly, let us know how pretty she used to be by simply repeating how others would marvel at her beauty. She even composed a little couplet about her looks, drawing on the words of others: "they called me a little golden doll". Her neighbours confirmed what a desirable person she was: "whoever gets her will be truly blessed". She did not have to say outright that she had been a great success as a housewife. She simply said that folks in her new home and village had never uttered a word of criticism, she had nothing but praise from all quarters. Indirect speech or reported statements would say far more than she could have conceivably said about herself.

Rashsundari attained a level of sheer mastery in signifying

something very different from what she had said directly or overtly. She did this by a very careful framing of her direct statements. She would conclude an episode with pious statements, resigning herself to divine will without protest. At the same time, she surrounded it with vivid details that described the very painful consequences flowing from her obedience. As a result, the surface message got scrambled and confused, so that she appeared compliant, and also a victim figure precisely as a result of that compliance. She had been most eager to help and please others when she was a child. She helped out an infirm aunt with the housework. When her own family got to know, they were overjoyed, and she did even more, to make them happier. Soon, she realised that she was doing all the work, she played no more. "My days of playing were over. Now, I worked all the time." This was a precise prefiguration of later times in her affinal family when she took over all the housework without letting anyone know how much it cost her. She lost all leisure, the kitchen became her prison, she had no one to look after herself. Social approval was bought at terrible cost.

The strategy was deployed with meticulous, long-term planning, spread over three chapters, in the course of which she breaks us to information about her secret reading. She prefaced the event with long, vivid and richly-detailed accounts of the gruelling household labour that she had to perform without respite. She shapes that account in a circular fashion, from bed to kitchen to bed, from dawn to midnight to dawn, to suggest the eternal motions of the wheel, the endless repetitions, the ceaseless activity that makes nothing happen but stills the movement forward, towards an end or an escape. She saved the narration from any taint of reproach or self-pity by frequently inserting phrases like: "Why should

I talk of such matters, it is shameful even to think of them. I never mentioned it to anyone." She, then, had it both ways. Print gave her a way of letting the whole world know about it all while simulating a private monologue spoken only to herself. She came out of it not as one who protests, who rebels, but as the self-effacing Hindu wife who suffers all privations with smiling forbearance. She tells us how she held out her uneaten meal to an unexpected guest—the supreme test of the good wife. *CB* has an episode where Chaitanya's wife does exactly that and proves that she deserves her husband. Rashsundari then goes on to show that, she had to continue her fast for the next two days even when she was dying of hunger because of the sheer pressure of work, and because this selfless housewife had no one who might have noticed her urgent needs.

The most poignant and powerfully written sections relate to her wedding and to the subsequent transplanting on alien soil. It then seemed to her that she had been served a life sentence, that God had consigned her to a fate that resembles the helpless sacrificial goat at its moment of execution. In fact, the tense and heaving prose where the moment of separation is described, joins together the two acts of ritual and religious prescription to make a powerful oblique critique of their shared inhumanity: the sacrificial goat, crying hopelessly for its mother before the axe falls, and the little girl clinging to her mother for the last time before she is forced out of her family. The rest of her life is spent in the prison. Indeed, she says exactly this. "I have been imprisoned within this household. There will be no release for me till the end of my days." But she hastens to follow this up with a song of praise: "Such is your custom, and I shall praise it." She describes her life of labour in her new home, but she thanks God because he gave her a strong and healthy body to stand up to the strain. Had her health broken down, she says with all its cruel implications, she would have had none to take care of her. She also slips in the significant word 'subjected' when she talks of herself in relation to God. For it was the strength of the slave that God had blessed her with, so that her labouring body would not fail others. Words, intentions and effects are conjoined in a curious syntax to produce mutiple meanings, all at odds with one another. The long-range effect was to build up a strong sympathy base for her act of disobedience, her reading, which follows this account. The final impression is one of insidious, delicate, masked expressions of pain that complicate her gestures of compliance but that also stop short of overt criticism.

At one place alone, does the dialectic between the submissive devotee, the good wife and the self-aware victim-figure break down, or, rather, Rashsundari chooses to snap out of the endless transactions between them. Towards the end of the third composition, she expanded the prison-house metaphor with deadly thoroughness. Her new home would not relieve her to visit her mother. She candidly tells us why: they could not do without her endless labour inputs. The few occasions when she did get permission, she was let out for a few days like a prisoner out on parole. Even when her mother was dying, she was not allowed to pay her a last visit, she was serving the house of strangers while the loving mother lay dying. She concluded this chapter with an unambiguous reproach, a hurt cry: "Dear God, why did you make me a part of humanity!" This is one statement that ends without a single recuperating word of praise.

IV
Godly Designs

Whenever she refers to the social order, Rashsundari describes it as God's design. God is, therefore made the author of the patriarchal discipline, responsible for her sufferings. There were two alternative ways of assigning responsibility that she chose to avoid. One was to stress the inexorable logic of *karma,* or of deeds committed in past births, whose consequences were stronger than divine mercy. The other way was that of liberal reformers. Whenever they campaigned against a social abuse, the reformers would castigate it as something that was contrary to God's will, as evils inflicted by human cruelty. Rashsundari avoided both resolutions. She ascribed all her sufferings to God's will, not to *karma* or to social and human imperfections. The choice indicates the way she read her relationship with God. The more smilingly and patiently she described her submission, the better she underlined the tyranny of his rule. The devotee's willed surrender accentuates divine despotism rather than absolves it. The precise space of her relationship may be clarified through contrasts with two other statements from 19th century women's writings.

Saradasundari Debi, in her memoirs, ascribed a coherent and convincing reason to the suffering that God inflicted on her. It was to round off her experiences, to give her a taste of all that human beings may feel, to make her a more complete person.[8] Binodini Dasi was a late 19th century actress who stormed the public theatre. Trained by the legendary playwright-cum-director Girish Ghosh, and personally blessed by the saint Ramakrishna, she was most remembered for her devotional roles through which she rendered the stage into a pedagogical space which taught the audience about *bhakti.*

At the end of her career, with a life full of suffering behind her, she exchanged letters with her guru about what God had done to her as a reward. She refused to believe that she had been a religious instructor on the stage, she said it had been mere entertainment, and no more than that. She had thereby not established a close relationship with God. In any case, God was either all-merciful but not omnipotent, or he was omnipotent but unkind.[9]

AJ occupies a middle space between the two. It is, in intention, closer to the latter position, but it does not draw out the implications of the stance at all. On the contrary, it surrounds itself with exclamations about divine mercy.

Rashsundari's devotion, then, had a more complex design than either willed submission or critique. That ambiguity and tension inform her manipulation of the folk theatre or *yatra* metaphor. These theatres, with their travelling companies, their elaborate stage props and musical accompaniment, had acquired tremendous popularity in 19th-century villages.[10] The director-cum-manager was called *adhikari*. Rashsundari calls God the *adhikari* of the theatre of life. He directs a play which is about her life, where she is the audience and where she is also called upon to play the key role. God is the scriptwriter, the director, the manager. He is the active agent who causes the entire process, whereas she is passive, directed, commanded. She has no idea, as either spectator or actor, of what is coming next, nor can she influence the course of the play—even when it is all about herself. God, on the other hand, is not only omniscient and omnipotent, he is also completely whimsical, inscrutable. He has written the cruellest script. He calls her out to play the role of the mother and puts a little baby in her arms. Merged into the role, she loves it dearly until God comes on the stage as death and takes it away, leaving the mother helpless with empty, aching arms. Rashsundari sees no reason why he did any of that, but she presumes that he would have got some amusement from this spectacle, this certain hour of maternal sorrow. As she accepts his will, she also understands that such is the inscrutable, unaccountable nature of God, such is the play, the *leela,* which gives him satisfaction. Acceptance is tied into this cruel characterisation.

In *AJ, leela* has a meaning that is substantially different from the way it occurs in the Vaishnavite religious imaginary. In the latter, it refers to episodes in the life of Krishna, to God assuming human shapes and aspects to play with. They, therefore, evoke enchanting, fulfilling, wondrous associations. In *AJ,* in radical contrast, the primary site of *leela* is a poor, mangled, helpless human life, marked by many sorrows, losses, frustrated desires. *Leela* takes on a new set of implications as a consequence.

On the other hand, God enacts his many lives before her eyes. He frequently changes roles—as Krishna, as Ram, as Chaitanya. He is in complete command, he begins a new role the very moment he begins to weary of the old one. His control over the scripts, the direction, the acting is in total contrast with her helplessness, ignorance. The metaphor derives its valences from the theological concept about the origin of creation: all appearances are *maya* that God has invented to amuse himself with. It has personal resonances as well. It expresses not just the spiritual helplessness of the devotee—a sense that derives from Shakta devotional traditions—but also the social helplessness of the woman whose passivity and fatalism are not existential conditions alone, but are deeply scored over with specific gendered experiences.

A sense of marginalisation probably accompanied the spread of the new art form of *yatra* in the 19th century, marking out within the spectacle the boundaries between the play on the stage and the passive spectators facing it. A mid 20th century novel tried to describe the first destructive impact of this new art form upon a local community. It completely disrupted the older, more collective and participatory modes of devotional singing and acting where the boundaries were far more blurred. This now gave way to a spectacle, alien and distanced, which could only be passively consumed.[11]

Rashsundari's self-alienated, reified and mystifying life was a thing of endless surprise, wonder and marvel for her. The devotee gains a purchase on the wonderful divine spectacle of *leela* at the cost of learning not to identify with her own life, to recognise it as a mere plaything in God's hands. The ability to aestheticise her own experiences through the act of writing is a consequence of this painful self-objectification.

The displacement of the site of *leela* from the life of the deity to the life of the devotee is a crucial reorientation within the key terms of Vaishnnav *bhakti,* a shift, however, that goes unnoticed since it is couched in the old language. It is further compounded by the inversion of the concept of *tatastha bhakti* that I have referred to earlier. Gaudiya Vaishnavism enjoins upon the devotee a mode of absorbed contemplation of *leela* that would leave her transfixed on its shore. Ideally, this is facilitated by assuming the persona of one of Krishna's lesser companions at Vrindaban. Rashsundari uses the mode of transfixed contemplation, but she contemplates her own life as manifestation of *leela*. The language of adoration, of absorption in *leela* continues in *AJ,* so the fundamental break within the object of contemplation remains hidden. And so are the consequences of this shift.

We might argue that humanity and creation have been contemplated earlier as well to understand the nature of divinity. And *dehavad* has used the workings of the human body as evidence of divine designing. But in both of those, we have abstracted and generalised models of the human life and the human body. With Rashsundari, a concrete, sensuous, specific individual life is selected for inspection— the life of the everywoman, one might say, marked out by inevitable experiences of deprivation and constraint. From the making of such a life the nature of the maker is deduced. It is curiously akin to the argument from first cause: you deduce the existence of the potter from the existence of the pot, and of his perfection from the perfection of the created object. The values, however, are switched around here, for far from a perfect creation, she has before her a sad and deprived life. Even the considerable gains and power that came her way when she reached middle age, were advances that were thrust upon her: she had no hand in their making. She underlines the lack of control, of command, as much when she talks of the good times as when she recalls the times of distress. Both indicate her passivity, her helplessness. She returns to the same point when she talks of the different stages of her own body, or of their sudden betrayals. If she is ignorant of the workings of the very body she inhabits, how would she have anything in the world to call her own?

There are resonances of this mode of contemplation in Shakta traditions, especially in songs. Paradoxically, the pessimism of these 18th-century songs also engendered a conviction in the individual life as an adequate and appropriate theatre for the enactment of divine purposes. Charles Taylor locates in the exaltation of everyday life a sure beginning of modernity.[12] In early modern Bengal, that life was a ground of testing divine intention in a very different way: it derived value and significance from its status as exemplar of the goddess Kali's wilfulness, her arbitrary decisions. In our earlier sections on 18th and early 19th century antecedents to some strands in Rashsundari's thinking, we have touched on how these times—more conscious of change, history and the individual self—reoriented earlier modes of constructing experiences. We shall return to the theme in the last section.

In his attempt to see how experience came to be constituted in modern western societies, Michel Foucault has defined experience as the correlation between fields of knowledge, types of normativity and forms of subjectivity in a particular culture; from this correlation, the individual would derive resources to subject himself to an aesthetics of living.[13] The nature of Foucault's exploration is especially important in the intimate areas of individual life where the processes of ideological interpellation are less structured than they are in more public forms of identity. I do find, however, two major problems in his method. In the first place, the emphasis is uniformly on activities, practices and behaviour through which the individual may reconstitute experience. Modes of understanding, arguments, intellectual lineages and their reformulation receive secondary attention. Secondly, the place of transformations, conscious selection and breaks that the individual performs on himself, and the struggles with a given culture that go on continuously during the process, remains weak and unaccented in this scheme. A sense of both of these would be very important for understanding *AJ*.

V

Early Fears, Mother and God

AJ does not belong to a distinctive theological tradition, radical or plebeian. Nor does it proclaim the religious vision born of solitary ponderings of the autodidact. It does not, for instance, improvise a new and challenging cosmology as did the miller Menocchio in mid 16th century Friuli.[14] One of the most vexing things about *AJ* is that, having narrated the thrilling story of her self-taught reading, Rashsundari does not pause for even a moment to tell us what her reading of *CB* did to her mind. Nor does she say at any point what thoughts occurred to her after she had gone through all the religious manuscripts that the household possessed. As usual, she is wary of dwelling at all on any influence that came from outside. In the scheme of things in the *AJ*, the sole importance of the *CB* lay in stimulating her desire to read, not in giving her religious instruction. What, then, does Rashsundari do with her religious understanding?

AJ proceeds on two different axes on this question. In the first place, there is a long, chronological and systematic account of how and why she heard of God in the first place. The second, more implicit and oblique concern, is to show what she had heard and expected from God, and what she found out for herself.

AJ elaborates and clarifies an entire process of God-formation by a human mind. Step by step, piece by piece, we see him being constructed. We trace out the needs that lay behind the enterprise, we find laid out before us the purposes that are ascribed to him.

A possibly exaggerated account of childish fears creates the space to let God into the narrative. It also is the structuring principle for the entire section on her childhood, and it continues to dominate the sections on her youth. In most other 19th-century autobiographies, childhood is remembered as a sanctuary. In fact, time itself is patterned in mythologies and in histories, as a steady decline from an early golden and happy age. Although some modern liberals did posit the new times as one of recovery and growth, many others ruled out such possibilities and viewed the past years of childhood, as well as the ancient times of history, as a treasure beyond recovery.[15] Debendranath's autobiography, for instance, begins with marking out a warm, close, loving space inhabited by his pious and loving grandmother and himself. It was a small and infinitely precious world, filled with delights of feelings, taste and sight. For one of the most public figures of his times, it is surprising that the opening section has no mention of lineage, property or connections—though, of course, in his case, they would hardly need a mention. It is also the only time when he talks of family, of intimate relationships, of love and of the domestic space. With men—especially of public importance, who would be inspired to write autobiographies—their childhood would be the last time when they would remain ensconced within the world of women. The small space was thus something like the safety of the womb, when they looked back at it from their adult male vantage point.[16]

Not so with Rashsundari. It is only later that she talked of the great love and security that surrounded her in her "father's house", a recapitulation that came at a time when she had already lost it. *AJ* begins with the terror that she secretly harboured about child lifters. The fear made her comply with the tyranny of her playmates for she thought that if she complained then child lifters would come and take them away. So she put up with all their oppression and subjected herself to yet more terror.

Two things get immediately established and they form a pattern for self-narrativisation. First, for some unspecified reason, she needed to keep all her fears to herself, she suffered in silence. Second, her sufferings were induced by her consideration for others, a consideration that brought her no return from them. In this way, she went on suffering for others. She fed her friend with her own food, and the friend beat her up. She helped out an infirm aunt and, gradually, she found herself doing all the work at home: and she played no more. There were other causes of distress. Her house got burnt down, the children got lost at night, she lost a dear cousin whom she had practically brought up. There is, in fact, no mention of playmates who were fun, of games she played, of any experience that was unconnected with fear or with loss. The moment one set of fears is assuaged, a new and bigger set comes to take its place. Her mother's words about God calmed her fears about her dead father and about kidnapping. But she was confronted with marriage, a terrifying prospect of loss and uncertainty.

The stark picture of childhood is very hard to account for. In a number of ways, Rashsundari was luckier than most girls of her times. Even though she was fatherless her relatives loved her, and she was brought up by a wise, serene and adoring mother. Since the family was affluent and the girl pretty, fixing a match for her proved no problem at all—a headache that otherwise plague natal families of most girls and renders the daughter a liability. In fact, she was kept at home well beyond the customary age of marriage, for her mother could not bear to let her go. In Bengal, the 16th-century lawgiver Raghunandan had tightened up injunctions about the *garbhadhan* ceremony which required ritual cohabitation between the husband and the wife as soon as she reaches puberty.[17] Girls were married off well before menarche which, in the warm climate of Bengal, tended to occur quite early. Even in her affinal home, the new family loved her and she was initially made much of. Her first encounter with her mother-in-law is a sharp contrast to the more typical recollection by Saradasundari: "Every time my mother-in-law looked at me, a pint of blood would dry up in my body."[18]

Fears would have constituted a necessary organising principle for the narrative for several reasons. Rashsundari does not strive to project a selfhood that is firmly centred, unified, continuous. On the contrary, she repeatedly talks of a fragmented self that goes through fundamental breaks and transformations, a mind and a body each stage of which is foreign to the others and a striving to attain a whole sense of the self which is constantly thwarted. Two circumstances, however, never shift: one is the sense of a radical uncertainty of everything and the consequent fears that mark her entire life, and the other is the continuous relationship with God which arises out of the fears. These two appear as something like a fixed point in her identity, and by making them so, Rashsundari locates an ordering device to narrativise a self that must otherwise seem disjunct and broken.

We had remarked earlier that 19th-century debates on reform had rendered the home and the family—the only spaces to hold on the woman—deeply problematic ones. Issues around which reformist agitations revolved—sati, widow remarriage, age of consent, *kulin* polygamy—would underline the fact the family was more a site of oppression than sanctuary. *AJ* obliquely draws upon and confirms the understanding, through a reiteration of fears, great and small. In contrast to male narrativisations of childhood or youth, these were not times of happiness.

Does the narrative render her a victim, a figure of abjection through a constant reference to fears? From the first reading, it certainly seems to be a predominantly whining voice that is speaking. Thankful praise is, often, a masked complaint. Yet, the implication is quite transformed when we look at the central event in the text: her mastery over the word. She then emerges as an active agent, determined in her opposition to custom and one who revolutionises her own mind. The complaints then assume a different function in the narrative—they frame the moment of oppositional action, they justify her defiance, they conceal its magnitude by reminding us of how much she accepted and how grievously she suffered. The praise, too, takes on new relevance, for she had, indeed, been able to achieve the impossible.

In a world filled with troubled apprehensions, the first words about God came from her mother who tried to remove her fears. This, incidentally, was the first extended presence of the mother in the text. She, in fact, had caused the fears to sprout, for she had told Rashsundari about child lifters. Now she calmed her terror by telling her about the omnipresence of God. It was as if the mother gave birth to the idea of God. The idea was invoked two more times—once when Rashsundari first came to know about her departed father and was terrorised by the thought, and next, when their house was burnt down and she and her brothers got lost. Each time, the notion of omnipresence and omnipotence was expanded and in the last discourse, the mother explained the relationship between the family deity and the Supreme Lord, the master of the universe. Rashsundari was given the classic concept of advanced theology: the different grades within divinity which were interconnected but sedimented layers within a single truth. As we have seen, this chain of arguments occurs in different versions within all major philosophical systems in high Hinduism.

The first mention of God came as a family idol, as a strictly localised person. This seems to suggest a polytheistic divinity, many gods for many people. Eventually, however, a monotheistic understanding is affirmed. From the third section of the book, he is called Parameswara, the Supreme Lord. Although not entirely unknown to Vaishnav invocations, this name is somewhat unusual. Bengali Vaishnavs use names of Krishna that suggest qualities of the divine life or some mythological feat. When they refer to Chaitanya, Gour or Gouranga (the fair-bodied one) are the common appellations. Parameswara or names that suggest the abstract quality of ultimate power or grace is used only occasionally, not as the main designation. Rashsundari, however, makes it her preferred mode of address, abstracting divinity, thereby, from sensuous qualities, concrete events, legends, mythology. For most of the book, he is a curiously faceless, abstract figure without any of the lush and vivid attributes of either Krishna or Chaitanya. The world of mythology and hagiography is generally missing, except in a couple of sections at the end of the book, in the revised second version. The family idols, central objects of daily adoration for Vaishnav householders, are never described. We are just given their two names—Dayamadhav and Madanmohan—and in one episode she tells us that she donated an ornament to the idol. The preference, then, is for a god without stories, without familiar associations, for someone who manifests himself entirely through his interactions with Rashsundari's life. This indicates a deity who is very different from what is usually associated with women's devotion. This is also a god who can only be understood by Rashsundari, no mythological lessons or theological commentaries can reveal him. Individual understanding through serious and autonomous intellectual effort is the key to this religion—very different from the female world of ecstasy, mysticism and wild and excessive emotions and sensuality that Julia Kristeva ascribes to true feminine writing.[19]

It is noticeable that the name of God was bequeathed to her by her mother. Bereft of rights to natal property, this was the only inheritance she could retain in her new home. This was also the only bit of her old identity that remained with her. Marriage changed everything—her family, her place, her lineage and even her name. In the new home she would be designated according to her relationships with various people: "Here I have no name." The name of God did not change. It is also important to note that her own name was finally returned to her with the publication of her own book.[20]

Once Rashsundari came to know about God, "on that very day, my mind sprouted the first seeds of intelligence." Her way to God lay through thinking, it was not instinctive nor spontaneous. It was the cerebral way, not pietistic, emotive, ecstatic or ritualistic. It had to necessarily express itself through reading and writing. It was, for a woman, a very modern way.

God came to Rashsundari not as an icon or as myth and ritual, but as words spoken by the mother. The mother came into the text to bear the words of God. Her mother was, above all, her *guru,* her access to God. Rashsundari took great care to establish that she had none other. In contrast, Vaishnavism in all its variants—orthodox as well as deviant, esoteric—emphasises the supreme importance of a godlike guru, ritual purification by whom cleans the body and the soul. Each family has its own *kulaguru.* Rashsundari must have gone through the ritual act and the sacred word—*mantra*—with which the guru initiates the disciple into the pure state. She, however, neither mentions her own, nor the guru's discourses. She mentions religious readings and discourses that went on in the village and even in the outer quarters of the household, but only in order to underline her exclusion from them, to point out that she got nothing out of them. The mother would also have taught her how to perform various female rites or *vrats,* but in the text she is entirely a pedagogic voice who discourses on God. This mode of instruction is strikingly different from conventional female ways of influencing religious belief. Debendranath, too, holds his grandmother responsible for his religious life. However, whereas his religious life was preeminently a matter of spiritual and theological discourses, his grandmother had been an example of piety, of the devotional practices that are enjoined upon a virtuous Hindu widow. Her chanting of sacred *mantras,* her acts of decorating and worshipping the idol, her ritually pure cooking and offerings of food to the deity, stimulated his aesthetic and sensory feelings which got connected with religious meanings. Above all, her death opened the door to his momentous realisation about the transience of life, it led him onto metaphysical speculation. Very different, then, from the regular lessons, the reasoned explanations that Rashsundari received from her mother about the nature of divinity.

By making her mother bear the entire weight of a complete religious instruction that must have been acquired piecemeal and from a variety of sources throughout her entire life, Rashsundari endowed the mother with a specifically 19th century role. In Vaishnav hagiographies, the mother is a source of nurture and indulgence, but not of instruction. Nineteenth century reformers, on the other hand, believed in the modern pedagogical principle that an enlightened and educated mother was the best guide for early instruction as well as for morals. Hindu revivalists had a different perspective on the centrality of women. The woman, in their view, had escaped colonisation far more surely than the man, being ruled by traditional norms and discipline and by remaining untainted by western values and education. For both groups, the woman was, for different reasons, a major inspiration.

Obliquely, this move of Rashsundari's made a larger point about herself. The mother's teaching, however potent, had ceased to reach her from the time of her marriage—that is after she was thirteen, and had been settled in her new home. From a very early age, then, Rashsundari's spiritual growth would have been self-made. *AJ* is a jealously individualistic narrative, shaping the material of her life around the lonely efforts of a heroic individual. In this sense, it is a typically 19th century *bildungsroman*. Debendranath's autobiography is similarly patterned on a lonely spiritual quest where he gathered the ingredients of his religious life all by himself. The difference lies in the organisational, mobilisational, institutionalising imperatives that structure the later part of Debendranath's book. Rashsundari's gender-constrained religious activism, in contrast, had to be confined to reading and writing.

VI
Childhood in *Amar Jiban*

Mother and God are linked together in the narrative within a single structure, to remove a nervous child's constant fears. We have seen that even after learning about God, her childhood had not been free from anxieties. In fact, *AJ* has a peculiar relationship with the intertwined themes of the woman's childhood and the child-like woman. On the one hand, Rashsundari's childhood was never marked by the usual associations of that stage: she was not carefree, fun-loving, adventurous. She worried too much, she played no games, her one attempt at a picnic ended in fiasco. She also learnt how to look after a child, how to cook and how to do household chores far too early. We find in the child of ten a little adult woman, already doing most of the things that she would be doing later in life.

On the other hand, all through the narrative, she seems to foreground the essentially unchanging, child-like condition of her mind. She remained fearful and nervous, she hardly understood the wordly implications of her station in life, she never cared much about the things that preoccupied most householders. Even when she acquired a keener sense about her possessions in her more power-laden middle age, she would constantly distance herself as narrator from the narrated self of the successful householder by two devices. First, she would laugh at the changes that had befallen her, she would make it sound like a little girl playing at being grown-up, without having internalised this state. She spoke about it with the detached irony of the observer, whereas, the narrating voice merged more effortlessly with the narrated one when she described her more helpless and subordinated states. Second, she would constantly remind us about the continued lack of control, about a wilful fate that might take all this away in a second. She invoked the concept of *maya,* the fundamental non-materiality of earthly states, the transience of all states.

Of course, part of the intention behind such self-portrayal was to emphasise her unwordliness, her innocence, her freedom from material attachments that are enjoined upon the good Vaishnav. But the narrative of ignorance, of uncertainty, had other functions as well. It was a way of indicating that in the larger, overarching design of her life, she remained a child without a sense of direction, helplessly dependent upon God's will. It represented the essential human condition.

The interpenetration of woman's childhood and the child-like woman grew out of a blurring of boundaries between the two states. Even when the body matured and the duties of a full-fledged householder were undertaken, the mind retained its essentially childlike characteristics. Conversely, the childish body and mind had been made to shoulder much of the experiences and responsibilities of the adult. Both were an imposed and gendered social condition that the woman confronted, as well as the existential condition of the human devotee. Loss of childhood, interrupted play is a constant theme in lullabies and nursery songs: "Let us have a last quick game together, my friend, for the son of a stranger is coming to take me away, and I will play no more." In post-Raghunandan Bengal, the accent on pre-pubertal marriage meant very early weddings and an effective and abrupt end to childhood. Rashsundari was, in fact, married at a somewhat unusually late stage. Anticipating the exile in the home of harsh, critical and unforgiving strangers, little girls were trained in housework from a very early age. That was why Rashsundari's family had been delighted to discover that she had picked it up so effortlessly.

On the other hand, as we have seen earlier, the woman was not meant to grow up into an autonomous agential capacity, to develop moral or intellectual autonomy. The impulse for *strishiksha* was, indeed, a protest against this enforced childhood. Rashsundari thanks God for at least relieving her of the burden of total ignorance: "Had I not known even this much, I would have needed to depend on others." As the ultimate horizon for this abject child-like dependency, the eternal dependence of the human being upon God's arbitrary will is invoked. It underlines and extends the gendered condition of the woman into an overarching human condition.

If the introduction of God had temporarily assuaged some of her worst childhood fears, the structure of reassurance that mother and God held in place, broke down completely when Rashsundari realised that she was to be married off. Terrified, she rushed to her mother for a denial. Her mother tried to rise to the occasion, but this time her words rang false and she was crying.

Rashsundari's world—tenuously held together by her mother's comfort—crashed around her as she realised that her mother was lying, that she was as helpless and vulnerable as Rashsundari herself. She was a woman. In utter terror, her words choking her, she tried to salvage something from the old structure: "Would Parameswara come with me?" Her mother replied that he would go with her wherever she went. Bereft of the living, precious, human mediation of the mother, a male divinity was left to Rashsundari as the memory of her mother's speech, as the promise of a reassurance that had already been betrayed. He was, therefore, both a residue and an extension of the mother.

In her early fatherless family unit, God might have been a symbol of the missing father. It is extremely significant that Rashsundari's god is almost invariably male—she obviously cannot imagine an authority figure that is not phallic. More, he is addressed as the father, even though the Vaishnav imaginary practically never visualises Krishna in that role. Krishna is either the lover or the child. His adult maleness in *AJ* is released from the limitedness and vulnerabilities of the mother. At the same time, he was entirely a creation of the mother. The narrativisation of God seems to bear out, in important particulars, a Lacanian characterisation of the child's entry into the symbolic world of the father's law. The differences are, of course, more important. Here we have a constructed and narrativised entry rather than an experiential stage within a developmental process. The transition, moreover, is not from pleasure to discipline or from plenitude to loss, as one from absolute terror to a relative though fragile security.[21]

When the terrible, unbelievable ordeal of parting arrived, and the little girl lost her home, her birthplace, her mother and every single face she had known, Parameswara was the only bit of identity that she carried with her from her old life. A new place was reached after three interminable days' of boat journey—when she literally did not have the ground under her feet. It was filled with total strangers, and even the spoken dialect would have been somewhat different. She went over his name in her heart again and again: "I admit it was only out of fear that I called out to you." She makes it clear what location and function she had ascribed to God— deliverance from pain and terror. What she is silent about, and, yet, what comes through from her subsequent experiences, is how inadequate God was to the task. The pain did not go away, the fear was joined by many others. By the end of the book, the early expectation was gone. God now appeared as a powerful, whimsical figure who is not there to remove her fears, but who wants to amuse himself with the events of her life. He is the *adhikari* who made her play the roles that would entertain him. "Even if you are cruel to me, I have to call you the merciful one."

Mother and God failed her when she got married. Marriage began with great grief, with copious weeping. Rashsundari surely exaggerated her utter ignorance of the meaning and consequences of the event, in order to underline both her childish innocence and the trauma of unexpected separation. Most girls would be married off before twelve, she would have witnessed other weddings to know what it involved. Writings of other women echo the pain of separation.[22] Another autobiography recorded how a mother was blinded by her ceaseless weeping after her little girl was taken away from her.[23]

The pretended ignorance about the wedding ceremony
gives the narrative its profound shock value. The event is
preceded by the trappings of merriment: red silk and shining
jewellery, music and guests, a little girl happily trailing after
her mother, excited by the ceremony. The image of plenitude
is then given a harsh and piercing counterpoint in the image
of the sacrificial goat crying for its mother when it knows
that it is going to die. We, subsequently, have a series of animal
metaphors—helplessly manipulated by cruel humans—to
recall the fate of women: the sacrificial goat, the caged bird,
the netted fish, the blinded bullock. It is immensely significant
that the entire wedding is described without a single reference
to the groom, although the bride and the groom go through
a prolonged ritual sequence together. There was no way that
Rashsundari would have failed to register the presence of the
groom at her side. The only figure is that of the little girl
crying her heart out. The description is slippery with tears.
They are the metaphorical blood that is shed at the time when
the little girl is physically severed from her family.

VII
A Life of Trials—Early Married Life

Rashsundari wrote out her life as a series of trials that she
survived with God's grace. The real ordeal was married life,
although childhood, too, had been full of tribulations. She was
married at twelve, in all likelihood before her menarche. She
was sent off to the new home immediately, for the completion
of ritual and ceremonial rites at that end. After that, she was
brought back home, where, following custom, she remained
until she reached menarche. She tells us that she was sent
back to her in-laws after a year, though she does not mention

why, for reasons of modesty. At her new home, her husband was the only son and her sisters-in law had been married off already. Much later, once they were widowed, they came back to this household. There were few close or senior relatives at home, so discipline was not very severe. Her mother-in-law was loving and indulgent and allowed her a year's grace when she was encouraged to play with the village children—but not outdoors. When she describes the household, it seems to be smaller than the usual size of joint family residences. Describing a 19th century rural joint family household of means, W.J. Wilkins says that it could contain up to three hundred people living together.[24] The village, however, would have many more of kinsfolk, living in separate houses. Home was mainly populated by the servants some of whom became very close to her. The day labourers and the outdoors servants, who were connected with the family plots, were fed at home. Altogether, there were twenty-five mouths to feed at each meal.

Rashsundari, at no point, described her home. Dineshchandra Sen has described old prosperous houses in Faridpur as being largely thatched cottages, supported by bamboo poles. They were often works of art, intricate weavings in cane and bamboo decorating the walls and the ceilings, the supportive poles being highly coloured and painted. Terracotta figurines would decorate the walls and the poles. Woven cane mattings and hanging shelves made of ropes and studded with painted shells brightened the rooms. Very often, the women of the family would make these themselves. The houses were beautiful pieces of architecture and Sen mentions one at Madhukhali village at Faridpur that was completed over a hundred years and that was designed by a famous Muslim mason in the early 19th century.[25] Passages in *AJ* does suggest a similar architectural plan and room furnishing. As was customary, the female parts of the household were segregated from the outer male parts which would contain the sitting room as well as the estate offices. The female parts would have the kitchen, the living rooms and the domestic shrine. They would also have an inner courtyard.

Rashsundari proudly mentions her skilled handicraft products. These objects were, according to Sen, manufactured by women for decorating the interior, and Faridpur, indeed, was famed for its women's handicrafts.[26] She also played with her companions, or rather, they played and she watched them. Soon such occupations began to bore her. She was growing up, her mind needed food, but she could not read, could not listen to serious religious discourses, was not allowed into discussions about non-domestic matters.

From the way Rashsundari described him, her husband was a big, heavily-built man, most probably considerably older than her and already established as the *karta*, the only adult male of the home and the master of the household. Women might run it, but his would be the final decisions in household matters. He also ran the family estate. Being the only man of the family, he must have acquired an authoritative manner even at that stage. Rashsundari retained a sense of deep awe about him till the end of her life which would have been planted by their earliest contact: the nervous child would have found such a man frighteningly awesome. Intimacy would not have come easily or at all. In any case, their contact would be restricted to bedroom meetings at night. In daytime, the new bride was not even meant to converse with him.

Hers was a pious, deeply orthodox upper-caste Hindu family, untouched, as yet, by new education or reforms. This was precisely the authentic, uncontaminated Hindu space that

Hindu nationalists have valorised as the true site of freedom and that, even now, fetches nostalgic sighs about an idyllic happiness that modernity has compromised forever. There is a long tradition in modern Bengali literature that very lovingly paints and reaffirms, almost in every generation since the 19th century, the beloved icon of the good Hindu woman: with her ritually-sanctified conch-shell bangles and the vermillion paste in her hair-parting and on her forehead, her simple cotton sari and her veiled, beautiful face. She is immersed in service, in nursing babies, above all, in cooking. Recalling the prodigious feats of cooking by East Bengal women, Sen has written: "It was through this, above all, that women expressed their love... Love enabled them to make such a fine art out of cooking."[27] An immense aesthetic and cultural load is invested in this figure who is equated with Annapurna, the goddess of food and of nurture. In his preface to *AJ*, Sen recalls these associations and extends them to the figure of the bounteous Motherland. Rashsundari is made to stand in for that beauty, for those gestures of service and nurture, for that love. We need to take up the constituent elements of the icon to explore what Rashsundari said about this image that she struggled to fit into.

As we have seen earlier, her new home was not, in most respects, as harsh as it might have been. Nonetheless, grafting remained a pain-filled, incomplete process. Incarceration was its recurrent image: "I was caged for life... in this life there will be no escape for me... I was snatched away from my own people, I eventually became a tamed bird." She accepted her new family, but the love she gave them was no spontaneous affection. It was the result of training and necessity, the habit of the tamed bird. She praised their indulgence, she was thankful that she passed all the tests and earned the reputation of a flawless new wife. But she was careful to explain what it cost her to earn this. She was also quite clear about the limits of their affection. They would not let her visit her beloved mother despite her best efforts, not even when she lay dying: her labour at home was indispensable, she explains, not herself as a person.

She described *sekal*—those times—with uncharacteristically outspoken criticism. "I am filled with loathing when I look back on all that... the coarse clothes, the heavy cumbrous jewellery, the conch-shell bangles, the vermillion mark..." The marks of the good Hindu wife, so pleasing to cultural nationalists from Dinesh Sen to Dipesh Chakrabarty,[28] generated such repugnance in her that for once her language was cleared of all equivocation, double-voicedness. She used images of blindness, of dumbness, of paralysis, to describe the gamut of injunctions that governed the young woman. She was condemned to silence, to awkward, limited movements, to interdictions on spontaneous gestures, clear utterance, free speech. Above all, she was condemned to endless service, to crippling gestures of deference. She was condemned to ignorance, to illiteracy. The young woman was not meant to talk to most grown-up older male relatives, to several categories of older female relatives, and she needed to observe carefully graded degrees of voice modulation and movements with regard to all inmates of the household. The boundaries of permitted movements and speech, of expected observances, were very fluid and varied with each family. No new bride could ever be quite sure of the exact scope of restrictions. The plurality of custom was not liberating, it created perpetual puzzles and endless anxiety about transgression. As a much older wife, with several children of her own, Rashsundari was not sure whether she could be seen by her husband's horse.

This was definitely carrying the strictures of modesty to its *reductio ad absurdum,* but it does outline the inherent problems of the system.

Her life of leisure came to an abrupt end when her mother-in-law became an invalid. The very absence of senior women relatives and guardians that had contributed to relative ease and comfort for the new bride at first, turned into a major problem. Rashsundari had no help at home, she had to take over the nursing of the invalid, the meticulous tending of the family idol, the cooking and feeding of twenty-five mouths twice every day and the general supervision of an elaborate and complicated household mechanism. She was fourteen at that time.

To put it differently, she now truly filled out the slot where generations of Bengali men had so lovingly placed her. And she was a singular success in her appointed role, for she came out of the ordeal with flying colours. Nobody could fault her—she was immersed in housework, she was ideally self-sacrificing and she neglected her own needs in an exemplary fashion. Of course, with a lifetime of unbroken record as the good wife, she still could not be sure that she would die unblemished, for the minutest of lapses could defame her for ever even when she was in her eighties. As the popular Bengali saying has it:

> The woman will burn, the ashes will scatter
> Only then we know that she had been good.

Meaning, that as long as she lived, she could always err, for her very nature was flawed.

AJ deconstructs the iconic figure of the ideal Hindu woman in two very crucial ways: the work that is meant to be emotionally satisfying, aesthetic activity is taken up one by one and shown as work: tending the family idol, cooking and feeding others, serving guests, mothering. They are listed as labour, not as works of art or emotional release. Moreover, they are described as punishingly hard work. She evacuated the image of nurture of all associations with emotional fulfilment.

This is very obvious with the theme of mothering. She started her fertile phase at the age of eighteen, when she was already overburdened with responsibility and work. Between eighteen and forty-one, she conceived twelve times, and she brought up eleven children. She gave birth roughly at two-year intervals, for a continuous span of twenty-three years. This time coincided with the period of the most relentless household labour, before she had a daughter-in-law to assist her. Childbirth was a particularly draining and dangerous process. Lying-in rooms were insanitary, a lot of exacting ritual taboos had to be maintained and post-natal care was notoriously undeveloped. Census figures show that female mortality was particularly high in these fertile years.[29] At the same time, it seems that Vaishnavs had somewhat lenient regulations and better post-natal custom: for instance, they gave cooling fluids to mothers rather than hot food that others wrongly believed to be invigorating.[30] That, along with the mild climate of her birthplace Pabna, probably account for Rashsundari's unimpaired good health. Had it broken down, she wondered, with (probably) unconscious irony, who would have looked after her? She was also lucky that most of her children were born without mishap and most of them were sons. That would have considerably improved her status within the family.

Parenting was the mother's exclusive responsibility. Rashsundari's husband resented it when the babies cried at night and disturbed his rest. She herself felt guilty, remiss. In *AJ*, the early years of the children are a time of painful whirl. She thus restored the feel of slog to the icon of smiling motherhood. A common problem of overworked motherhood is that mothers hardly have the time to enjoy that most magical of times—the years when their children are tiny infants, growing up into full human beings. Rashsundari would have few spare moments to savour that incomparable experience, since she remembers that period simply as a time of great trial: "The Lord alone knows what I went through all those years." A popular Bengali lullaby sums up the frustration of the young mother who, tied to the household machine, hungers in vain for uninterrupted time to be alone with the precious baby:

> I'll run away to the forests with my treasure
> And there, all by myself, I'll simply gaze at its enchanting face.

Rashsundari recalls with formal pride the good qualities of her sons after they had grown up. One of them helped her to write, another one posted her the first printed book she had come across. But she talks of them with great depths of feeling when she describes their death. It was as if she experienced the concentrated emotions of motherhood at their fullest at the moment of their termination, when she lost her sons one by one. It was as if the most vivid meaning of motherhood to her was its loss.

VIII
Food and Eating in the Woman's Life

The most prominent field of the woman's labour was cooking, the making of food. *AJ* establishes a very peculiar relationship between the woman and the food that she cooked and served. Rashsundari spent an overwhelming part of her life cooking and feeding others. In the prosperous countryside of East Bengal, affluent rural families acquired legendary reputations for the dishes that their women cooked in immense variety and with excellent skills. Food signified far more than its immediate meaning: it was love, it was womanliness, it was the metaphor for family life. Women were graded and family memory organised, according to the grand meals that had been served. Bengali literature and post-Partition recollections of refugee Hindus from East Bengal are luscious with evocations of the sweets that were prepared with milk and coconut, the many kinds of fish, deployed in innumerable shapes and tastes, the hundred different vegetable dishes that no two families ever cooked alike. Even the historical scholarship of Sen turns delectable with those recollections.[31] This was the arena where female creativity, talent and emotion found optimal expression. To be a woman is to be a happy and excellent cook.

On the other hand, there was an equally strong normative insistence on the indifference of the good woman towards food. Ritual fasting and a loudly expressed preference for non-eating, for minimal and shoddy meals, for leftover food were enjoined as a sign of virtue. Bengali hospitality was dominantly defined as the woman's willing surrender of her meal to the unexpected guest. In the sacred popular verses that are read out at the daily worship of Lakshmi, the goddess of fortune, the goddess tells the woman:

> I regard that woman to be my equal in virtue
> Who starts chewing the betel-nut as soon as she has had her
> bath.[32]

The lesson is that the virtuous woman is one who habitually misses her lunch, for the betel nut is consumed after a meal.

Her eating was a peculiarly non-structured, uncertain

activity for the woman. In orthodox families, even now, meals are not a collective event, but are sharply hierarchised. Men are served first, then children and old women. Whatever is left after that would constitute the food of young women who have cooked the meal. In rural, upper-class families, women of the family would have done the cooking by themselves, even if they might have some help for other kinds of work. They ate generally in the kitchen and there was much male joking about the choice bits that they keep hidden just for themselves. In actual fact, however, leftover food, the dregs, were what they served themselves, straight out of the cooking utensils, any old how, while the meals that they served others were elaborately and beautifully set out. Rashsundari was the only young wife in her family, so she ate alone and nobody ever got to know whether she ate anything at all. The professed indifference to food, conjoined to the tradition of eating leftover food, ensured a great propensity to ill health and high mortality that is so marked among Indian women even to this day—a fact that is primarily caused by serious malnutrition. This, of course, was something that happened inside the female domain, in the kitchen, and something that was primarily decided by women themselves, for they were in sole charge of the distribution of food.

The kitchen-centred politics, and distribution of power that was articulated through the division of food in joint families, are vital dimensions of the interpellation of women into patriarchal ideology. The whole process is ideologically conditioned through normative procedures that are, moreover, expressed and taught as aesthetic and emotional preferences. At the end of the process, women produce the food and the food is expropriated from them. Once the dominant male/female division has been worked out, then within the female

domain, it is further hierarchised according to age, status and
domestic importance of various categories of women. The
widow or the dependent kinswoman and the youngest wife
constituted the lowest end of the pole.

AJ is a striking example of the workings of this interpellation
where the woman alone takes the decision to deprive herself.
Rashsundari was the only wife in the family, without any
senior woman to pressurise her. Her family was affluent and
caring, so she was under no moral obligation to go without. Yet
such was the force of prescription, and so firmly had it been
internalised, that she would not take care of her own pangs of
hunger. She also indicated something quite interesting: except
for rice, the basic minimum ingredient of a meal, she would
not allow herself to eat any other kind of food, even when no
one was looking. This rigidly minimalist decision was shaped
by a fundamental uncertainty about what and how much a
woman was allowed to eat, especially in upper-caste families
where a whole lot of food taboos operated. Nineteenth-
century behaviour manuals that purported to teach young
wives proper deportment, confessed their helplessness in the
matter: "My child, I can give you no good advice on this. If
you serve yourself, you will be called shameless. If you wait
for others to serve you, you may have to go without food."[33]
Even in urban enlightened families, brides faced the same
anxieties.[34]

Interestingly, the same prescriptive authorities that had
relegated women to a lifetime of non-eating in the midst
of endless feeding, and had fixed this role in the image of
Annapurna, the goddess of food, had also imagined the
terrifying counter-image of Kali, the primal female force that
devours Creation itself. Female saints often exercised their
saintly privilege with bouts of voracious eating and with

demands of being physically fed by others.[35] Rashsundari made fun of her appetite and greed in a poem on her old age, a stage which, in a sense, had defeminised her and set her free from compulsory inhibitions. Her senility alone would let her articulate her desire for food.

Rashsundari described her acts of cooking and serving uncompromisingly as hard work. She made no reference to any possibility of excitement about cooking, of the gratification of feeding the loved ones, of the aroma and flavour of the memorable dishes she surely would have prepared as a successful housewife. Whenever she wrote about food, she always called it rice—reducing food to its basic, irreducible and dullest minimum. She thus emptied out the act of cooking from associations of creativity and filled it with hard labour. She refused the iconic privilege of Annapurna.

She mentions only two items of food in an account of a life that was primarily involved in handling and creating different varieties of it. One were the mangoes that her mother had packed up for a picnic for her and her friend when she was a child. The other was the rice that she cooked every day for at least twenty-five people for lunch and dinner. It is significant that in both cases, she described her failure to eat that food. In the first event, her friend had both the mangoes. In fact, Rashsundari happily fed them to her. In the second case, Rashsundari not only shrinks and reduces food to the colourless, flavourless rice, she describes her relationship with it as one of perpetually interrupted and deferred eating. After a whole day's cooking, she sits down to eat and then is obliged to hold out her uneaten meal to an unexpected guest. Suffering pangs of hunger, she waits for her delayed dinner, but the lamp blows out, a storm begins, the babies howl and she is afraid that her husband might wake up. So she does without. The next meal is washed away by the pee and the shit that her baby leaves on the plate. "Forget about being cared for in other ways, most days I did not even get to eat two proper meals." Food, for her, remained a source of anxiety, not nurture.[36]

IX
Middle Age in *AJ*

Rashsundari lost her husband when she was fifty-nine. We find a self-consciously formal obituary report about him in *AJ*, but little else. He was a man of considerable local importance and was ideally suited to be a masterful *Karta*—a fact that she records with awe and trepidation rather than with affection. We are told that he would be impatient when babies cried at night, that bound as he was by ties of custom, he was of no help to her in her desire to read. He certainly was not told about the desire, nor about its secret fulfilment. He cried when she was seriously ill, but he also said stoically: "Is she gone? So let it be then." There are no recollections of the time when they were young together. His own death was described as a social catastrophe, not as personal tragedy—loss of a crown of gold was how she described it. She made an extraordinary statement in this connection: "I do not regret what God had willed." This certainly was carrying resignation and submission beyond the bounds expected from a good Hindu wife. She departed from the norms of a widow's expression in yet another small but significant way. Whereas widows are expected to see their prolonged life as a curse, Rashsundari thanked God for her long life.

Yet, widowhood was a social disaster, and here *AJ* is quite close to the reformist discourses about the plight of the Hindu widow.[37] There are some veiled and bitter words in *AJ* about the ritual inauspiciousness of the widow, of her dishonoured state. However, when her widowhood arrived, Rashsundari was already the seniormost woman in the household, the mother of many sons and with daughters-in-law subservient to her. In her case, she would have been quite cushioned from the deprivations of the state.

Rashsundari was forty when her first son was married off. She did not conceive after that. It was customary for parents to terminate the sexual relationship at this stage and we may assume that this must have happened, for forty was too early for menopause. Rashsundari described her middle age that was presumably free from sexual activity, as a period of ease and happiness. Initiated into sexual life very early—probably at thirteen—with a stranger who was much older and an awesome person, the nervous girl might not have experienced much pleasure or intimacy from the contact. In any case, the sexually active years would coincide with the time of hardest labour, minimal freedom and draining childbirths. Her youth and her sexual body would have been a liability rather than a source of pleasure. It is striking that in her imaginings, there are no erotic associations for Krishna.

Middle age, in sharp contrast, was a time of power and privilege, a point when she emerged as a figure of considerable authority within the household. Her fears fell away, the taste of confidence was sweet. For the first time, she used the words, my *sansar*. It was a time of integration. The new perspective of life coincided with a new view of religion. At the very end of her book, she gave conventional and familiar names, mythological associations to her God. For the first time, too, she addressed him in the name of the family idol. A self-created God, wrested and saved from her mother's home, was merged into a collective, shared devotional activity. Her reading was now known and respected, she began to read out to groups of women openly, she was writing a book about her life. She allowed herself, for the first time, to describe her involvement with the permitted range of religious practices that are followed by a Vaishnav woman of comfortable means—pujas, arranging ritual congregational feasts, buying ornaments for the family idol. Her religion now expressed a family of property and status, and no longer the lonely struggles of the *bhakt*. Yet, there was something very new about her practice. The money for them came not out of family inheritance but from the proceeds of her own book.

X
Her Body, Her Dreams, Her Reading

In hagiographical conventions, closeness to divinity is established through the intensity and frequency of trance-like states and through miracle-making powers. *AJ* does not ascribe a touch of the divine to Rashsundari, but it does imply a special relationship with God. It marks her out as a chosen person, manifesting some unique purpose of God through her life events. The signs of such a state had to be in some ways located within the realm of the marvellous, if not the miraculous. For this purpose, *AJ* identified four areas of her life and redefined them as divine manifestations: changes in the states of her own body, her ability to dream strange dreams that either foretold events or narrated an extra-mundane reality, the unexpected retrieval of lost objects and her ability to read and write.

It was strange and somewhat outrageous for a domesticated woman like Rashsundari to refer so often and at such length to her own body and its changing forms and purposes. She, however, does not explicitly mention the functions of her female body, she focuses on the fit between the altering demands of life at various stages and the wonderful way in which her body changed to adapt to them. This fit is designated as the sign of the attention that God has paid to her. Here her body again stands in for everywoman's, for the human condition as such. Her own exceptionality lay in her ability to interpret the signs which few may understand.

Her youthful body had been healthy, pretty and fertile. It had also been an exceptionally strong and resilient body. In middle age, the strength remained but the fecundity dried up, as befitted the seniormost woman in a large and important household. As the home filled up with a younger generation of women, ready to shoulder the burden of daily labour, her responsibilities dwindled, and her strong body began to age and decay. She now awaited her last journey across life with a lightened load of capabilities. With detached irony, she contrasted the present decay and senility with her old beauty, capabilities, functions. Rashsundari defamiliarised a normal female life-cycle by imparting a sense of deep wonder to it. The known body was made strange, exotic and holy, the sign and site of God's handiwork: "Plain eyes can see it quite clearly."

The supremacy of sense perceptions as the primary source of religious knowledge, and of the human body as the object of this knowledge, ties up with strands of body-centred, popular esoteric cults. Yet, in sharp contrast to these, Rashsundari did not seek to manipulate and stretch the limits of the ordinary body. To her, its normal states were wondrous enough. The cultic practices often involved a relationship with a male body and their chief purpose was to impart supernatural powers to it. In a way, then, it was a replication of the patriarchal order, albeit through deviant sexual activities. Rashsundari's religious project, in total contrast, was autonomous and self-centred.

Her dreams are recorded eloquently and vividly. Some were, in part, replication of events that were happening elsewhere at precisely the same time. Later, the dream sequence would be confirmed by news of real events. At the same time, she would dream on beyond the actual event. When she dreamt of her son's death, she partly witnessed events as they were occurring at a different place—with the difference that she was present as an observer within the dream. But she also dreamt of an entire sequence of the son's life beyond his moment of death—again, with herself as an observer, passive and commanded. Some other dreams are symbolic events, requiring interpretation— as when she dreamt of a shower of golden flowers and the next day a grandson was born. Here, interpretation hinged on the contiguity between the dream and a succeeding event, and the common ambience that united the two—the advent of something precious. Certain dreams or sightings are left unexplained: the curious episode of the ghostly dog or the occasion when she supposedly went through and came out of her own physical death. She described them as happenings that were entirely unusual and inexplicable and did not try to interpret them, for their importance lay in their undecipherability. Dreams and such events combined to constitute a privileged access to a superior reality. They were tame, domesticated, minor marvels.

The unexpected return of long-lost precious objects has always been a part of miracle tales associated with holy places or holy men who are sought out for this purpose. In her old age, Rashsundari got back a gold nose-ring that she had lost in her youth. Even though the owner had lost her youth, the lost object was still bright and shining, totally unblemished. It was as if some essence of herself had remained unchanged in God's custody, retaining its old lustre, although her mortal life had been irreparably altered. Its return was a divine message to remind her of that. The rendering of this event into a sacred tale depended on her act of interpretation, her allegorical narrativisation.

Her reading was the ultimate wonder, the most certain sign of her special relationship with God. This, indeed, was more than a sign, it was nothing less than a miracle.

Rashsundari had longed to read since she was fourteen. When she was twenty-five, and still illiterate, she dreamt that she was reading the *Chaitanya Bhagabat*. She chose to interpret the dream as a reality of a different kind: her dream was an accomplishment in itself, since dream reading, too, was a sort of a fulfilment, a sign of grace. Yet, soon that sense of accomplishment would not suffice, she longed to have access to it in her waking hours.

The day after the dream, she actually saw the *CB* and was able to identify it by the illumination on its wooden cover. Later, she took out a page and hid it in the kitchen. She also surreptitiously put away a palm leaf on which her son was practising his letters. Then, over a very long time, and in the most fearful secrecy, she recalled the letters she had heard being recited at the school in her old home, matched them with those on the palm leaf and on the page. Letter by letter, she taught her self to read, to become *jitakshara*.

For a very long time, her reading remained unsuspected. It was a forbidden pleasure. It was not a rebellion since it was secret and she did not let it interfere with her old life at all, although its duties and its responsibilities were now doubly irksome for they kept her away from her pleasure. On the surface, nothing had changed. In reality, a miracle or a revolution had taken place. And since it was one that she had made all by herself, it was really a revolution although she called it a miracle. The nervous little girl, the timid young wife who feared and obeyed everything and everyone, had vaulted across the forbidden boundary, knowing the risks, the interdictions.

It was a transgression of the deepest kind. She was now a woman with a double life. As a Vaishnav, she deliberately used the pattern or the narrative of transgression that was most familiar to her—that of the illicit or *parakiya* love between Radha and Krishna, the conflict between the woman's licit norms and a higher religious call that takes her beyond its bounds. She translated the theme as her given, prescribed household norms and a higher religious vocation that compelled her to disobey them. She used all the familiar tropes. The desire to read was constantly, though secretly stimulated through aural manipulation: Radha was impatient with longing when she listened to Krishna's flute, while Rashsundari heard of other women reading, she heard religious texts being read and expounded, devotional songs sung on her doorstep, but out of bounds for her. Her entire household was against women reading; her work filled up her day, there was no time for it. "I was forever yearning." She could satisfy the urge in broken snatches, in deep secrecy, at night. The occasional acts of reading were structured like secret assignations.

Rashsundari narrativised her transgressive reading as a higher religious calling, like Radha's illicit love, so glorified by Gaudiya Vaishnavism. Yet, however much the ultimate object of her desire was an access to divine knowledge, she chose to reach it through non-conventional means, she avoided the feminine paths to devotion, even the deviant ones that grew out of mystical or esoteric or ecstatic forms. She chose to reach it through reading a book. She thus inextricably aligned herself with the modern project of *strishiksha*. She openly says that her desire to read was implanted by news of this.

After she could, as a middle-aged householder, publicly announce her achievement to other women in the family, she gathered around herself a group of women. This was the only time spent with women, in a collectivity, that she describes with pleasure. Yet, it was a collectivity of such a new kind! It was reading-centred, and Rashsundari was its leader. It would occasionally practice yet another transgression that was forbidden to respectable women. They would sing to themselves. It is significant that these are the only solidarities, activities performed with women that she chose to remember, to recapitulate.

So what had to be hidden, what was considered deviant, constituted her point of individuation, the beginning of her authentic and autonomous self. It was, at once, the cause and the condition of the autobiographical enunciation.

XI
Kaliyuga or Modern Times

Rashsundari's desire came alive when she heard her elders discussing—with anger and fear—the new times. For them, the most disturbing thing about the dark new days was the fact that women were learning to read and write. "Now we are ruled by a female sovereign... this is the age of kali." Victoria's reign signified of the last and most degenerate of ages in a four-age time cycle. For Rashsundari, however, the reign would have carried very different significations, forcing a new view of the time cycle. If the new times and the Queen's rule heralded the possibility of the reading woman, then they were a resource and not a burden. Nor did she revise her opinion.

Late in life, she continued to look at the new generations of women with pleasure and with hope.

Possibly, a Vaishnav notion of time reinforced her choice. Post-Chaitanya *bhakti,* as we have seen, welcomed the kaliyug, for the saviour was born in this one. It was an age when the path to salvation had been made much easier and women and low castes were brought within its orbit. If this was an age of general decline of morals, purity and the right order, it was also an age of more generous hopes for the faithful. At the same time, however, it rejected the path of learning and knowledge as a false path. Interestingly, this view of time found strong resonances among the liberal reformers, who, on the other hand, saw the path to salvation in reform and education—the new *mantras.* Both were meant to purify religious life.

Rashsundari knitted up the two hopes and the two views of time together. Kaliyug was a time of salvation for all, it was a time when women could begin to read: "Blessed, blessed be this kaliyug." A Vaishnavite and a gendered construction of time met to contest a dark perspective on modernity that was shared by a brahmanical orthodoxy and an emergent group of revivalist-nationalists alike. And, in our times, that bleak view is reaffirmed by post-colonial cultural nationalists.[38]

Epilogue

If 19th-century processes enabled the writing of *AJ,* they were, nonetheless, incomplete, contradictory, botched-up. And here I have a personal debt to enter. A hundred years after Rashsundari, in the early decades of this century, a grand-aunt of mine was seized with a desire to read. Her affluent, educated, upper-caste family was non-cooperative, and she had to keep her desire a secret. The only reading matter that passed her way were paper bags carrying groceries from shops into her kitchen. The paper came from torn pages of schoolboys' exercise books, scored over with sums and spelling lessons. While cooking the evening meal, she would pore over them in the flickering light of the hearth fire.

There is a more contemporary tale to narrate as well. A few years back, a Government-sponsored literacy mission went into a village in West Bengal to teach the village women. A very old village woman came up to a member of the team and said, half in joy and half in accusation: "Where were you all my life?"[39]

Rashsundari's life and writing stood at the confluence of two orders—of patriarchy and of women's desires. On the one hand, was the tradition of *bhakti*. It allowed the woman, seeking an excess beyond *sansar*, a certain ambiguous space. On the other hand, there were her own times, when a new system of liberal pedagogy came to include women within its orbit. Both were crucially limited in their possibilities. Vaishnav traditions defined certain modes of devotion as the only sphere of excess. Liberal reform was most severely class and caste-bound and was, for most part of the century, confined largely to reformed families. Poverty and patriarchy combined to constrain change, growth of autonomy. For other women, seized with the hunger for the word, it had little to offer beyond stray pages torn out of school exercise books.

Notes

1.   I prefer the word hagiography rather than myth, since Krishna was seen as human incarnation of Vishnu, while Chaitanya was a historical figure. Myths would deal with entirely non-mortal, divine figures.

2.   These late 19th century autobiographies have been reprinted in the *Atmakatha* series, op cit.

3.   Debipada Bhattacharya, *Bangla Charitsahitya, 1801–1941,* Calcutta, 1964, pp. 79–81.

4.   Steedman, *The Radical Soldier's Tale,* History Workshop, Routledge, London and New York, 1988, pp. 2–3.

5.   Preface to the 1957 edition, op cit.

6.   Chatterjee, *The Nation and Its Fragments,* Oxford University Press, Delhi, 1994, pp. 140–44.

7.   Steedman, op cit, p. 19.

8.   Saradasundari, *Atmakatha,* reprinted in the *Atmakatha* series, op cit, p. 17.

9.   Asutosh Bhattacharya, ed, *Nati Binodini Rachana Sangraha,* Sahitya Sangstha, Calcutta, 1987; letter from Girishchandra Ghosh, p. 180.

10.   See Subir Raychoudhury, *Bilati Yatra Theke Swadeshi Theatre,* Jadavpur University Press, Calcutta, 1971.

11.   See Advaita Mallabarman, *Titash Ekti Nadir Naam,* Calcutta, 1957.

12.   Charles Taylor, *Sources of the Self: The Making of the Modern Identity,* Cambridge University Press, 1989, pp. 266–74.

13.   Foucault, *The Use of Pleasure: The History of Sexuality,* Vol 2, New York, 1986, Introduction.

14.   Carlo Ginzberg, *The Cheese and the Worms,* Penguin, 1982.

15.   I have no direct evidence from these writings that Darwininian ideas about the death of the species contributed to notions of inevitable and unstoppable decay—a sense that the experience of political subjection would augment in colonial India. This would, however, be a very productive field to explore. On 19th century, post-Darwinian English understandings about the flow of history, see Gillian Beer, *Darwin's Plots: Evolutionary Narratives in Darwin, George Eliot and 19th Century Fiction,* RKP, 1983. On 19th century Bengali patternings of time, see Sumit Sarkar, "Renaissance and Kaliyuga: Time, Myth and History in Colonial Bengal", *Writing Social History,* op cit.

16. Debendranath Tagore, *Swarachita Jiban Charit,* Calcutta, 1898.

17. On the practice of *garbhadhan* in the 19th century, see Monier-Williams, *Religious Thought & Life in India: Vedism, Brahmanism & Hinduism,* originally published 1883, first Indian edition, Delhi 1979.

18. Saradasundari Debi, *Atmakatha,* First published, Dacca, 1913. Reprinted in *Atmakatha* series, Calcutta, 1981, p. 7.

19. Ann Rosalind Jones, "Inscribing Femininity: French Theories of the Feminine" in Gayle Greene and Coppelia Kahn, eds, *Making a Difference: Feminist Literary Criticism,* Methuen, London and New York, 1985, p. 86.

20. On the shaping of the woman's religious experience by her day-to-day events of privation, see Caroline Walker Bynum, *Holy Feast & Holy Fast: The Religious Significance of Food to Medieval Women,* University of California Press, Berkeley, Los Angeles & London, 1987, p. 25.

21. On Lacan's influence on feminist analysis, see Toril Moi, *Sexual/Textual Politics: Feminist Literary Theory,* Methuen, London and New York, 1987, pp. 97–107.

22. See Kailashbashini Debi, *Hindu Mahilaganer Durabastha,* op cit.

23. Gnanadanandini Debi, *Smritikatha,* in Indira Debi, ed, *Puratani,* nd, reprinted, Calcutta, 1957.

24. Wilkiris, *Modern Hinduism: Being an Account of the Religion and Life of the Hindoos in Northern India,* first published 1887, New Delhi reprint, 1985, p. 9.

25. Sen, *Brihat Banga,* Vol I, Dey's Publishing House, Calcutta, 1935, pp. 558–60.

26. Ibid, p. 360.

27. Ibid, pp. 56–57.

28. Dipesh Chakrabarty, "The Difference/Deferral of a Colonial Modernity: Public Debates on Domesticity in Bengal" in *Subaltern Studies,* Vol VIII, Oxford University Press, Delhi, 1994.

29. *Census of India,* 1901, Vol VI, The Lower Provinces of Bengal and their Feudatories; Report by E.A. Gait, Calcutta, 1902, p. 240.

30.   Wilkins, op cit.

31.   Sen, *Brihat Banga,* op cit.

32.   *Lakshmir Panchali,* Calcutta, nd, p. 3.

33.   Saudamini Gupta, *Kanyar Prati Upadesh,* third edition, Calcutta, 1917.

34.   There was a disconcerting uncertainty about the regularity and flow of meals in the Jorasanko Tagore family. See *Smritikatha,* op cit.

35.   See lives of Lakshmididi and Gopaler Ma in *Shri Ramakrishna Bhaktamalika,* op cit. Also June McDaniel, *The Madness of the Saints: Estatic Religion in Bengal,* Chicago, 1989.

36.   Both Peter Brown and Caroline Bynum have pointed out the productive aspects of renunciation—of food & of sex—in the life of a religious person. Caroline Bynum sees in such a woman's relationship with food, a way of manipulating her own life and the world around her—since food is the only object that lies within her control; Bynum is obviously talking of women who are holy figures, in lay or convent organisations, who have a measure of choice in their religious activity. Here, instead, we have a pious householder whose religious practice is a matter of imposed prescriptions. We find, therefore, a very different kind of relationship with food. See Peter Brown: *The Renunciation in Early Christianity,* Columbia University Press, New York, 1988, p. 442. Also Caroline Walker Bynum, op cit, p. 5.

37.   On socially perceived meanings of widowhood, and on womens' reflections on them, see Uma Chakravarti's excellent study, *Rewriting History: The Life and Times of Pandita Ramabai,* Kali for Women, New Delhi, 1997, chapter 5.

38.   For a powerful articulation of the bleak view, see Dipesh Chakrabarty op cit.

39.   I owe this episode to Prof. Jasodhara Bagchi who had been a part of the team.